COMPETITIVE STRATEGIES

FOR SERVICE ORGANISATIONS

Neil Botten and John McManus

First published 1999 by
MACMILLAN PRESS LTD
Houndmills, Basingstoke, Hampshire RG21 6XS
and London
Companies and representatives throughout the world

ISBN 0–333–71680–9 hardcover
ISBN 0–333–71681–7 paperback

A catalogue record for this book is available from the British Library.

This book is printed on paper suitable for recycling and made from
fully managed and sustained forest resources.

10 9 8 7 6 5 4 3 2 1
08 07 06 05 04 03 02 01 00 99

Edited and typeset by
Password, Norwich, UK
Printed and bound in Great Britain by
Creative Print & Design (Wales), Ebbw Vale

To our families and friends

Contents

Figures

Tables

Acknowledgements

The authors would like to acknowledge the help and assistance of the British Airports Authority (BAA) and their senior management team. We would especially like to thank Sir John Egan, Alan Osborne, Andrew Currie and Jim Brophy for their tireless effort and assistance in developing the case material with us. We would also like to thank Dr Paul Stonham, editor of the journal *European Management*, for his kind permission to reproduce Dr Jim Hamill's work, 'Competitive Strategies in the World Airline Industry', which is presented as a case study.

The authors and publishers are grateful to both the authors and publishers concerned for permission to reproduce copyright material. Every effort has been made to contact all the copyright holders, but if any have been inadvertently omitted the publishers will be pleased to make the necessary arrangement at the earliest opportunity.

Preface

The central concept of this book, that of Competitive Strategies for Service Organisations, was born in 1995 when my co-author John McManus, working on a document on service design, implied that a gap existed in the literature which failed to explain the influence and application of strategic management within a global service economy. During the following year, a number of discussion workshops were held with various friends and colleagues (managers, practitioners, and academics) to ascertain their views on strategic management and how strategic thinking influences the approach to implementing strategy in a service driven economy. The output from these discussion workshops provides the raw material upon which this book is largely based.

The picture that has emerged is a complex one, where strategic management theory and its practical application are, to some degree, out of sync in an emerging twenty-first century economy, where the global economic model based on the availability of capital is being replaced by the innovation and intellectual capital which is the corner stone of any service economy.

Without doubt strategic management is a challenge to the minds of practising managers and to do justice to our subject meant writing about strategy in all its practical dimensions, that is: political, economic, social, and technological. Though we take issue with some aspects of the management model – we do, however, keep an open mind and are conventional in our discourse on the use of strategic tools and techniques. Conscious of the limitations of conventional strategic management, the book explores future trends – and where these trends may take us.

In attempting to define the origins of service, special consideration is given to market dynamics and the management challenges it represents within service organisations. Service organisations by their very nature are dynamic, have different life-cycles, and changing portfolios of service offerings. Given these dynamics, managers must think beyond their current environment and arrive at decisions and actions that respond effectively to different market conditions.

Audience

In preparing this book for publication, we have paid special attention to the helpful comments made by reviewers and by practising managers employed within the service sector. We have also been fortunate in being able to draw on interviews with BAA senior managers over the last year. The book is aimed at both practising managers and students of management. The book may also be of value and interest to consultants. As well, the book should be of interest to academics specialising in strategic management and the service economy.

Objectives of the book

The principal objective of the book has been to provide an understanding of the major changes that will impact upon the players in the global service economy. Drawing on both academic and more populist literature, we hope to provide the reader with a better understanding of both the global economy and the service industry, and the shifting patterns within them. The relevance of the tools, techniques and approaches to strategic planning have been described with the intention of giving an insight into their applicability in this context. Despite our reference to the famous anonymous Arabic proverb: 'Anyone who says they can forecast the future is a liar – even if they are subsequently proved to be correct', in Chapter 6 we have attempted to give the reader our view on the most important drivers to affect planning in organisations. Since no two people will produce exactly the same view of the future, readers may feel that there are other factors that will affect their organisations and working lives. Hopefully, our thoughts, together with theirs, will better equip them to cope with a future in which the only certainty is going to be increasingly rapid change.

Overview of the contents

This book includes seven chapters devoted to the application of strategic management in the service sector. The text and case material are organised around the emerging service model. Whilst the book should be read holistically, each chapter is written from a stand-alone perspective.

1   Key themes in the global service economy

The primary objective of this chapter is to systematically address a topic that runs throughout the book, that is, the meaning of service and the purpose of strategic management in a service context. In this chapter, we discuss the evolution of the service economy and its impact on global competition. We examine trends in the service economy and how these trends will impact on strategic thinking. For example, competing in international markets requires a different perspective to competing in domestic markets. How to enter a foreign market, how best to interact with customers, how to manage joint ventures effectively, and how to determine vulnerability and risks are examples of considerations pertinent to strategic thinking – these elements are discussed in terms of external and internal environmental triggers.

2 Defining service organisations

This chapter explores the link between service, market, and strategy. Services have been traditionally described as intangible, having close relationships with consumers. Services are, in reality, market transactions where the object of the exchange is something other then the transfer of a tangible commodity. Service should be viewed along a continuum from complex to simple. In strategic terms, service design is critical to customer attention and market share. For this reason, a significant part of this chapter is devoted to the key components of service: intangibility, inseparability, heterogeneity, and perishability, including their relationship within the service design model.

3 The development of strategic planning

Following the various schools of thought since the early 1960s, this chapter considers the approaches to planning advocated by Classicists, Evolutionists, Processualists and the Systemic School of thought. Exploring the work of the principal authors under each approach, we have drawn together their contributions to the literature under each heading to arrive at a critical appraisal. A central tenet of the Systemic Approach is that any method used should be sensitive to the national culture in which the organisation operates. Similarly, no one of these approaches is entirely appropriate to all situations and each will have their proponents in different organisations, as will be apparent to the reader.

4 Strategic management models, tools, and techniques

The primary objective of this chapter is to focus on the principal models, tools, and techniques used by corporate managers in the formulation of strategy. A summary of the six most widely used models (or tools) is given – including the Boston Consulting Group (BCG) matrix, the General Electric/McKinsey matrix, the Seven Ss Framework, Profit Impact of Market Strategy (PIMS) model, Porter's Value Chain, and the Five Forces model. Each model/tool is described in detail in the context of the strategic management process, together with its uses and limitations. In describing these models and their usage, consideration was given to their applicability in a service context.

5   The application of strategic management

This chapter explores how strategic alternatives are generated, together with the formulation, implementation, and measurement of such alternatives. All those models and concepts discussed in Chapter 4 can be applied to all types of strategic problems. As previously discussed, managers must think beyond their current environment and arguably one of the best ways to assess the likely impact of alternative strategies is through the construction of detailed scenarios. Alternatively, Porter offers models which provide approaches to strategic choice. Porter's view on generic competitive strategies are deliberated and a discourse is given on his teachings.

6   Future trends in strategic management

Drawing on the changing nature of the economy that we have described in the first two chapters, Chapter 6 considers the main drivers of change which will impact upon organisations. Organisations will undoubtedly change their shape and, whilst there will be increasingly larger firms seeking cost effectiveness, they will need to be flexible and adaptive. Similarly, the nature of work will change and large organisations will have less and less core employees, releasing people who will sell their services to a number of organisations on a casual basis. Markets also will change – with the increasing use of e-commerce, national boundaries will be less and less impermeable, countries will need to find alternative ways to attract firms to operate within their boundaries, and retain them once they are there. The rapid convergence of telecommunications and media, together with spreading deregulation of these and other industries such as airlines, is described together with the implications for the players – a point which is again brought out in the second of our subsequent case studies. We also consider the impact of a more aware population and its impact upon the external relations which companies now have to spend much more effort in managing.

7   The Case material

We recognise that no single approach can be universally applied to all strategic management cases and problems, however, we are mindful that students often need examples of how to apply the concepts learned. For this reason, we have included two cases. The case studies included in this book are of BAA, a company that has demonstrated phenomenal growth since privatisation, and the World Airline Industry, where the effects of globalisation and deregulation have had a major impact upon the strategies that the players have been able to adopt.

Neil Botten and John McManus

1 Key Themes in the Global Service Economy

INTRODUCTION

The evolution of the service economy

The meaning of service historically has been ignored by Pan-European economies dominated by primary and secondary economic activities. Both managers and theorists have focused instead on refining management models for the industrial era. In the last decade, however, the service sector has come to dominate both UK and USA economies. Since this has occurred, the meaning of service – what a service is and how to provide it – has captured considerable attention. There is a general consensus of opinion that services are intangible and therefore invisible. The USA, by virtue of its trends in employment and economic activities, claims to be the first nation to have a service economy, approaching $3 trillion. In simple terms, 68 per cent of the nation's gross national product (GNP) and 75 per cent of its employment is derived from the service sector. European industrialised nations (such as Belgium, France, Italy, and the UK) report similar employment figures in their respective service economies.

In the last 50 years, we have witnessed a major evolution in our society from being manufacturing based to being predominantly service based. There are a number of explanations for this growth:

1. As industrial societies become richer, they choose to spend a higher proportion of their incomes on buying services rather then physical goods.
2. It has so far proved very much harder to draw out additional productivity from primary and secondary industries.
3. As countries become wealthy, they are able to 'export' their profits in the form of investments in other countries. Evidently, a number of countries have invested in manufacturing in other developing countries. The rewards are returned in profits, interest, and dividends that can be spent on leisure and other services.

4. As we approach the twenty-first century we are experiencing a new entre-
    preneurial renaissance.[1]

This new renaissance is being fuelled by advances in information technology, Government policies, and changes in corporate strategies. For example,
big companies and *economies of scale* succeeded in the comparatively slow-
moving world of four decades ago. But now, as we will discuss in Chapter 6,
only small and medium-sized companies – or big organisations that have
restyled themselves as networks of entrepreneurs – will survive to be viable
when we turn the corner into the next century. Already, 50 per cent of USA
exports are created by companies with 20 or fewer employees. Only 7 per
cent of USA exports are created by companies with 500 or more employees.
The fortune 500 now account for only 10 per cent of the American economy,
down from 20 per cent in 1970. Ninety per cent of the USA economy is
elsewhere: in small and medium-sized companies. Entrepreneurial individuals are creating the huge global economy. Ferris in his book says:

> The late twentieth century may be remembered in the history of science as the time when
> particle physics, the study of the smallest structures in nature, joined forces with cosmology,
> the study of the universe as a whole.[2]

Recent research has indicated that many entrepreneurs intend to keep their
organisations small and personally controlled. In general, they do not aspire
to be leaders of large quoted companies.

The entrepreneur was introduced into economic talk in 1755 by Richard
Cantillon in his *Essai Sur la Nature du Commerce en Général.*[3] Cantillon
described the entrepreneur as an individual who buys the means of production at certain prices, in order to combine them into a product that he is
going to sell, at prices that cannot be known at a time he commits himself to
costs. Cantillon's ideas were refined by the French economist Jean-Baptiste
Say in the early nineteenth century. Say's entrepreneur was the agent who
unites all means of production – the labour of the one, the capital or the
land of the others – and who finds in the value of the products, which result
from their employment, the reconstitution of the entire capital that he uti-
lises, and the value of the wages, the interest, and the rent which he pays, as
well as the profits belonging to himself.[4] This person was not an economic
automaton. To some extent he needed special human qualities, including
judgement, perseverance, and knowledge of the world, as well as of business. He is called upon to estimate, with tolerable accuracy, the importance
of the specific product, the probable amount of the demand, and the means
of its production: at one time, he must employ a great number of hands; at
another, buy or order raw material, collect labourers, find consumers, and at
all times give a rigid attention to order and economy; in a word, he must

possess the art of superintendence and administration. In the course of such complex operations, there are an abundance of obstacles to be surmounted, anxieties to be repressed or misfortunes to be repaired, and expedients to be devised.[5]

It is not difficult to imagine that a person responsible for such a wide range of critical tasks would stand at the centre of the study of economics and of economic history. But, this has not been the case. The main line of economic theory – that has as its parent Adam Smith's *The Wealth of Nations,* published in 1776 – has had little place in it for the role of the individual. In the classical and neoclassical view, the principal concern has been the examination of a general equilibrium between supply and demand resulting from the multiple reactions of business people, labourers, consumers, and investors to prices. The world of economic theory, to this day, is basically impersonal. Purchasers do not know other purchasers, purchasers do not know providers, providers do not know other providers; and there is perfect information. Individual variation is to some extent cancelled out in the total or it is suppressed by competition.[6]

Social or cultural considerations can be factored into this model only with difficulty and there is not much room for unique human insight, for the *neoclassical growth model* has been called 'perhaps the highest intellectual construction in the social sciences'.[7] Good work has been done within those assumptions, but those very assumptions presume away important aspects of what is plainly part of twentieth-century business. Some economists have departed from the neoclassical view and have attempted to find a place for the entrepreneur in their work. Most important among these is Joseph A. Schumpeter, who has recognised the importance of *innovation* and has suggested the part the entrepreneur played in its achievement. To undertake new things is difficult and constitutes:

> . . . a distinct economic function, first because they lie outside of the routine tasks which everybody understands and secondly, because the environment resists in many ways that vary, according to social conditions, from simple refusal either to finance or to buy a new thing, to physical attack on the man who tries to produce it. To act with confidence beyond the range of familiar beacons and to overcome that resistance requires aptitudes that are present in only a small fraction of the population.[8]

Neoclassical growth model: A theory or model for explaining long-term trends in economic growth in industrialised economies. This model emphasises the importance of capital deepening (i.e., a growing capital-labour ratio) and technological change in explaining the growth of potential real GNP.

Trends and future developments

A phenomenon is occurring in the world today – the smallest economic player, the entrepreneur, will merge with the global economy. The entrepreneur is also the most important player in the building of the global economy. So much so that big companies are decentralising and reconstituting themselves as networks of entrepreneurs, no more so than in the service economy. Writing in the *Washington Post* (24 July 1989), Elsa C. Arnett made the following predictions for the year 2001:

- Only 1 person in 50 will be promoted to top management, compared with 1 in 20 now.
- Firms with fewer than 200 people will employ 85 per cent of the workforce.
- The service sector will account for 88 per cent of the entire workforce.
- Approximately 70 per cent of homes in the USA will have computers, and an increasing volume of work will be done at home.
- About 63 per cent of new entrants into the workforce will be women.
- The retirement age for all will rise to 70.

These predictions of a decade ago are consistent with what is happening in Western economies. Today we can add to these trends by including the entrepreneurial talent of knowledge- (or Alpha-) based workers who have started their own businesses. When we examine the relationship between GNP and the number of new businesses started, it is apparent that enterprise formation is alive and well. This is substantiated by the growth in small and medium enterprises in Europe and the USA. In the UK there are about 3.5 million small businesses and 113 000 medium-sized enterprises. Why does this enterprise formation continue to grow? In part, it is the entrepreneurial spirit and in part, it is the individual's desire for independence. To some extent this is explained by the evolutionary school of strategy (see Chapter 3). Some authors, such as Tom Peters, applaud the high rates of business formations and failures that are a feature of Western economies, attesting that they are good for nations.

> Studies in the USA using the techniques of growth accounting break down the growth of GNP in the private business sector into its contributing fasctors. These sudies find that capital growth is only a modest contributor, accounting for about a fourth (20 per cent) of total GNP growth. Education, technological change, and other sources make up almost a half (50 per cent) of total GNP growth and 6 tenths of the growth of output per worker.[9]

Economic development and the emergence of the post-industrial society

Colin Clark, a well-known economist, argued that as nations become industrialised, there is an inevitable shift of employment from one sector of employment to another. Clark hypothesised that as productivity increases in one sector, the labour force moves into another sector of the economy. This observation, known as the *Clark-Fisher hypothesis*, leads to a classification of economies by noting the activity of the workforce. Clark limited his research to the primary, secondary, and tertiary sectors of economic activity. Foot and Hatt, however, suggested a subdivision of tertiary into quaternary and quinary. Table 1.1 describes the five economic sectors.

The predominant activity of the post-industrial society is the quality of life, as measured by those services within the quinary sector. The central consumer of such services is the professional (or knowledge-based) person because information, rather than energy or physical strength, is the key resource. Daniel Bell writing in *The Coming of Post-Industrial Society: A Venture in Social Forecasting* (1973) suggests that the transformation from industrial to post-industrial society occurs in many ways. Firstly, there is the natural development of services, such as transportation and utilities, to support industrial development. As labour-saving devices are introduced into the production process, more workers become engaged in nonmanufacturing activities, such as maintenance and repair. Secondly, the growth of population and the mass consumption of goods increases wholesale and retail trade along with banking, property, and insurance. Thirdly, as income increases, the proportion spent on necessities of food, energy, and clothing decrease, and the remainder creates a demand for durables and then for services. As already stated, consumption is the largest single component of the USA's GNP(see Table 1.2) constituting 68 per cent of total spending over the last decade.

Exchange between nations has grown steadily since 1950. In 1991, world trade reached three trillion dollars, of which about 74 per cent was accounted for by the Organisation for Economic Co-operation and Development (OECD) countries. Since 1980 world trade has increased at a faster rate than has world output. This means that the countries of the world have developed a greater inclination to trade goods and services with one another. Trading nations are now, more than ever, dependent on each other and those service organisations that are directly involved in foreign trade and those that are indirectly dependent on it have become vulnerable to changes in world conditions.

Moving to an invisible trade economy

For statistical purposes world trade is classified as either visible or invisible:

Visible trade: involves the exchange of physical goods and products.
Invisible trade: involves the exchange of services – such as financial, con
sulting, education, services, etc., and includes financial
transactions, profits, and interest payments.

Invisible trade accounts for about 26 per cent of the total world trade and is
increasing at a faster rate than visible trade. (This confirms the fact that the
world is being transformed from an industrial economy to an information-
based economy.) The USA is the world leader in invisible exports and when
both visible and invisible exports are taken into account, the USA is found to
have led all countries in world trade in 1989, with about 15 per cent of the
world total. (West Germany had 11 per cent, Japan 10.4 per cent, the UK 8.2
per cent, and France 7 per cent.) West Germany had a slight lead over the
USA with respect to visible exports (12 per cent), followed respectively by
Japan, France, and the UK. Many of these so-called advanced industrial nations would be better described as *service economies* based on the work activity
of their populations. Table 1.3 is a partial list of industrialised countries in
percentage order of those employed in service-producing jobs and contains
some surprising facts. Canada and Australia, for instance, although known for
their primary industries are high on the list. Several observations can be made:
global economic development is progressing in unanticipated directions, successful industrial economies are built on a strong service sector, and *competition
in services* will become global just as it has in manufacturing.

Table 1.1   Breakdown of economic activities

1. **Primary (extractive)** Agriculture Mining Fishing Forestry	4. **Quaternary (trade and commerce)** Transportation Retailing Communications Finance and insurance Property Government
2. **Secondary (goods-producing)** Manufacturing Processing	5. **Quinary (refining and extending** **human capacities)** Health Education Research Recreation Arts
3. **Tertiary (domestic services)** Restaurants and hotels Hair-care and beauty shops Laundry and dry cleaning Maintenance and repair	

Note: Service Sector includes: tertiary, quaternary and quinary.

Table 1.2   Major elements of consumption

Category	Contribution to GNP
Durable Goods Motor vehicles Household equipment Other	14%
Non-durable goods Food Energy Clothing and apparel Other	33%
Services Housing Medical care Personal business Education	53%
	100%

Source: USA Department of Commerce 1990.

Table 1.3   Selected industrialised nations – people employed in service jobs

Country	1980	1987	2000[10]
United States	67.1	71.0	78
Canada	67.2	70.8	75
Belgium	64.3	70.1	72
Australia	64.7	69.7	71
UK	*60.4*	*67.7*	*73*
France	56.9	63.6	69
Finland	52.2	60.1	66
Japan	54.5	58.1	62
Italy	48.7	57.7	61

Source: 1990 Statistical Yearbook, Department of International Economic and Social Affairs Statistical Office, United Nations, New York.

GLOBALISATION AND THE SERVICE ECONOMY

Worldwide service trade is growing largely due to the help of more flexible transport and communications capabilities. At the beginning of the 1970s, only 8 per cent of the USA economy (and 3–4 per cent in the UK) was exposed to foreign competition. Within two decades that figure had climbed to approximately 78 per cent, and is still rising. With the world heading towards a single economy, this trend toward greater international competition will continue for service organisations. Geographical distance is no longer a barrier between nations, however, and the challenges of ethnic diversity in the domestic market are multiplied by the difficulties of delivering a service in an international market with the added barriers of different cultures and languages.

Undertaking business in a foreign country poses an entirely different set of problems. For example, organisations often have difficulties in obtaining either competitor information or the requirements for operating in new environments. A change to the international environment in which business operates has been the development of gigantic regional groupings. There are now three main powerful trading blocks (see Table 1.4). As world markets shrink and countries become more intertwined both culturally and economically, service organisations must consider global assumptions about their markets. Kenichi Ohmae offers a theoretical argument for the need to become global. Dr Ohmae argues that organisations that have the right characteristics to become global players will succeed only if they operate in three geographical centres of the world: USA, Japan and Europe.[11] Those that stay in only one or two of these areas are unlikely to succeed in the long run, because the utilities that fall to those competitors that do penetrate the total trio will give immense cost advantage. The argument is based on the fact that these areas contain some 600 million people in the largest and most sophisticated markets in the world. UK companies have significant opportunities to expand and trade (with the trio) if they go about it in a manner compatible with the new cultures they enter. Different cultures have different attitudes to strategic planning and futurology as will be described later.

Table 1.4   Comparison of trio trading blocks

Trading Block	Regional Grouping
North American Market (North American Free Trade Area (NAFTA)	USA, Canada and Mexico
European Community (Western Europe)	The 12 Nations (EC, economically and politically integrated)
Japan and the Association of South East Asia Nations (ASEAN)	Thailand, Indonesia, Malaysia, Australia and New Zealand

The trio trading blocks

The three international regional trading areas account for 20 per cent of the global population and almost 80 per cent of the world output as measured by GNP. It is within this trio that most of the wealth of the world is currently created, consumed, and traded. As a result, more and more large organisations have service divisions in North America, Europe, and Asia. In such an interconnected economy, *the nationality* of organisations becomes an outdated idea, together with the view that national governments can obstruct or impede the process of internationalisation through protectionism or exchange policies. Governments are becoming partners in the economic process with their own multinational organisations. Using subsidies, reduced taxes, reduced antitrust regulation, cheap capital, research consortia, joint ventures, and so on, governments promote the cause of their domestic organisations. This is emphasised by the use of international diplomatic networks as sales offices for negotiating leverage. The role of government makes the new competitors more competitive. Deregulation is another force increasing the intensity of competition. Paradoxically governments are becoming both more, and less active. The financial markets, the media, and telecommunications are clear examples, which we will explore later in more detail in Chapter 6. The strategic responses of BAA and the Airline Industry to privatisation and deregulation are considered in the case material in Chapter 7. It is quite feasible for governments to regulate markets less, but help their organisations compete more effectively. It is reasonable to assume that the fear of trade wars among the three great trading blocks will continue to be the themes of editorials, political pronouncements, and academic theorists. Nevertheless, protectionist pressures will continue to be applied only in specific instances instead of across the board. Forces within the EC and North America will limit the attacks primarily to regulations against the Japanese.

Competitive and economic threats

The economic environment in which service organisations function is extremely complex. Operating within it are dynamic business fluctuations that tend to follow a cyclical pattern composed of four stages: *Depression, Recovery, Prosperity* and *Recession*. Each stage is characterised as follows:

1. **Depression**: heavy unemployment, low consumer demand, over capacity (unused capacity) in production, prices stable, or even falling, business profits low, and business confidence in the future low.

2. **Recovery**: investment picks up, employment rises, consumer spending rises, profits rise, business confidence grows, and prices stable or slowly rising.

3. **Prosperity**: consumer spending rising fast, output capacity reached: labour shortages occur, output can only be increased by new labour-saving investment, investment spending high, increases in demand now stimulate price rises, and business profits high.

4. **Recession**: consumption falls off, many investments suddenly become unprofitable and new investment falls, production falls, employment falls, profits fall, businesses fail, and recession may turn into deep depression.

No service organisation can disregard the economic climate in which they function, for the type, direction, and intensity of its strategy depends upon it. Organisations operating in the service sectors must be aware of the economy's relative position in the business cycle and how it will affect the position of the firm. By necessity, the service function differs with each stage of the business cycle. During affluent times, consumers are usually more willing to buy than when they feel economically threatened. For example, in the last few years we have seen growth in the financial service sector, where personal savings have climbed to record levels as consumers (fearing possible redundancy and short-term employment) cut back their expenditure on many services in the non-essential category. Organisations (and their managers) must pay close attention to consumers' relative willingness to purchase.

While organisational growth may experience cyclical variations (Figure 1.1), the successful organisation has a rising trend line. This, however, largely depends upon management's ability to foresee, correctly define, and reach new market opportunities. Effective strategy is only a partial solution. Equally important, is a need to develop an intuitive awareness of potential markets. This requires the organisation (or company) to correctly delineate opportunities.

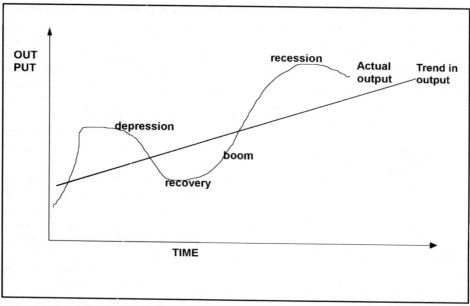

Figure 1.1   The business cycle

Competing in international markets requires a different perspective to competing in domestic markets. How to enter a foreign market, how best to interact with customers, how to manage joint ventures or subsidiaries effectively, and how to determine vulnerability and risks are examples of considerations pertinent to service competition on a global level. It is important to recognise that dangerous economic threats are mounting for service organisations. Such threats include:

- Government Policy and Legislation
- Macro Economic Environment Related to Fiscal Monetary Union
- Trade Policies
- Energy Costs
- Synergy with World Markets
- Expenditure on Research and Development (R&D)
- Time to Market of Competitor Services (e.g., experience curve)
- Competitor Pricing Policy
- Barriers to Entry (e.g., control over distribution, etc.)

Changes taking place within the international economy, and the economic threats that go with such changes, should not be ignored by service organisations. Statistics on import penetration for countries within the Trio make the threat clear. For the USA in 1970, imports represented 4 per cent of GNP. By 1980, the proportion had risen to 9 per cent and by 1990, it had further increased to over 18 per cent. During the same period, Japan witnessed imports increasing from 10 to 13 per cent of GNP. Rising import penetration across the major industrial economies of the world not only underlines the interlinked nature of the Trio, but also emphasises that the main competitors for native firms are increasingly likely to be foreign rather than domestic organisations.

At the turn of the century, those countries with access to natural resources became rich and tended to stay rich. With a higher income, more capital was saved and subsequently invested, raising productivity and generating more wealth. But the virtuous circle may be coming to an end, in a list prepared by MITI of the most rapidly growing industries for the 1990s,[12] all were far more dependent upon brainpower than natural resources. As such, they can be located anywhere in the world, it will depend upon who organises the brainpower and knowledge to be an attractive site. Hence, natural resources have fallen out of the competitive equation, as have sources of capital. Improved communications and technology mean that firms borrow in either New York, London, or Tokyo wherever the best deal happens to be.

Just as the pharmaceutical industry can be segmented into those companies that manufacture proprietary drugs and those that manufacture generic copies once the patents have expired, the same pattern can be seen with countries and improving technology. Whereas textiles were the backbone of the Industrial Revolution in the UK and USA, those economies have moved on and textiles are a standard third-world product. Products move from an initial, high-profitability, high-wage stage produced in highly developed economies to low-waged, labour-intensive and low-profit manufacturers. However, the speed of that transfer is increasing.

It is anticipated that by the year 2001, the Asia-Pacific international region will have a GNP comparable with NAFTA and Western Europe. This is largely attributed to the growth experienced in this region over the last ten years. Between 1991 and 2001, Japan, Australia, and the *Tiger Economies* are forecast to grow by 68 per cent (more than twice the percentage rate of NAFTA and Western Europe), while China and the Asia-Pacific developing countries are expected to achieve 126 per cent increase in GNP. As a result, while the USA, Western Europe, and Japan will remain important components of the world economy, the emerging *Tiger Economies* are likely to be increasingly significant.

Global triggers and the new competitors

It would appear there are characteristics in organisations that become global, in that there has to be the opportunity for high levels of demand for
service products that give rise to economies of scale. Globalisation is not a
naturally occurring state but is man made, and the triggers (external and
internal) that enable a service to be defined globally are the identification of
market segments countries. In turn, this enables supply sources to be consolidated so that the competitive cost advantages can be gained. For
example, the new competitors from Taiwan, Korea, India, and Brazil, among
others, are targeting industries and services, protecting home markets in
those sectors providing cheap long-term financing, and using exports to
provide economic growth. Many of them are following the Japanese model.
Initially, they use lower labour costs and an educated workforce to produce
a cost advantage. They then invest in the latest technology to reduce their
dependence on temporary labour-cost advantage, produce quality products
and services, and still maintain a cost advantage. They borrow, license, copy,
and even steal technologies, and avoid the costs of developing their own. As
a result, not only is there less volume to go around, but there are more and
more formidable competitors for that volume. Heller noted that the Japanese will go to any lengths, not to hide their weaknesses but to repair them.[13]
Heller cites the 'California Caper', the attempt to steal IBM secrets which
raised the possibility that some of Japan's brilliance in world markets rested
not on quality circles, or better strategies, or the spirit of Zen, but on simple
theft of Western technology. Even more than other examples, the behaviour
of Hitachi in this respect offends against the principles of truth and fairness.
Such practices usually carry a cost: in this case, the $300 million Hitachi
allegedly had to pay IBM.

It has been observed by Ellis and Williams that, in all enterprises (including services), a pressure exists between those factors driving an enterprise
towards globalisation and those working in an opposite direction for localisation.[14] By deciding the size and direction of external drives impacting on a
particular industry (see Figure 1.2), it is possible to determine the extent of
the globalisation process. An external-change factor is considered as such
when it relates to developments which are outside the organisation's control. For external factors to bring about change, they must be defined by the
organisation and acted on in a way which results in that organisation gaining access to global markets. Often, external triggers may have existed for a
number of years, but have not been acted upon because of the organisation's internal context. Internal triggers normally enable a fundamental
reappraisal of the organisation's strategy and internal development.

External and internal environmental triggers

The external environment consists of two variables: Threats and Opportunities, both of which are outside the organisation and not within the short-term control of management. These variables form the context within which the organisation exists. The external environment has two components: Industry Environment and Societal Environment. The industry environment includes those elements or groups that directly influence, and are influenced by, an organisation's major operations. Some of these are: shareholders, governments, suppliers, competitors, customers, creditors, trade unions, special interest groups, and trade associations.

The societal environment includes more extensive forces, that is, ones that do not directly touch the short-term activities of the organisation, but which can and often do influence its long-term decisions. Such Political, Economic, Societal, and Technological (PEST) forces are depicted in Figure 1.2. The societal environment for corporate decision making has both expanded in scope and increased in importance. At the end of the 1990s, no organisation can initiate a strategy without taking the societal environment into account and managers must develop an awareness of the manner in which it affects their decisions. The constant pressure from social issues requires that managers place more emphasis on solving PEST issues than merely concerning themselves solely with the standard questions.

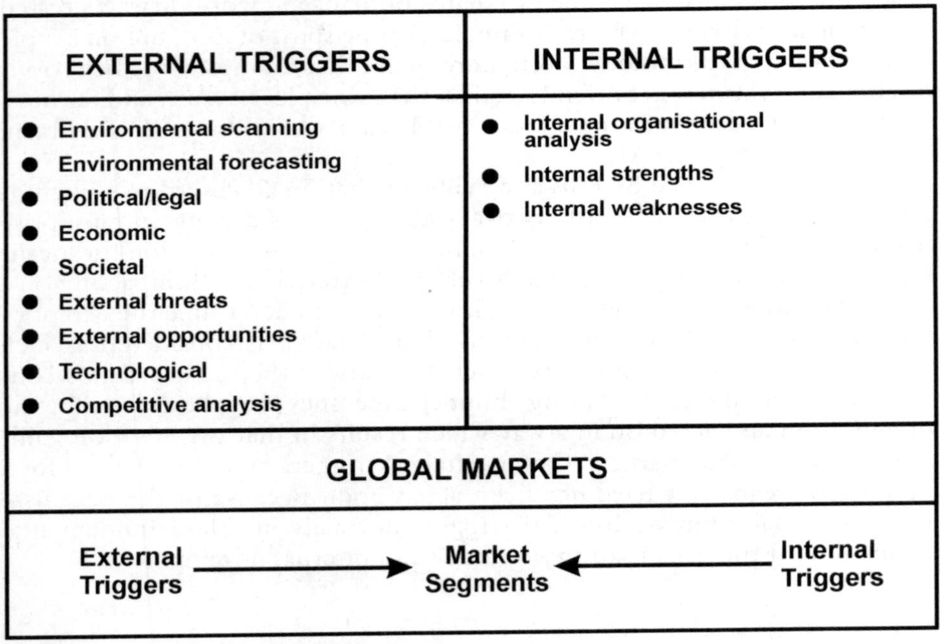

EXTERNAL TRIGGERS	INTERNAL TRIGGERS
• Environmental scanning • Environmental forecasting • Political/legal • Economic • Societal • External threats • External opportunities • Technological • Competitive analysis	• Internal organisational analysis • Internal strengths • Internal weaknesses
GLOBAL MARKETS	
External Triggers ——→ Market Segments ←—— Internal Triggers	

Figure 1.2   External and internal triggers

Defining the meaning of PEST

Political: any government plays a number of roles which go beyond the making of laws and raising taxes. All types of industries and businesses are affected by government policies, not least those in the public domain. Within the context of a global economy, the power which is government will set the climate for business and for business confidence. A change in government can dramatically alter the nature and structure of organisations both domestically and internationally.

Economic: almost without exception, government policy influences the nature of business competitiveness and company profitability. For example, deregulation of the world's capital markets in the 1980s and the removal of exchange controls have resulted in many global mergers and acquisitions, and a leaner and fitter world economy. Conditions in the world economy do cascade down into both national and domestic economies. The importance of international events in recent years has increased the need for economic intelligence. Businesses which are reluctant to search out and take advantage of the new trading blocks, single markets, and the GATT may soon find their (profitable) markets exposed to new competitors.

Societal: some strategists consider this to be the most difficult environment to identify, judge, and respond to. It includes demographic changes, culture, educational standards, lifestyles, values, and beliefs. Social and demographic changes often appear to move at a slow pace, yet their impacts are likely to far outweigh the result of political decisions in the long term. Continuing trends in world unemployment, the fall in European populations, increasing age differentials, and culture change will impact on business and profitability.

Technological: in the last 25 years, we have witnessed phenomenal change in the areas of technology and know-how. Accelerated rates of change in information technology, telecommunications, medicine, and defence have altered the nature and structure of our working and domestic environments. This is how a competitive weapon – the lead time between invention, innovation, and market introduction – has shrunk significantly with the application of computer technology, while the development of telecommunications has combined to make the global economy a reality.

Internal environment: this consists of two key variables, those of Strengths and Weaknesses, that are within the organisation itself and are not usually within the short-term control of the senior management. In the main, these variables form the context in which work is achieved. They include: the organisation's structure, culture, and resources:

1. Corporate structure refers to the way an organisation is organised in terms of authority, chain of command, and processes.
2. Corporate culture refers to the organisation's values and beliefs, and the expectations shared by management and associates.
3. Corporate resources refers to the organisation's assets. Such assets include: people, know-how, skills or abilities, and finance.

Twenty-five years ago Stern succinctly pointed out: 'the more educated society becomes, the more interdependent it becomes, and the more discretionary the use of its resources; the more strategy and marketing will become enmeshed in social issues'.[15] A quarter of a century on, one key issue facing contemporary service organisations is how to measure the accomplishment of socially oriented objectives. An organisation that is attuned to its societal environment must develop new ways of evaluating performance. Traditional cash flow, return on capital employed are no longer adequate. This issue will be further developed in Chapter 5, in 'Measuring strategic success', as one of the most important problems facing contemporary service organisations.

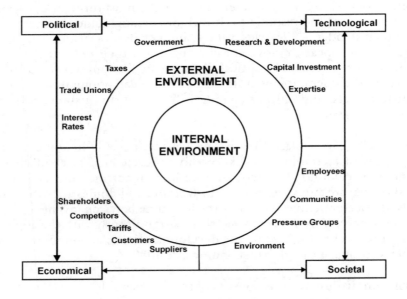

Figure 1.3   A summary model of environmental variables

Succeeding in the global economy

One of the key empirical studies of the late 1980s was undertaken by Cvar into patterns of success and failure in global competition (see Figure 1.4).[16] Cvar argued that successful global companies had five factors in common. They had all:

1. Developed a pre-emptive strategy.
2. Managed their companies on a global basis.
3. Measured their performance on a global basis.
4. Had higher than average R&D compared to the sector norm.
5. Demonstrated a measure of single mindedness in overcoming obstacles to globalisation.

The phenomenal, and global, success of *In Search of Excellence* spawned (certainly in the USA and the UK) an awakening of the meaning of quality, value, and beliefs.[17] Peters and Waterman's study was fundamental in emphasising the soft aspects of global management, including those internal attributes of the organisation such as shared values, loose-tight structures, and the anticipation that an excellent firm will find environments appropriate to the exploitation of its excellence. The authors also found that the philosophies of successful companies included the following ideologies:

- Belief in being the best.
- Belief in the importance of the details of implementation, the nuts and bolts of doing the job well.
- Belief in the importance of individual people.
- Belief in exceptional quality and service.
- Belief in individual innovation and its inference, the willingness to support failure.
- Belief in the importance of freedom to enhance communication.
- Belief in a recognition of the importance of economic growth and profits.

INDUSTRIES WHICH BECAME GLOBAL	TRIGGERS FOR GLOBALISATION
• High levels of Demand for standardised Products • Economies of Scale	• Common Segments Identified • Products Defined Globally • Supply Sources Consolidated

SUCCESSFUL GLOBAL COMPANIES

- **Pre-Emptive Strategy**
- **Performance Measured Globally**
- **R&D Higher Than Average**
- **Manage All Elements Globally**
- **Overcome Barriers To Globalisation**

Figure 1.4   Success factors in global competition

Source: Adapted from M. R. Cvar, 'Case Studies in Global Competition: patterns of success and failure', in M. E. Porter (ed.), *Competition in Global Industries*, Harvard Business School, Boston, 1986.

Researchers (past and present), such has Ansoff, Moss-Kanter, and Quinn et al,[18] who have examined so-called excellent organisations largely agree with Cvar's findings with respect to maintaining a global perspective within their markets. How do they achieve this? According to Johnson and Scholes, managers do not reinvent their organisational world every time they face a new challenge.[19] They have to employ some set of assumptions or guiding principles to make sense of the world – what they refer to as a recipe. However, if the recipe is necessary so that managers can operate effectively, it is also dangerous because it is likely to create the sort of drift that the organisation must avoid. Organisations must be able to challenge the status quo and change beliefs – excellent organisations appear to have this ability.

Multinational service operations

In true services, which exclude receipts and payments on investments and government transactions, the USA has been maintaining a trade surplus for the past 20 years. Leadership in the *knowledge-based* services such as software, telecommunications, and information services has proved to be very mobile. However, not all services travel equally well, and considerations of **cultural transferability, network development,** and **host government policy** must be taken into account.

Cultural transferability: commercial banking would seem to be culturally neutral because financial needs and the associated business transactions are relatively homogeneous worldwide. Indeed, the exception to this is the Middle East, where paying interest on a loan is not recognised by the Muslim faith; thus, banks must adjust by creating service charges that include, but do not mention, interest costs. Customer services are faced with obvious language barriers and behavioural customs that might affect the service delivery (e.g., the need for nonsmoking areas in USA restaurants). However, in food service, the desire is often to emulate the cultural experience of a foreign land. The success of Benihana of Tokyo in the USA is partly due to creating the illusion of a Japanese dining experience while still serving familiar food. Likewise, for many non-Americans, eating at McDonalds and drinking a Coke is an opportunity to experience something American.

Network Development: many service organisations reluctantly expand into global operations, forced by the desires of their customers. For example, in the case of holders of VISA card and MasterCard, customers expected to use their credit cards wherever they travelled. In both cases, the original concept was designed for a domestic market, but the customers eventually insisted on a global network. Maintaining operations control and standards of quality becomes difficult, however, because staffing is usually accomplished with nationals of the host country, and thus there are inherent language and cultural differences.

Government Policy: governments around the world have played a significant role in restricting the growth of multinational services. This includes but is not limited to making it difficult to repatriate funds, that is, to take profits out of the host country. Discrimination has taken a number of creative forms: banning the sale of insurance by foreign firms, giving preferential treatment to local shippers, placing restrictions on the international flow of information, and creating delays in processing licensing agreements. A major reason for this situation is the continuing refusal of countries (with the exception of the USA) to recognise the importance of services in international trade.[20] It was not until 1982 that trade barriers on services were placed on the agenda at a meeting of the General Agreement on Tariffs and Trade (GATT), a group of 88 trading nations that for decades has been establishing codes of conduct for trading goods. In 1993, the GATT agreement considering financial services was held hostage by several Asian countries wishing to protect their domestic firms from global competition. For example, Korea has an outright prohibition on foreigners selling mutual funds to local investors, and Japan requires a multilayer application process with no clear objective criteria for approval.[21]

The nature of the borderless world

Kenichi Ohmae argues that we now live in a borderless world where customers worldwide are aware of the best products and services, and expect to purchase them with no concern for national origin.[22] In his strategic view, all firms compete in an interlinked world economy, and to be effective, they must balance the five Cs of strategic planning: customers, competitors, company, currency, and country.

Customers: when people vote with their pockets, they are interested in quality, price, design, value, and personal appeal. Brand labels, such as the *golden arches*, are spreading all over the world and news of performance is hard to suppress. The availability of information, particularly in the industrialised Trio markets of the USA, Europe, and Japan, has empowered customers and stimulated competition.

Competitors: nothing stays proprietary for long. Equipment and software vendors supply their products and services to a wide range of customers. The result is the rapid dispersion of technology available to all firms. Two factors, time and being the first mover, have now become more critical as elements of strategy. Furthermore, a single firm cannot be on the cutting edge of all technologies. Thus, operating globally means operating with partners.

Company: automation during the past years has moved firms from a variable-cost environment to a fixed-cost environment. Management focus has thus changed from boosting profits by reducing material and labour costs to increasing sales to cover fixed costs. This is particularly true of many service firms (e.g., airlines and communications business) which, to a large extent, are fixed-cost activities with huge investments in facilities and equipment. The search for a larger market has driven these firms towards globalisation and cross-border markets. However, the nature of a firm's corporate culture may determine how effectively its service will travel overseas. The domestic success of Federal Express was built on a go-it-alone attitude, on rewards for nonunion employees who propose cost-cutting ideas, and on direct access to Fred Smith with any complaints. In contrast, UPS, which works with a union labour force and strict work standards, has moved overseas with fewer problems.

Currency: global companies have tried to neutralise their exposure to fluctuating currency exchange rates by matching costs to revenues and becoming strong in all regions of the Trio so that if any single one is negative, it may be offset by others that are positive. Companies have also employed international finance techniques such as hedging and options. Thus to become currency neutral, a firm is forced into global expansion.

Country: having a strong presence in all the Trio regions provides additional strategic benefits beyond currency considerations. First, as noted above, exposure to economic downturns in one region may be offset by operations in other economies. Second, selling in your competitor's domestic market neutralises its option to employ a strategy using excessive profits earned in a protected domestic market for expansion overseas. For example, with government co-operation, Japanese companies have exploited this strategy, and recently they have been criticised for this by their trading partners. However, only truly global companies achieve *global localisation* (a term coined by Akio Morta of Sony), and thereby acceptance as a local company while maintaining the benefits of worldwide operations. To reach this level, a firm must become close to the customers in the foreign country and accommodate their unique service needs. For fast-food restaurants, discovering the drinking and eating habits of the host country is crucial for success. Thus, instead of expecting the Germans to enjoy a Big Mac and a Coke, McDonalds added beer to the menu. Permitting local management to modify the service within limits to accommodate local tastes should be encouraged, even at the risk of introducing some inconsistency across locations. An extreme example, is Mr Donut's in Japan, which changed everything about its product and service except the logo.

Pull and push factors in cross-border markets

Marketing services in foreign territories used to be treated as an indicator of prosperous, large organisations which had potentially outgrown their own home markets. In the 1990s, such a perception is misleading because involvement with markets is an option available to most organisations. Values, attitudes, and lifestyles are changing. Extensive consumer travelling, exposure to international media, removal of trading barriers between nations, and changing consumer perceptions and expectations worldwide make cross-border marketing a logical extension of operations in the home market rather than an expensive luxury.

Organisations are drawn towards cross-border markets either for market pull or market push considerations (or even a combination of push and pull). Market *pull* factors are defined as factors which seduce organisations away from their existing domestic markets because of the perceived attractiveness of the market. In contrast, *push* factors usually originate out of difficulties in an organisation's present markets plus opportunities to overcome such difficulties by transferring into cross-border markets where competition may be less ferocious. Examples of pull and push factors are summarised in Table 1.5.

Table 1.5   Summary of key pull and push factors

Pull Factors	Push Factors
Expanding market opportunity which offers considerable levels of sales revenue. Attractive levels of entry – due to lower labour costs or political climate. Potentially higher levels of profit for investing shareholder funds.	Congestion of domestic market opportunities. Increasing costs of labour and raw materials (if applicable). Unfavourable political climate. Unfavourable profitability levels.

International markets operate on the premise that the world is a potential market or series of markets. Beginning with its own set of needs, each country and region will offer a different range of marketing opportunities and challenges. A recent survey undertaken by Professor Kashani identified a number of key challenges faced by European managers.[23] Kashani asked managers to peer into the future and indicate how the market environment of their business was likely to change. More specifically, respondents were asked to rate the degree to which a diverse set of developments would affect their organisations for the rest of the 1990s. So, based on Kashani findings, what does the rest of the decade hold for the world market? According to the general survey, three developments stand out as the most unsettling:

1. Consolidation of competition (fewer and fewer players).
2. Changing customers and their requirements.
3. Globalisation of markets and competition.

Significantly, fewer, but larger competitors appear at the top of the list. Kashani's survey shows that, for a wide cross-section of industries (including services), no other development comes even close in terms of its relative importance. This development is followed by the other two as having the most potential to have an impact on the future market environment. While consolidation of competition remains a top development of general concern, others tend to be more sector specific. In services, changing customers and their requirements, and globalisation of markets and competition were identified as developments with the most impact. Across the board, there is a certain commonality of likely developments in the market place: fewer and stronger competitors; ever-changing customers; and persistent pressure from changing technology and globalisation.

Screening cross-border opportunities

When considering ventures into cross-border markets, a mechanism is required to filter out unsuitable market investments. A well-planned market strategy cannot, on its own, guarantee success. This is dependent on how well the organisation manages those variables defined in Figure 1.3. Entry into a new market involves risk – risk is obviously far greater when a totally unknown environment is faced. At the same time though, many opportunities can (and do) arise which encourage companies to accept the identified risks and assist in justifying management's decision to allocate physical, human, and capital resources to a foreign market.

According to Chisnall, careful examination should be made of the likely impact on trade of political developments in countries envisaged as export markets.[24] Trade is more likely to develop where political stability is evident. Economic and political factors are often inextricably linked: devaluation; floating rates of exchange; political strategies aimed at maintaining balances of power; and so on – all these are sophisticated influences which make international trading complex, difficult, and exciting. Typical strategic questions relating to the market PEST are summarised in Table 1.6.

As discussed earlier, the Trio trading nations have focused attention, some of it harshly critical, on the influence of big business on the political, social, and economic environment of many countries. Multinational organisations have injected vast sums into technological development and have contributed to the growth of national economies not only directly, but also through the multiplier effect, which has generated substantial wealth. Critics of multinationals draw attention to the power they allegedly have to transfer production (and resulting services) across national borders – the economic and social consequences of such disinvestment is particularly disliked by the trade unions. But freedom is largely mythical as any radical business move of this nature would be in collision with government policies and would alienate public opinion. The multinational firms tend to develop highly sensitive political antennae which are even more vital in expanding economic and political structures such as the European Community. The liberalisation of industry and trade and the opportunities for employment which are embodied in the Treaty of Rome depend on the most effective use of the resources of several countries. Within member countries, national business firms, while retaining a considerable degree of managerial autonomy, frequently have the backing of the immense financial and other resources that are available to subsidiaries of multinational corporations. Political intervention in business affairs will emanate from national governments and increasingly be at a federal level in Europe. Commercial activities will take place within a far more complex and regulatory environment. Take, for example, the restrictions on advertising in Europe and within the European Community: the use of the word 'free' is legal in Germany only if the item is of small value; in France, it is illegal to advertise books on TV; Sweden requires that your advertisement spells out the total cost of your item – thereby hindering creative introductory offers. These restrictions are already in place, but the greater danger is that the European parliament could appear to be identifying the most severe restrictions in national laws and then adopting them for all member states. In 1990–91, Greece banned toy advertising on TV and, at that time, there was an expectation that such a ban would be extended to all European member states. Not too long ago, the European parliament considered banning all health claims by food advertisers, including the citations of medical experts and any mention of nutritional quality. Some would argue that we need to oppose European restrictions on marketing throughout the member states. That must also include restrictions here in the UK.

To quote Barrie Morgans, CEO IBM UK: 'in the late 1990s our innovative ability and the need to compete have never been more important.'

Table 1.6   Summary of market political, economic, societal, technical (PEST) considerations

Political Considerations Is the political climate stable? Does the government provide assistance to foreign companies? Is there a possibility that the present or future government will change attitudes to ventures by foreign companies within their borders? What ethical stance is adopted? What local powers do officials have?
Economic Considerations Is there economic growth? How is wealth distributed? What tax regime is operated? What are the rates of income, sales, and corporation tax? What are the labour costs for different levels of expertise? Do trade unions exist? If so, what is their role and structure?
Societal Considerations What are the society's attitudes, beliefs, and behavioural patterns, and are they changing? What types of socioeconomic groups exist? What are the habits of such groups? What attitudes are prevalent, e.g., democratic, religious? Is the society ready to embrace new ideas? What is the purchasing power (current v projected)?
Technological Considerations Is there sufficient expertise available for running a complex operation and for product and service development? Is there an adequate infrastructure system, e.g., transport, shipping, etc.? Are there any suitable sources of data and information? Are there good research facilities? What is the quality of higher education? What test markets are there? What would be the cost of undertaking R&D?

Michael Boskin, chairman of the Council of Economic Advisors to George Bush, is quoted as saying: 'It doesn't matter if a country makes potato chips or computer chips.'[25]

Under the classical theory of comparative advantage this was perhaps true, there is no role for the government in the location of industry, natural resources would dictate where production occurs, and everyone would benefit from the increased trade, or suffer only small losses. Rates of return are assumed to be equal wherever production occurs, as labour rates and capital rates equalise in the long run. This, of course, is not true. Just as manufacturing industry, with its lower rewards, will migrate to less-developed countries where labour is cheaper, we will see a segmentation within service industries. Pundits, in both the UK and the USA, bemoan the excessive growth of the service sector and the demise of the manufacturing industries which their countries have traditionally led, whilst in truth, the average wage for the service sector is lower than that for most manufacturing. In 1992, average American hourly wages were about $20.00 for those manufacturing beer and cigarettes, $6 for those manufacturing women's clothing, but only $5 for those working in cafes and restaurants.

But this is not a fair comparison, within the service sector there are those industries where high rewards are achieved, both by individuals and by firms. Where there is a reliance upon R&D and the expert application of knowledge, the rewards are far higher. Countries have to make investments in knowledge and skills, and make it easier for companies to make the same investments if they wish to attract them. Whilst an economy is buoyant and there is high discretionary disposable income, there will be a steady rise in the low-waged service sector as consumers demand more and more personal service. However, unless a country is able to maintain a base of companies who are paying superior returns to knowledge workers and encouraging the growth of that service sector, then that discretionary disposable income will be eroded and the future will be bleak. The higher the 'personal' content of the service, the less likelihood of it becoming truly global. Conversely, the higher the knowledge content, the easier it will be for that service industry to transcend national boundaries via enhanced communications technologies.

2 Defining Service Organisations

INTRODUCTION

Classifying service organisations

As discussed in Chapter 1, the tertiary, quaternary, and quinary sectors can broadly be broken down into two classifications of service organisations – commercial and consumer services – which are not mutually exclusive. *Commercial services* are provided to organisations to enable them to achieve their corporate objectives that, in the case of industrial and commercial companies, generally relate to profit targets. However, services are also consumed by nonprofit organisations because the entire economic system requires services of many kinds to keep it viable. According to Chisnal,[1] financial, insurance, legal, transport, security, and communications services typify those which are indispensable to organisations, whether profit motivated or not. Buyers in the public sector and in industry may differ in their prime motivation, but share the same responsibilities: to procure goods and services of use in their organisations as opposed to personal consumption. *Consumer services*, on the other hand, are those provided directly to satisfy personal needs. As noted earlier, there are many kinds. Some kinds of service are used for both personal and organisational benefit, although for different tasks. Despite these differences between services and goods, many companies exhibit both manufacturing (tangible) and (intangible) service characteristics (see Figure 2.1).

Services should be viewed along a continuum from complex to simple. At one extreme, there are, for example, providers of electrical power and at the other extreme, suppliers of fast-food. According to Lovelock,[2] the act of service can be examined across two dimensions: who or what is the direct recipient of the service and the tangible nature of the service. This gives birth to four classifications (see Figure 2.2):

1. Tangible actions directed to the customer, such as passenger transportation and personal care.

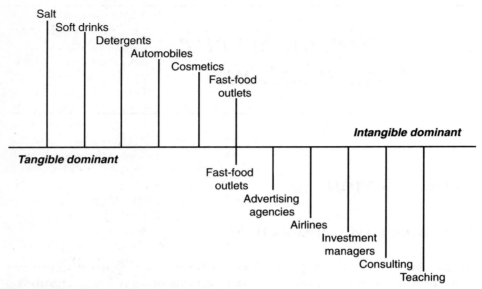

Figure 2.1   Scale of service tangibility

Direct Recipient of the Service

Nature of the Service Act Tangible actions	*Services directed at people's bodies* Health care Passenger transportation Beauty salons Exercise clinics Restaurants Haircutting	*Services directed at goods etc.* Freight transportation Industrial equipment repair & maintenance Janitorial services Laundry & dry cleaning Landscaping/lawn care Veterinary care
Nature of the Service Act Intangible actions	*Services directed at people's minds* Education Broadcasting Information services Theatres Museums	*Services directed at intangible assets* Banking Legal services Accounting Securities Insurance

Figure 2.2   Understanding the nature of the service act

Source: After Christopher H. Lovelock, 'Classifying Services to Gain Strategic Marketing Insights', *Journal of Marketing*, Summer 1983.

2. Tangible actions directed to the customer's possessions, such as laundry, cleaning, and janitorial services.
3. Intangible actions directed to the customer's intellect.
4. Intangible actions performed on the customer's assets, such as financial services.

Lovelock's classification system raises a few interesting questions about the traditional way services have been managed and delivered. For example, does the customer need to be present physically throughout the service, only to initiate or terminate the transaction, or not at all? If consumers of the service need to be present physically (e.g., rent a hotel room), then they must travel to the service facility to become part of the process, or the server must travel to the customer (e.g., ambulance service). This has significant implications for facility design and employee interaction because the impressions made will influence the perceptions of the service. In many services, the design of the service is determined by the person/persons who actually provide the service. The individual provider of the service must equate the service to the client's needs while providing the service. In some cases, the understanding required by the service supplier needs to be high. For service providers, such as fast-food restaurants and automatic teller machines, providing the service involves very little discretion.

It may be argued that an understanding of service is related to the degree of individual customised service. Such examples (see Table 2.1) include education which requires a high degree of personal judgement, but is not customised to the individual student. Health care also requires a high degree of judgement on the part of the doctor, but is customised to the patient as well. Public transport, on the other hand, is low on both measures. It is often stated that services should be situated as close as possible to the point of sale. Over the years, this has resulted in a proliferation of small, decentralised service units geographically dispersed across the customer-service region. It is not surprising that retail banks and building societies have embraced the automatic teller machine, and other forms of electronic and direct banking, to ease service intensity.

Thinking strategically and creatively about the nature of the service may identify more convenient forms of service delivery or identify a product that can substitute for the service. For example, video-tapes of educational programmes and compact-disc recordings of concerts represent a convenient alternative for physical attendance, and they also serve as permanent library records of the events. Research undertaken by Hollins and Hollins identified 13 factors which help keep a service dynamic.[3] They are:

1. Adequate time allowed for design.
2. Customers willing to change.
3. Change in service design specification.
4. Flexible machinery, subcontracting features of the service.
5. Many small procedures.
6. Increasing number of producers.
7. Wide, effective market research (innovation seeking, market pull).
8. Technology change.
9. Ill-defined market infrastructure or infrastructure incapable of accepting a new design.

10. Changing external environment (legislation, economic climate, resources).
11. No conformity of standards.
12. Open management design guidelines.
13. Organisations seeking new concepts.

Table 2.1   Customisation and judgement in service delivery

Extent to which customer contact personnel exercise judgement in meeting individual customer needs	Extent to which service characteristics are customised	
	High	**Low**
High	Legal services Health care/surgery Architectural design Executive search firm Real-estate agency Taxi service Beautician Plumber Education (tutorials)	Education (large classes) Preventative health care
Low	Telephone service Hotel services Retail banking (excluding major loans) Good restaurants	Public transport Routine appliance repair Fast-food restaurants Movie theatres Spectator sports

Source: Reproduced from C. B. Lovelock, *Services Marketing,* Prentice Hall, Englewood Cliffs, NJ 1984.

Defining service characteristics

The argument centring on the differences between goods and services began with an attempt to define services (Regan[4]) and the resulting question of how we classify them. The debate over the last 30 years led to the identification of four characteristics that are now commonly cited as the components that distinguish services from goods: intangibility, inseparability, heterogeneity, and perishability.

Intangibility

Services have been traditionally described as intangible, having close relationships with consumers. Judd has defined services as: 'market transactions where the object of the exchange is something other than the transfer of a tangible commodity'.[5] Such transactions involve the provision of transport systems, cash security, and transfer (banks), public utility undertakings, tourism, legal, management consulting, fast food, and so on. In academe, the meaning of service is described from the perspective of organisation dynamics, marketing, and operations. In the business world, excellent descriptions of the meaning of service are to be found in Zemke, Desatnick, and in Kotler.[6] These recent works share the common focus of describing the unique attributes of services and service organisations. They have begun to clarify the meaning of service as it is provided by many Pan-European organisations. Kotler, for example, states that:

> A service is any activity or benefits that one party can give to another that is essentially intangible and does not result in the ownership of anything. Its production may or may not be tied to a physical product.

Intangibility implies that a service is experienced; it is rendered; physical ownership cannot occur. Thus the conceptual boundaries of marketing (and operations) must be expanded to accommodate this property of services. Scholars such as Zeithamel[7] have identified weaknesses in the literature as needing adjustment to achieve this accommodation. One such adjustment arises from the consumer's difficulty in evaluating an intangible service offering. Service strategies must therefore make the offering more tangible, an opposite approach to the one commonly used for physical goods.

The encouragement of the provider-client relationship becomes increasingly important to service companies, as interaction is very often the only impression customers retain of the company. Gronroos has stated that the consumer interaction process must be carefully managed to lessen the effect of intangibility.[8] By controlling the tangible aspect – the delivery phase of the service in which the customer is involved – a service company will help ensure the client retains a favourable impression of the service and of the provider. This increases the probability of developing a lasting relationship and repeat business.

Inseparability

Inseparability of production from consumption is another key characteristic of service. Again Kotler offers a statement:

> A service is inseparable from the source that provides it. Its very act of being created requires the source, whether person or machine, to be present. In other words, production and consumption occur simultaneously with services. This is in contrast to a product which exists whether or not its source is present.[9]

As stated, service organisations tend to be organised differently from manufacturing due to a greater degree of interaction between the service provider and the customer. This interaction derives from the fact that *production and consumption are more likely to occur simultaneously* with services than with goods The peculiarity of inseparability in services has led to the identification of several problems that arise when formulating strategic plans. Very often, a service is first sold, then produced and consumed. This is different from the process that occurs with goods, which are usually produced first, then sold and consumed. Consequently, means must be devised to market the service successfully before the consumer has had any experience of it. Organisations (or service providers) must consider that in service sales and production personnel are one and the same, and that the customer of a service may also participate in its production.

Customer contact occurs because service operations typically depend on the customer to make a contribution in the form of behaviour or information – the raw material to be transformed to service output. The consumer is required to take action when depositing money in a bank (a form of behaviour), for example, and an airline requires information in order to fly its passengers. For these reasons, service customers have been called (or referred to as) 'partial employees' of the firm by Bowen.[10] The customer's participation in the production of the service, then, adds to the already greater labour intensity of service firms as compared to the capital intensiveness of manufacturing firms. When customers become partial employees, it is necessary to manage their performance. Performance is viewed as a function of a person's motivation, role clarity, and ability; these determinants hold for both employees and customers. That is, customers can be expected to perform in their roles as partial employees to the extent that they obtain rewards through their efforts (motivation), they understand the nature of the task (role clarity), and they have the necessary competencies (ability).

If customers are involved in the product-design stage, for example, the company needs to demonstrate that customers obtain higher quality or lower cost from exerting this effort (motivation), clarify the terms and conditions defining the customer's inclusion in the design process (role clarity), and select or train customers to participate effectively in product design (ability). As a consequence, there is a need for a high level of attention to the service encounter and for internally oriented, strategic service planning or internal marketing. Through these steps, greater importance is placed on controlling the service encounter and on the development of high standards of service quality (an aspect we will return to later in Service Design); practices that have also been identified as important in overcoming the intangibility problem.

Heterogeneity

Services are often described as acts or experiences directed toward consumers; products are objects that are possessed. Moreover, services tend to be more nonstandardised, heterogeneous, and customised at the point of sale than products. Zeithamel et al. have provided a definition of heterogeneity that reflects the interpretation put forth by most writers on the subject:

> Heterogeneity concerns the potential for high variability in the performance of services. The quality and essence of a service can vary from producer to producer, from customer to customer, and from day to day. Heterogeneity in service output is a particular problem for labour intensive services.[11]

This lack of homogeneity in services creates difficulties throughout the entire product-development process, including the design, production, and service delivery stages. This makes it harder to control the output of service organisations, and thus to control the output of those producing tangible products. As with intangibility and inseparability, one approach to minimising the effect of heterogeneity is by controlling the service encounter. One means of control consists in adopting uniform production procedures and increasing the amount of automation. This approach has been repeatedly advocated by Levitt[12] as a means of reducing the degree of variability in each service offering, thus gaining more consistency.

Perishability

Services have been described as being perishable in nature (unstockable), that is, they cannot be stored for use at a latter date. They therefore must be consumed when produced or be lost. For example, a hotel cannot store a room. If it is not rented, then the lost revenue is forfeited forever. Rushton and Carson have summed up the impotence of perishability:

> Services cannot be produced before required and then stored to meet demand. If a service is not used when available, then the service capacity is wasted.[13]

Without the ability to stockpile and achieve the flexibility toward fluctuating demand that physical goods allow, service organisations are more seriously affected by changes in demand. For example, peak loads, excess demand,

and scheduling difficulties need to be addressed within strategies for services. Sasser suggests that demand and capacity be managed to better meet the needs of service organisations.[14] Possibilities include using peak-period and off-peak pricing, developing non-peak demand, developing complementary services, creating reservation systems, and using part-time employees. Matching supply to demand is an important aspect of developing strategies for services. A word of caution is, however, offered by Nicouland,[15] who points out that in an international global economy, these techniques cannot always be applied, due to the legal and cultural differences that might not allow some procedures to be used.

Distribution channels are also affected by the perishable nature of services. This has been cited as one of the reasons for the development of short distribution channels in service industries. However, not all service channels are short – indeed, it could be argued that service-channel management is necessary, although approaches are required that differ from traditional channel management. The inability of many service firms to develop effective barriers to entry from competition, because of the difficulty in obtaining patents, has also been attributed to the perishability of services.

Service design

According to Voss et al. a service can be split into two parts, the physical items and the service's intangible elements.[16] The physical items can be directly specified in terms of attributes such as sound or taste, or in terms of variables, such as size and volume. Service elements can be subdivided into service attributes (Table 2.2) which are soft measures, and service variables which are hard measures. It is errors between elements, especially where they make up a complicated process, which can give rise to service performance issues. Schonberger identifies the variation pile-up problem,[17] where errors between stages in a process may fit within the tolerances defined for that stage, but when added up, create a final offering which is outside the tolerance. Whilst it is easier to set and measure standards within the manufacturing processes, techniques are now becoming available to allow similar functions to be measured in service industries, for example, key performance indicators or activity-based service levels.

Service design assumes a significant importance in the pursuit of quality. According to Shoestack in Czepiel et al.:

> Every detail of the overall design is important and can affect the service encounter. I have seen corporate reputations undone by envelopes containing confidential customer data that popped open in transit due to inferior glue.[18]

An alternative mechanism for defining the components required by the service-design process is the design core methodology developed by Hollins and Hollins. The methodology considers not just the elements which make up a service, but the environment within which it will operate. According to Schonberger: 'quality of service was traditionally considered too hard to pin down, was poorly defined and thought to be manageable more by art than by principles.' This perception is changing. Zeithamel et al. have examined and applied mechanisms which can be used to measure service performance.[19] Figure 2.3 summarises the primary factors in their model. As can be seen, five gaps can exist between the perceptions of the parties involved. Gap five is the combination of gaps one to four and represents the overall differences between the perceptions of the service provider and the customer. The remainder of the gaps are described in detail.

Gap one

This occurs as a result of service providers not knowing their customers' requirements. The key contributing factors to the existence of this gap are lack of marketing research orientation, that is, the extent to which managers make efforts to understand customers' needs and expectations through formal and informal information gathering activities . This includes:

- Insufficient market research.
- Inadequate use of research findings.
- Lack of interaction between management and customers.
- Inadequate upward communications, that is, the extent to which top management seeks, stimulates, and facilitates the flow of information from employees at lower levels.
- Too many levels of management, that is the number of managerial levels between the topmost and bottom-most positions in the organisation.

Strategies for resolving the problems created by these factors include using information from customer complaints, researching customers desires in similar industries, research on intermediate customers, key client studies, customer panels, transaction-based studies, and comprehensive customer expectation studies. The discrepancy between managers' perceptions of customers' expectations and actual specifications they establish for service delivery defines Gap two, and is wide in many organisations.

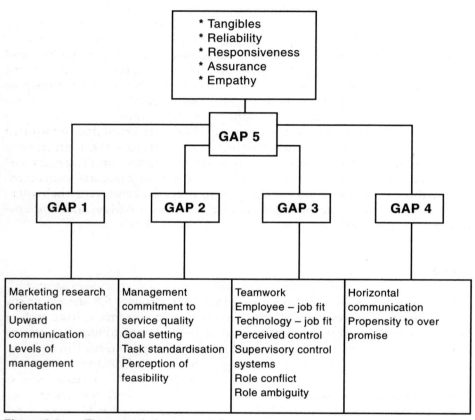

Figure 2.3 The extended gaps model

Gap two

The key factors contributing to the existence of Gap two are:

- Inadequate commitment to service quality, that is, the extent to which management views service quality as a key strategic goal.
- Perception of feasibility, that is, the extent to which managers believe customer expectations are to be met.
- Task standardisation, that is, the extent to which hard and soft technology are used to standardise service tasks.
- Goal setting, that is, the extent to which service quality goals are based on customer standards and expectations rather then company standards.

Resolution of the first two factors requires senior management commitment to provide necessary resources and leadership in promoting and driving the necessary change. Issues of change management and leadership are covered more fully below. The second two factors should be a natural part of the change process frequently required to solve the first two. On their own, they can and should be developed as part of the service provision process.

Gap three

A service-performance gap may exist between service specification and actual delivery. This is Gap three of the model and arises for the following reasons stated below. Solutions to these issues include training, both technical and interpersonal, feedback on performance, defining roles, generating standards, applicable recruitment, and remuneration policies.

- Role ambiguity, that is, the extent to which employees are uncertain about what managers and supervisors expect from them and how to satisfy those expectations.
- Role conflict, that is, the extent to which employees perceive that they cannot satisfy all the demands of all individuals (both internal and external customers) they must serve.
- Poor employee job fit, that is, the match between skills of employees and their jobs.
- Poor technology-job fit, that is, the appropriateness of the tools and technology that employees use to perform their jobs.

- Inappropriate supervisory control system, that is, the appropriateness of the evaluation and reward systems in the company.
- Lack of perceived control, that is, the extent to which employees perceive that they can act flexibly in problem situations encountered in providing services.
- Lack of teamwork, that is, the extent to which employees and managers pull together towards a common goal.

Gap four

The final gap results from the difference between what a company promises and what it actually delivers. Factors affecting Gap four include: horizontal communications (communication occurring both within and between different departments) and a propensity to over promise. The first factor is influenced by corporate culture and forms a significant part of any strategic programme. The second factor requires a clear understanding of what is possible on the part of people who deal directly with the customer. As Peters identifies,[20] it is better to under promise and then deliver a better service than the other way round. Accurate communications are therefore vital to avoid misrepresentation or over promising, and to educate the customer about the overall aspects of the service provided and effort involved. Some care must be taken in the methods used to measure customer satisfaction. Peters offers a warning about five seemingly innocuous issues which can cause major problems if overlooked:

1. A determination that a customer complaint is not symptomatic of a larger problem.
2. Insistence that an issue is subjective rather then objective and therefore not measurable .
3. Measuring results on the basis of what is achieved rather then what is not achieved.
4. Using averages rather then worst case to measure performance.
5. Always measure performance systematically.

The importance of leadership is heavily emphasised in virtually all texts on strategy and associated subjects, such as quality and service design. Teboul considers that a low level of senior management involvement, interdepartmental barriers, and a cumbersome chain of command will result in piecemeal quality improvements.[21] As McManus identifies,[22] change cannot be successfully implemented without:

1. An awareness of the customer's requirements at all levels in the organisation.
2. Continuous improvement as the only way forward.
3. A clear vision of the direction to follow.
4. Top management will and determination.

Zeithamel et al. consider it important that top management exercise service leadership by replacing incomplete, incorrect, superficial criteria with leadership-based criteria and a willingness to promote the right people to middle-management positions. Smithy emphasises the dual aspect.[23] Firstly, management is seen as catalytic with power to improve key business processes, to set policy and objectives, and a style which other staff adopt. Secondly, leadership is required to set clear direction: that is, to set priorities and apply disciplined, organised improvement; to lead by example and set standards; to remove waste and excess that inhibits fast responses to customers' needs; and to create an environment where staff feel encouraged to improve and are given space to do so. Pugh defines an effective manager as someone who: anticipates the need for change; diagnoses the nature of the change required and carefully considers the options available; manages the change over a period of time so that it is both effective and accepted.[24] Johnson takes this one stage further by outlining that effective change managers:[25]

●   Make clear the broad objectives of, and key issues relating to, the required change.
●   Explicitly contrast the old and new, to highlight tacit assumptions about the old.
●   Dramatise change to aid understanding at an emotional as well as an intellectual level.
●   Effect substantial changes in power structures.
●   Demonstrate change by their own actions, through changes in operating procedures and routines, and through top management's visible association with change.
●   Employ symbolic mechanisms to dramatise the need for ardent change.
●   Make sure that key employees at all levels are involved in change decisions and implementation.

The last factor is reflected by Pettigrew and Whipp who consider that leading change involves action by people at every level of the business.[26] Two factors which contribute to two different gaps in the service model developed by Zeithamel et al. relate to organisational structure. They argue that a flat hierarchy, broad-span organisation built on a network basis is more flexible at handling the changes required by customer orientation and quality. They consider it necessary to eliminate levels of management thus allowing the remaining managers to be closer to customers, and to understand their needs and expectations. The type of organisation best matching the above criteria is akin to the organic form described in Dawson where people are essentially cosmopolitan,[27] working in an environment where communication is both lateral as well as vertical, with task definition from network sources and with control which allows considerable individual flexibility and initiative.

KNOWING YOUR CUSTOMERS AND MARKETS

The majority of marketing literature supports intangibility, inseparability, heterogeneity, and perishability – the four distinguishing properties of services – and maintain the need to market them differently to goods. What is 'market'? From some points of view, talking about markets is dangerous because it encourages us to take an intellectual stance towards customers, who themselves respond individually and emotionally. Some strategists see markets as a sociological abstraction. Their purpose is to help us (the consumers) to think about something which is otherwise too complex to imagine. The essence of the service marketing concept is to be responsive to customers and their many needs; this cannot happen unless quite a lot is known about customers (both present and prospective). It is 35 years since Marion Harper wrote: 'To manage a business well is to manage its future: and to manage the future is to manage information.'[28] This statement is certainly true today – more so than ever for those businesses engaged in the provision of services. Information on consumer needs and the motives of individual buyers (or groups of buyers) is crucial. Market research can provide useful data and information on purchasing habits. Without valid and reliable data, the organisation cannot be successful. Through systematic marketing research, present and emergent needs will be identified, analysed, and evaluated. Such an evaluation must cover:

1. Strategic situations and possibilities

- The purpose of the service?
- What needs does the customer currently have that are not being adequately met by available services?
- Potential competition (who are the market competitors)?
- Which markets will it serve?
- Will it replace an existing market?
- What demand will there be for the service?
- How will the service be provided?
- What will be the critical performance criteria (i.e., how will market success be measured)?

2. Purchaser situations and possibilities

- Who will be the purchasers?
- When will they purchase (e.g., time of day, seasonality of the service, etc.)?
- How and where will purchasers procure the service?
- What components of service will they purchase?
- How often will they purchase the service?
- What innovations will alter customers' buying habits?

These questions cover both quantitative and qualitative assessments related to specific markets considered to be of value to the service provider. Table 2.3 summarises the various purchaser situations. The interpretation of market needs carries intense responsibility: it demands, among other managerial qualities, the ability to assess risk and to cope with uncertainty. Defining exactly what the service is to be will enable the organisation to state what the competition is and on what market the service is to be focused. It is considered advantageous for service organisations to identify key purchaser groups and devise strategies to win business by offering customised services. Research and information databases should enable profiles to be developed of customer buying patterns, and so on. For example in the UK, banks and building societies typically have two types of customers – borrowers and lenders. In recent times, banks and other financial institutions have put together strategies designed to satisfy a range of low-volume customer needs, whilst keeping the cost of servicing them at acceptable levels.

However, the evidence from a large European bank shows what can happen when customised products are offered in the mass market or when poorly planned, but high quality products are introduced to a market that may not even recognise or appreciate their expensive features. A detailed analysis of the bank's economics uncovered differences in the cost-revenue structures of two important market segments: small individual customers accounted for 6 per cent of all revenues and 14 per cent of all costs, while small commercial customers accounted for 39 per cent of all revenue and only 15 per cent of all costs, Rosier.[29] Another example involves the USA company Sears and Roebuck, which became a financial services giant by exploiting its customer information database. Unlike American Express, Sears and Roebuck was in a position to use its credit card and customer buying pattern database for the delivery of new services. It has had a long presence in the insurance industry with its Allstate division and, more recently, it has had companies, such as Dean Witter and Coldwell Bankers, to establish itself as a one-stop financial services centre with retail hours.

Davis refers to such use of information as *informationalising* – that is, figuring out what information might add value to an existing service and providing it for a price.[30] To emphasise his point, Davis discusses the case of Rosenbluth Travel – a small company that has grown into an electronically facilitated micro-market organisation that is both centralised and decentralised. Over the past decade, the company's annual sales have grown from $40 million to more than $1 billion. Based in Philadelphia, this family-owned business now has more than 300 offices in the US, plus associates (through Rosenbluth International Alliance) in 30 agencies in 33 countries, adding over 1000 global locations. The alliance structure allows flexibility to gear up or down, yet promotes a spirit of partnership that not only encourages high service performance, but provides corporate identity and shared rewards.

At the beginning of Rosenbluth's expansion the founder (Hal Rosenbluth) spent a number of years at the sharp end gaining a bottom-up perspective on his business. His experiences led him to believe that the public was confused. No one knew what air fares were available. That's when the founder realised that Rosenbluth was in the information business, not just the travel business. Rosenbluth focused on the market in corporate travel and came up with such innovations as listing flights by fare instead of the standard listing by time and departure, which required an agent to look across different screens and make decisions based on whatever fares appeared. Rosenbluth also introduced a number of further innovations which included:

- A database of client information that allowed travel clerks to personalise services.
- An electronic transactions tracing system that compiled a wide range of travel data, letting customers analyse their travel patterns more closely.
- Guaranteed savings programmes through partnerships with corporate clients (rather than competition based directly on price, which was the industry norm).

The US travel industry is going through radical change as consumers look towards travel agencies to provide dollar value as intermediaries in the service supply chain. Changes within the air travel industry are forcing travel management companies to look at alternative means of supplying services such as travel tickets. In the past, airlines have looked to distributors to be as low-cost as possible. Travellers, however, look to travel agencies to provide a value-adding service. According to Hal Rosenbluth, airlines are also looking to continue to eliminate cost inefficiencies in the operations and marketing of their products.

The widespread growth of ticketless travel, Internet booking sites, and stiff commission gaps in the USA appear to parallel the airlines continued attempt at cutting operating costs. Ticketless travel (or *electronic tickets)* involves the traveller obtaining a confirmation number and an itinerary, while the actual ticketing information remains in the airline computer system. Clients purchase electronic tickets as they normally should paper tickets – through their travel agent or with an airline over the phone. With electronic ticketing, however, tickets do not have to come back to an originating office if they need to be changed and reissued. Instead, travel agents' or airlines' reservation booking staff make all changes in the airlines' computer systems and passengers can check in with their original confirmation numbers. On the day of travel, electronic ticket purchasers simply show a photo ID at the airport to board their aeroplane.

Rosenbluth believes that armed with the right technology travel companies are uniquely positioned to gather information on the entire travel experience. They have the ability to gain an intimate knowledge of the consumer. They are not, like airlines, limited to only a segment of the traveller's profile. Current technology, in the form of proprietary databases and information-management systems, enables a full understanding of the consumer's needs.

The use of electronic commerce to target customers at a micro-market level is one key aspect of service strategy, for example, bar coding and checkout scanner technology creates a wealth of consumer purchasing information that can be used to target customers with accuracy. New technology (such as electronic commerce) is playing a significant role in the way services are marketed. By opening up electronic commercial customisation, new technologies like the Internet and Intranets have shifted the way the business operates, creating new markets, blurring sector definitions, and redefining the meaning of products. In the USA and Europe, deregulation of telecommunications markets will allow telephone companies to deliver everything from telephone and mobile services to Internet access and video on demand. Changes in information delivery mechanisms will also lead to changes in content in order to exploit fully the potential of these new services (for example, the global Internet market is now worth an estimated £460 million). Convergence of broadcasting, telecommunications, and computing markets will enable electronic commerce to flourish on a global scale.

The USA Direct Marketing Association (DMA) estimates that goods and services worth $600 billion yearly will be sold over the telephone by the year 2000. It may be argued that the future lies in a micro market, where the unique selling point for companies is the individuality of the company's product for each customer. This concept is enabled by advances in information technology, where companies across the world can now contact consumers individually and market their services on that level. Retailers, banks, legal services, and hotels are customising down to the individual and this is having a fundamental impact on marketing, advertising, and distribution. The growth of these new technologies cannot be ignored. The future will not just be about more sophisticated products and services, it will be about new markets, new customer expectations, and fundamentally new ways of working. Successful service organisations of the future will be those that identify emerging business opportunities, apply enabling technologies effectively before their competitors do, and be first into a first-mover-advantage position. A lot of that advantage is tied into future developments in telecommunications and chip technology – for example, SMART cards could pave the way for a whole new range of services, such as pay-as-you-view TV, currently being looked at by the electronic giants. Another big growth area for the SMART card is coin-operated machines, from parking machines to arcade games, and may eventually replace high-street cash machines.

Table 2.3   Characteristics of purchasing situation

Type of Purchasing Situation	Newness of the Problem	Experienced Information Requirements	Consideration of Purchasing Alternatives
New purchase	Problem or requirement is new to purchasing decision makers	Past experience is not considered relevant, much information required to make purchasing decision	Purchasing alternatives not known and solutions considered are new
Modified purchase	Problem or requirement is not new, but is somewhat different from previous situations	Past experience relevant, but more information required before making decision	New alternative solutions, known or unknown, will be considered before making purchasing decision
Straight purchase	Continuing or recurring requirement	Past experience considered sufficient to make purchasing decision, with little or no additional information required	Alternative solutions may be known but are not given serious consideration

Source: Adapted after M. Cameron, A. Rushton and D. Carson, *Marketing*, Penguin 1988, p. 72.

The marketing mix within services

The extent of marketing and its associated activities is defined by a concept called the *marketing mix*. An organisation's marketing mix consists of all the variables that are controllable by the organisation in communicating with and satisfying its target market.

Once a particular customer group (or market) has been identified and analysed, the organisation can begin to direct its activities to profitably satisfying the market needs. Although there are many variables involved in marketing services, research would seem to indicate that such variables can be classified into seven strategic elements:

1. Product (re service)
2. Price
3. Place (location add distribution)
4. Promotion
5. Physical evidence (symbols, e.g., buildings, uniforms, etc.)
6. Participation (employees and customers)
7. Process (procedures, etc.)

The seven Ps

Product (re service)

The product component of the marketing mix for services refers to the variety and depth of services offered within a particular area of service operation. It is concerned with the matching of services to target markets. The quality of service to be supplied is determined by market demand and competitive positioning. The size of the potential opportunity (i.e., market) for new services will depend upon the degree of domestic and global demand. As we have already discussed in relation to Rosenbluth Travel, innovation plays a significant part in exploiting service opportunity. The size of a potential opportunity produced by a particular market is clearly an important consideration, as is the likelihood of a sustained overall growth of market revenue. Service providers should seek out those markets which offer the greatest opportunity, knowing that if they can become established in such markets, significant revenues can be expected. Like products, successful services pass through four distinct stages, namely: *Service Development, Growth, Maturity,* and *Saturation and Decline.* The service life cycle identifies and explains the stages that a service goes through from the moment it is launched to the moment it is withdrawn. Understanding the pattern and movement of the cycle can help identify important marketing environmental factors that organisations need to be aware of before they decide upon an effective course of action.

Service development: this is when a new service is first brought to the market, before there is a proven demand for it, and often before it has been fully established in all aspects. Revenue is low and sales creep along at a slow pace.

Service growth: demand for the service begins to accelerate and the size of the total market expands rapidly. The emphasis is on market penetration and promotional campaigns to market the service.

Service maturity: demand levels off and grows, for the most part, only at the replacement and new family-formation rate. Subtle differences between competing services become significant to consumers, who have more knowledge of the variety available in the market.

Service saturation: there are now many competitors in the market, revenues have further declined and their is little consumer growth. It is time to consider new service markets and strategies.

Service decline: the service begins to lose consumer appeal and revenue drifts downward, the service is in decline. The provider may have to accept the gradual decline and ultimate withdrawal of the service from the market. When decline occurs, the consequences are traumatic. Major losses of market share occur, profits are marginal at best, and a fatal inability to compete in the market becomes apparent to investors and competitors. Figure 2.4 highlights some of the activities that become important during the five stages.

By adopting different strategies at different stages of the service life cycle, and by anticipating shifts from one stage to the next, service providers can maintain adequate profit levels. Difficulties arise in anticipating future developments. There is evidence to suggest that the length of the life cycle is contracting (or accelerating depending on your point of reference). The time between the introduction of a service concept and the point at which it reaches maturity is growing progressively shorter. The life cycle is not the only facet of economic activity that is accelerating. Futurists such as Toffler, Kahn, and others have documented the accelerating pace of change in American society.[31]

Area of Concern	Stages of the Service Life Cycle			
	Development	*Growth*	*Maturity*	*Decline*
Number of Competitors	Very few	Average	Many direct competitors	Many indirect competitors
Rate of Sales Growth	Very rapid	Rapid	Moderate to slow	Slow
Level of Profitability	Low to moderate	High	Moderate	Very low
Duration of new Development	1–2 yrs	2– 3yrs	Indefinite	Indefinite

Figure 2.4   Activities within the service life cycle

Price

Price may be defined as the *exchange value of a good* or *service*. The value of a service, then, is *what it can be exchanged for in the marketplace*. The ancient Greek philosophers recognised the importance of price to the functioning of the economic system. Early written accounts refer to attempts to develop a fair or just price. The limited understanding of time, place, and possession utilities, however, foiled such efforts. At the end of the 1990s, price serves as a means of regulating economic activity. The employment of any or all of the factors of production and service (labour, land, capital, and entrepreneurship) is dependent upon the prices received by each. For an individual firm or organisation, prices represent the revenue to be received. Prices therefore influence a company's profit as well as its employment of labour and capital. The basic economic model in classical and neoclassical economics states that demand falls in response to prices rising. At the simplest level, a choice must therefore be made – is it cheapness and volume that is being sought in the market? Alternatively, is it higher price exclusivity? Neither system has intrinsic advantages over the other. Both are equal in their power to create profits. If a product or service is to be highly profitable in one of the few high-cost markets it must be unusually glamorous and select (e.g., the fashion industry). The real challenge is to get the best of both worlds by selling in volume at high prices with low production costs as well.

In the preparation of policy and strategy, pricing should be seen as a key component and not merely in a subservient role. With this aspect in mind, some specific pricing objectives may relate to drawing quick cash returns without profit maximisation, acute pricing may be pursued in order to enhance market share, prices may be set to achieve minimum levels of return on investment, there may be instances where unusually high prices can be charged because of scarcity, product patents, technological supremacy, and so on. As pricing is a key enabler in achieving market share, every effort should be made to identify those influences which impact on the service and the resultant price offered (Table 2.4).

Market and price elasticity

In some markets, cheapness is indisputably the main purchasing determinant and nothing cam be achieved without a competitive price. The insurance and mortgage sectors provide obvious examples. The marginally cheaper product will immediately outsell the others. This is because the service product is uniformly strong at any one price band. The main appeal on the other hand of a Rolex watch has nothing whatsoever to do with its cheapness. Quite the opposite, in fact. It stems from its intrinsic value as a perceived high-value commodity. Further, it is beyond most people's reach, the owner may fulfil personal desire and gain valuable reputation. Price thus depends on the way that the customer perceives the product or service. It is not an objective commodity or a simple question of adding a percentage mark-up to costs. Marketing, as we have established, will influence the customer's point of view. In contrast, price elasticity is the measure by which the relationship between demand and price are measured. An elastic market responds readily to price changes, but an inelastic one does not. A breakdown of the degree of elasticity present in any particular market is consequently an essential component in any pricing equation (Figure 2.5).

Pricing strategies

As one would expect, pricing strategies vary from organisation to organisation. In fact, multiple objectives are common among many organisations. Pricing strategies can broadly be classified into three groups, namely:

1. Profitability objectives: these include profit maximisation and revenue goals.
2. Volume objectives: these include sales (or service) maximisation or market-share goals.
3. Social and Ethical: these include *status quo* objectives and prestige goals.

An alternative division of these strategies is based on the premise that pricing strategies do not represent a specific price, they simply identify the type of approach which may be necessary to achieve a defined market share. As each policy is considered, you are encouraged to consider carefully the situations which favour the application of that policy. Such policies include:

- **Market-oriented policies**: policies determined as a result of market conditions and or expectations.
- **Cost-oriented policies**: related to the integral cost of the service.
- **Competitor-based policies**: revolve around competition between purchasers, competition between providers, or both. The prices charged by competitors are closely monitored and the market is divided into categories that reflect the levels of quality, service, or reputation that are provided. Each segment has a price leader which determines the current going rate. If the price changes in either direction, the rest of the market is likely to follow suit. The following subsidiary policies are involved:
    - **competitive pricing**: a direct attempt is made to compete with the market leader by demonstrating superior product and service quality, a lower price, or attractive discounts.
    - **penetration pricing**: sales volume is boosted by undercutting competitor's prices by significant margins.
    - **discount pricing**: prices are set at deliberately high levels, but large discounts are then offered.

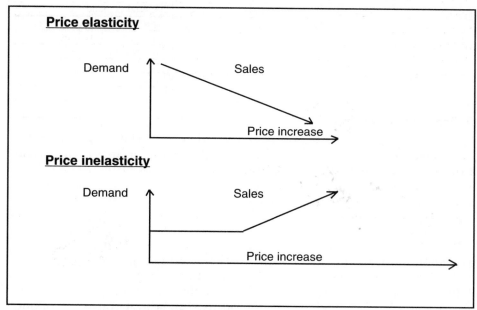

Figure 2.5   Price elasticity and inelasticity

If prices can be determined individually, then every transaction is, in principle, undertaken in a distinct economic market; and if the unit value of transactions is sufficiently large, there is a real sense in which this is true. Although it is generally true that the ability to segment markets enhances profits, enforced segmentation of this magnitude does not. In fact, PIMS evidence shows unit size of sale as one of the strongest negative influences on structure and on profitability. The advantage of distinguishing many distinct economic markets is mostly (although not necessarily) offset if the firm faces only a single monopolistic customer in each one.

Discrimination between groups on bases other then geography generally encounters customer resistance and practical difficulties. A few service industries offer lower prices to the old or to the young. In some industries, ingenious ways of achieving group discrimination are available – the airline requirements of a Saturday-night stay is an elegant, if fallible, means of distinguishing business from leisure travellers.[32]

Table 2.4   Internal and external influences on pricing strategy

Market Factor	Internal Influences	External Influences
Nature and extent of demand	Business objectives	Customer expectations
Competitors' activities	The other six Ps	Potential demand
Costs of promotion	Resources (e.g., capital)	Reputation of the company
Business policy	Attitudes of management	Competitors' activities
Service life-cycle	Current cost structure	Competitor knowledge
		Legal constraints
		The economy
		Taxes
		Incomes

Some pricing strategies are not related to either profitability or revenue volumes. Nevertheless, these other objectives are important in the pricing behaviour of many firms. They include:

1. Social and ethical considerations
2. *Status quo* objectives
3. Prestige goals

Social and ethical considerations: are the determining factors in particular situations. For example, in some parts of Europe, the USA, and Canada some medical practitioners used a sliding scale based on relative income to set patient fees. Essentially, these doctors used an ethical evaluation of one's ability to pay as an input to their pricing formula. Social and ethical considerations are playing a larger role in the pricing policies of companies.

Status quo objectives: are the foundation of the pricing philosophy for many enterprises. The philosophy usually stems from a desire to minimise competitive pricing. In general, the maintenance of stable prices allows the firm to concentrate its efforts in other areas of marketing, such as product improvement or advertising. For a long time McDonald's, with its 15 000 restaurants worldwide serving 28 million customers daily and its annual sales of £16 billion, de-emphasised price competition in their advertisements in favour of developing product features that differentiated their products from the competition.

Prestige goals: are another type of objective, separate from either profitability or sales volume. The desire for a prestige image spells out the pricing policies of some firms. Comparatively high prices are established so as to maintain a prestige and quality image with consumers.

Market share

Gaining market share is a common pricing objective in American business. A firm's strategy must adapt to its market share position in a particular market.[33] Some organisations with high market shares may prefer at times to reduce their share because of external influences such as government action in the area of monopoly control. There are several reasons why organisations adopt a type of market-share objective:

1. Market-share objectives are more readily measurable than other aims and therefore can be used as an evaluative mechanism.

2. Market-share goals may also provide the firm with a preferred competitive positioning within an industry, an established market for a service may make them less sensitive to competitive efforts.

3. Increased sales may result in more profit. The extensive Profit Impact of Market Strategies (PIMS) project, conducted by the Marketing Science Institute, found a link between market share and profitability.[34] Pretax profits as a percentage of sales were 3.42 per cent for firms with 10–20 per cent of market shares, but they climbed steadily to 13.16 for firms with market shares of over 40 per cent.

The PIMS research findings are considered controversial. PIMS research has consistently reported that a large market share should lead to greater profitability. The underlying reason seems to be that a high market share results in low unit costs because of economies of scale. However, several studies have found that a high market share does not always lead to profitability. Firms selling products of high quality relative to the competition have been found to be very profitable, even though they do not have a large market share.[35] PIMS researchers respond, however, that the single most important factor affecting a business unit's performance relative to that of its competitors' is the quality of its products or services. They also state that market leaders tend to have products of higher quality relative to those of their competitors and market followers.[36]

Place (location and distribution)

At a macro level, the USA, the UK, and Switzerland are the nations with the greatest number of international positions in service industries.[37] Geographical location plays a significant role in (some) service industries. For example, Singapore's strength in ship repair benefits from its location on shipping lanes between the Middle East and Japan. Switzerland's position astride Europe's trade routes is part of its success in a number of trade-related services. Akin to a nation's location is its time zone. London's status as a financial and trading centre is aided by its location between America and Asia, which means that personnel based in London can communicate with both regions during a normal weekday. The USA, the UK, and Switzerland are the nations with the greatest number of international positions in service industries.

Location and distribution are key aspects of the service supply chain. The role of location is often a misunderstood characteristic. The importance of different distribution channels and the presence or absence of types of intermediaries varies enormously between nations. As a result, for many nations distribution channels need to be customised to ensure products and services are made available to a wide variety of consumers. At a micro level, services may be transportable, location-bound, or a combination of both depending on the degree to which the service, or parts of it, may be separated from its production.[38] For example, the Internet may serve anyone anywhere there are telephone lines. On the other hand, a restaurant is physically bound. A financial service such as First Direct may require local representatives, but the major part of the service may be performed anywhere. Channels of distribution for services include service representatives (agents) and franchises (like Avis). In franchising, outlets are contracted to an organisation which not only supplies products of service, but also dictates trading policy.

Promotion

We have already discussed the nature of homogeneity in service design which presumed that offerings between services could not easily be differentiated by consumers. Promotion is connected to communication which aims to influence the consumer (and/or user markets) about the benefits of purchasing the company's products or services. Promotions therefore attempt to persuade consumer behaviour to respond in a manner desirable to a company and, to accomplish this aim, a wide variety of communication methods are used. Consumer behaviour results from individual and environmental influences. Consumers often purchase goods and services to achieve their ideal self-image and to project the type of self-image that they want others to accept. The four basic determinants of consumer behaviour are the individual's *needs, motives, perceptions,* and *attitudes.* The interaction of these factors with influences from the environment causes the consumer to act.

Promotional strategy is linked to the process of communications. A definition of communications is the *transmission of a message from a sender to a receiver.* Marketing communications, then, are those messages that deal with purchaser-provider relationships. Marketing communications is broader than promotional strategy since it includes word-of-mouth and other forms of irregular communication. However, a planned promotional strategy is, of course, the most important part of marketing communications. The principle phases of strategic communications concern four interrogative aspects – *Who, What, How, To whom?* Namely:

1. Who – the sender (i.e., marketing).
2. What – the input (i.e., marketing message).
3. How – the media (i.e., mass media).
4. To whom – the receiver (i.e., target audience).

The communication process is originated by the sender (the provider of the service). From this origin, messages are directed to selected markets (i.e., purchasers) through media of various types, for example, commercial television and radio, cinema, the press, direct mail, trade fairs, point of sale, and sales literature. Established service providers who wish to continue to grow will usually choose promotional methods that enable them to repeat the message regularly as repetition is almost as important as the promotion itself. For example, research has shown that 95 per cent of people forget the exact message of a television advertisement within six weeks of seeing it.

Promotional strategies should be aligned to corporate strategies and may be classified as long or short term. In organisational markets, for example, immediate reaction to advertising is most unlikely. Companies generally have several objectives in mind when communicating with their markets and these should be lucid, because this will help in planning an effective promotions strategy.

Physical evidence

This is an important element of the marketing mix because the customer is usually in contact with at least some part of the service production facilities, equipment, and personnel. In addition, since services are intangible and thus difficult to evaluate, physical evidence provides clues as to service quality. A simple example, is the gold credit card that promotes a superior package of credit services. The grade of paper and print, form and language of letters and statements also affects the perception of service quality. Similarly, credentials indicated by diplomas hung on the wall or certification initials in advertisements are physical evidence of service quality.[39]

Airlines are well known for their ability to create service identity through consistency in the decor of their planes, their graphics, their advertising, and their uniforms. As another example, Fred Smith of Federal Express does not want anyone to have a neutral reaction to the brazen purple, orange, and white emblem on his planes, delivery trucks, and advertising material. He also stresses the personal grooming of his employees – clean-cut, no beards, no trendy hairstyles. Even the selection of courier uniforms is a major corporate event. Physical evidence adds substance to the service concept. Service marketers should therefore be involved in the design, planning, and control of such physical evidence.

Participants

Refers to any and all people who play a role in the service encounter. This includes both employees and other customers. The attitudes and actions of employees can certainly affect the success of a service encounter. It is also likely that the behaviour of other customers, for instance, in a movie theatre, restaurant, or classroom, can affect an individual's service experience.

Employee behaviour must be strongly customer oriented in services. Employees in contact with the customers should truly be considered salespeople. Throughout its development, AT & T has been noted for the friendliness of its telephone operators. Florida Power and Light is another example of a company where the employees do their utmost to answer queries and assist customers. In contrast, most of us have had contact with uncaring sales people, rude service people, and discourteous managers.

In services, marketing is everyone's job. Thus it is important to have employees with the skills, attitudes, commitment, and ability to use discretion in dealing with customers. Sometimes employees are even called on to sub-due unruly or out-of-place customers so that the service experience may remain positive for other customers.

Process

A major objective of marketing is to identify the needs and wants of the marketplace so that the service may be designed to fulfil those needs. This, in turn, includes the design of the service *process* and how the service is delivered. Ultimately, it reflects how all the marketing-mix elements are co-ordinated to provide a consistent, quality service for the customer. Poor attention to the service process leads to poor service quality. Overworked sales clerks, whose jobs include inventory management, difficult paperwork, sales-floor maintenance, and many other operational tasks, cannot be ex-pected to respond warmly and proactively to customers. The system neither allows them to do so nor rewards them for doing so. Speed, not interaction quality, is the prime performance criterion. Bank tellers operate under simi-lar conditions. In these examples, the design of the service process, which dictates the design of the job, does not support service quality. It is one of marketing's tasks to ensure that the service encounter is a positive one and that service quality is maintained. Thus marketing must be involved in de-signing the service process and is often involved in, or responsible for, quality control in services.

The nature of target marketing in services

A market is comprised of many consumers (and stakeholders such as govern-ments, etc.) but consumers alone do not make a market. A market requires not only purchasers and a willingness to buy, but also needs purchasing power and the authority to buy. Services and marketing services for international markets are established activities for many organisations. It is true to say, however, that both the changing scope, and composition, of international markets and the emergence of new organisational forms are creating new pressures for evaluating strategies for existing markets and for those compa-nies entering new markets. The global or transitional service corporation is a new concept for competing in world markets. Global companies (such as IBM, Microsoft, DHL Worldwide, McDonald's, American Express, etc.) con-sider the whole world as their competitive arena. The challenge faced by global organisations is how to satisfy the individual consumer under diverse global marketing conditions. It is often impossible to develop one product or service which will be equally appealing or will satisfy all consumers in the market. This is due to the fact that consumers buy different services according to their gender, age group, income, occupation, or geographic location. It is therefore evident that organisations operating in the global service arena must attempt to develop or adapt services to satisfy specific groups of consumers. This need brings forward the concept of target marketing. The process of target marketing needs to be carried out in an orderly and scientific manner to be effective. Kotler states that the process of target marketing has three discrete phases:

- Market segmentation
- Market targeting
- Product positioning

Market segmentation

The objective of market segmentation is not to complicate a firm's operations – the nature of an effective marketing segmentation strategy is that it should result in increased market penetration and more efficient use of corporate resources; at the same time, customers' needs should be more fully satisfied. According to Michael Porter, segmentation is necessary to address the central question of competitive scope within an industry, or that is to say, what segments of an industry a firm should serve and how it should serve them.[40] It is also the basis for the choice of focus strategies since it exposes segments that are poorly served by broadly-targeted competitors and in which focus can be both sustainable and profitable. Broadly-targeted competitors must also understand industry segmentation because it reveals areas where they are vulnerable to focusers and may suggest unattractive segments that are best left to competitors. Attention to segmentation from a strategic perspective is increasingly important because new developments in technology are altering some of the old rules of segmentation, with implications for both focusers and broadly-targeted firms

Firms must think both about the full range of environments in which they will compete and the entire economic spectrum of a business activity, including operations, suppliers, marketing, distribution, and customer service. Only then can an organisation identify strategic market segments, or economic activities, through which the company may:

- Establish an advantage comparative to the competition.
- Define its market and competitive advantage over time.
- Secure stable profitability levels.

The question here is: In which parts of the industry can the firm expect the highest long-term returns? In practical terms, within which market segments will it be possible for the organisation to:

1. Develop a supportable advantage relative to competitors in other, possibly neighbouring, segments?
2. Dispute competitors' attractive returns on any investments required to enter the chosen segments?

The most important attribute of a strategic market segment is its defensibility. Evidence that a segment exists consists in the barriers to competition that surround it. The higher the barriers, the higher the profit potential in that segment. Such barriers can (and will) include:

● Trade barriers and taxation.
● Capital investment.
● Technology (patents and proprietary technology).
● Location and infrastructure (closeness to natural resources and transport facilities).
● Existing goodwill.

The nature of market segmentation involves organisations designing services that satisfy smaller homogeneous groups of the total market. Once these groups have been identified and their needs understood, an organisation may be able to develop a market mix appropriate for servicing a subgroup it considers a potential and profitable market. It could be argued, however, that as we head towards the year 2000, organisations should stop thinking of customers as part of a homogeneous market and should instead consider customers as distinct, each of whom requires their own unique strategies in product policy, in promotional strategy, in pricing, in distribution methods, and direct-selling techniques (i.e., the Everybody Markets – the philosophy of maximising the value of contact with each customer).

Future strategies will need to be directed towards constantly changing market needs. Under such conditions, market awareness, organisational flexibility, strategic vision, and external relationships are important strategic capabilities. Getting closer to the customer requires assessment of the customer's needs and wants. The purpose of this assessment is to find an actual or potential competitive advantage. The actions essential in matching customer expectations to the organisation's capabilities are shown in Figure 2.6. Similar to the Extended Gaps Model, this figure highlights one approach to maximising competitive advantage in the market place. Although not unique the process involves:

1. Ensuring that the service is customer focused (both input and output should be directly related to the customer and meet expectation, perception, and satisfaction factors) .
2. Analysis of customer requirements which should consider demographic, geographic, buyer behaviour psychographic (or lifestyle segmentation) subdivisions. See Tables 2.5 and 2.6.
3. Advantage opportunities occur when gaps exist between purchaser expectations and provider performance.
4. Gaps are identified by comparing the capabilities of the competition and the organisation's customer requirements.
5. Analysis should identify the best market-segment opportunities for the organisation to create service value.

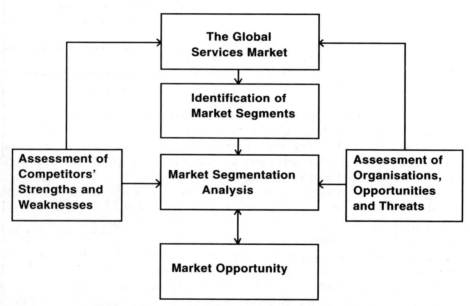

Figure 2.6   Determinants of market opportunity

Table 2.5   Methods of market segmentation

Segmentation Methods	Physical Attributes
Demographic	Sex, Age, Income, Occupation, Social class
Geographic	Countries, Counties, Cities Towns, Rural areas
Buyer Behaviour	When purchases are made, Reasons for purchasing, Purchasing influences, How purchasing is done
Psychographic	Belongers, Achievers, Emulators, I-am-me group, Experiential, Societal conscious, Survivors, Sustainers, and Integrated.[41]

Qualitative Dimensions of the Market
Identification of Best Prospects by Focusing on Best Segments: • Heavy users   • Frequent purchasers   • Firm intentions to buy soon   • Good brand loyalty   • Favourable attitudes towards brand   • Segmentation, pinpointing best   • Prospects (from above)

Conditions of Market Segmentation
Differences between Markets: • The degree of competition   • The availability of substitutes   • Consumer attitudes to the product   *Degree of Market Power:*   • Few providers (or sellers)   • Product differentiation   • Barriers to entry   *Trade barriers:*   • Standards and legislation   • Control over distribution

Table 2.6   Key segmentation criteria used in EC countries for direct marketing

Factors	Belgium	Denmark	France	Germany	Greece
Most commonly used consumer segmentation criteria	Social class Neilson zones Geographic database	Demographic from census database	Socio-demographic database	Age Profession Income Family status Lifestyle	Urban/rural profession database
Most commonly used business segmentation criteria	S.i.c. Size VAT	S.i.c. Location Size Turnover Decision maker	S.i.c. Size Turnover	S.i.c. Size Turnover	S.i.c. Size Turnover

Source: Ogilvy and Mather, Belgium 1992.

Market targeting

Not to be confused with the overall process of *target marketing*. Market targeting is the action whereby one or more of the market segments identified are evaluated and selected. Strategies adopted here include *Undifferentiated, Differentiated,* and *Concentrated Marketing.*

Undifferentiated marketing (approaches the market as a whole rather than in segments). This strategy involves the introduction of products and services and promotional material designed to reach a consumer critical mass. The approach is high risk, and will usually involve the firm in brutal and sustained competition with companies operating in a number of segments within the total market, which could prove costly inasmuch as marketing operations will need to be geared towards total market coverage.

Differentiated marketing (aims at a number of segments with separate offers for each). A firm may consciously decide, or may be forced by its competitors, to operate in many segments of a market. In such cases, the firm will adopt multiple strategies around the seven Ps previously discussed. For example, the strategic options facing such an organisation will be:

- new entrants into their market
- threats from new substitutes
- reactions and actions of their current competitors

This approach may also involve the introduction of a singular product or service which can appeal equally well to more than one segment, for instance, McDonald's fast-food restaurants appeal to the young and the retired alike.

Concentrated marketing (attempts to achieve a large share in one or a few segments). A firm may be determined to concentrate its resources and activities on one or more market segments rather than diffusing its operations thinly over many large segments (e.g., the Bodyshop adopted this strategy in the 1980s). Research would suggest that this approach is favoured by small to medium companies which specialise in one area of the market rather than contesting with larger companies on unequal terms. Although successful for some firms, this approach is risky because small markets are prone to unexpected changes, which could prove problematic to the provider who has specialised in that one market segment.

Product positioning

Where a market is considerably fragmented an organisation (or service provider) would be advised to focus on a relatively small segment, especially if only limited resources are available. Philip Kotler (the marketing guru of MBA culture) terms this a niching strategy and suggests:[42]

1.   The niche should be of sufficient size and purchasing power to be profitable.
2.   The niche has growth potential.
3.   The niche is of negligible interest to major competitors.
4.   The firm has the required skills and resources to serve the niche in a superior fashion.
5.   The firm can defend itself against an attacking major competitor through the customer goodwill it has built up.

You will recall, from our discussion in Chapter 1, the emergence of the entrepreneur and the expansion of small businesses within the global economy. One derived benefit of market segmentation is the development of small or specialist firms which can cater for the needs of relatively small markets. Unlike the big service providers (such as the UK's Royal Mail) who need to invest huge sums of money in equipment, buildings, and the like in order to deliver a small range of products and services, small enterprising providers can avoid headlong impact by concentrating on those sectors of the global market demand which are seemingly insignificant to the large service provider. Although they are vulnerable to market downturns, the entry of rival niches, and the sudden attention of the major players in the market, niche providers can generally gear-up a marketing mix that matches their target customer's needs. However, shifting from a primary commodity to a specialised niche marketing position requires expertise, direction, and management throughout a business. Economies of scale and universal marketing approaches are traditional in undifferentiated product and/or service firms. Penetrating specific segments and offering services adapted to certain customers' needs demands sets of attitudes and a degree of versatility which are likely to be novel to many old, established companies.

In theory strategic market position is related to the concept of niche. This is so because each position implies a fundamental niche (in which firms could exist in the deficiency of competition from neighbouring positions) and a realised niche (in which firms can exist given a specific set of competitors). Since the success of any firm in any position is determined by competition within that same competitive position from firms in positions nearby, positional markets are very complex. Strategic positioning provides an essential frame of reference for guiding management decisions. Swift environmental changes, shifts in buyer preferences, new products and services, and increased competition demand that firms continually update their strategy positioning to exploit new opportunities and to avoid potential pitfalls. An understanding of the concept of strategic positioning and its implications for marketing decision making is important for several reasons. Firstly, changes in marketing environment, both nationally and internationally, are increasing at a rapid rate, so making strategy development significant to the success of an organisation. Secondly, strategy positioning analysis produces important guidelines for decision making and provides a basis for effectively linking corporate and marketing strategy. And thirdly, appropriate shifts in marketing strategy must be based upon a thorough comprehension of a firm's present positioning.

Any organisation entering a new market with a new product or service faces a marketing challenge that is practically different from one operating in an existing market with a credit in product and services in the bank. An essential phase in the marketing management decision process is an assessment of the marketing strategy positions already occupied by the organisation, and those into which it may venture. Differences in the maturity of markets and products, coupled with the base of experience of a given firm, will probably affect the specific activities of management with regard to environmental analysis, target market selection, and market strategy design and profit over time. Paramount to the requirement for strategic positioning analysis is a recognition of market-product dynamics. Clearly, the last decade has adequately demonstrated that change is a central component with which management decision making must contend, now and in the future. Changing environmental conditions such as style changes, economic monetary union, political unrest, declining birth rates, and ageing populations represent both opportunities for and threats to particular organisations and individual firms. Consequently, strategic positioning is an essential frame of reference for the variety of management decisions which must be made.

Selecting positioning strategies

A firm's marketing strategy position is influenced both by the effective market-product situations it is pursuing by the firm and by factors beyond the firm's control, such as product life-cycles, environmental forces, and competition. Ansoff identified five different marketing strategy positions.[43] The five alternatives are discretionary since a continuum of possible variations exist. Nevertheless, this division seems appropriate in terms of characterising the essential differences as they affect marketing decisions.

1. **Balancing strategy**: in this position, a firm seeks to balance revenue cost flows to achieve desired profit and market-share targets. Both existing markets and products are typically at mature levels and competition is well established. Management has amassed a broad base of knowledge and experience about familiar markets, products, and services. Associationships between functional areas of the firm are well established. Market opportunity analysis (see below) within a balancing strategy is aimed at refining the firm's knowledge of its markets. Market segmentation strategies may often be suitable to enable the firm to concentrate its efforts upon certain groups of product end-users, thus achieving advantage over competition through specialisation.

2. **Market retention strategy**: this position relates to a situation in which a product or service is being changed or a market is being increased; it is therefore a logical extension from a balancing strategy position, triggered by management's desire to improve corporate performance or to sustain historical sales and profit levels. It is the typical strategy position occupied by mature firms.

3. **Market development strategy**: pursuit of this strategy may extend a firm beyond existing market-product capabilities, and is likely to require realignments of organisational relationships and procedures. Market development is a major undertaking, and is unlikely to fit into existing operations.[44] Careful assessment of the feasibility of pursuing this strategy should be made in terms of environmental influences, market potential, competitive situation, and financial viability.

4. **Growth strategy**: moves the firm into higher levels of uncertainty than any of the three strategies above. Either a new product or a new market is involved, in combination with a market expansion or product modification. Significant resources are required to pursue this strategy, and a variety of

new operating relationships must be established. The size and arrangement of resources among the various components of the marketing mix must be carefully planned; changes during the initial stages of schedule implementation may be required. An understanding of prospective markets is crucial, indicating a possible need for acquiring information through marketing research and intelligence activities.

5. **New venture strategy**: this position strategy represents an entirely new undertaking by the firm. Whilst high risk, the opportunities for success are very attractive. Direct competition is not often present (e.g., Bill Gates's company, Microsoft, when it first introduced PC Windows). The market in a new venture situation is often not well defined. Management's understanding of customer characteristics and perceptions must be developed over time. Segmentation strategies often need to be deferred until the market gains some maturity and a sufficient degree of permanence so that similar customers can be identified. Initial revenue-cost relationships may be negative during the period that the firm is seeking to build market acceptance.

Market analysis

A market analysis should help to answer two simple questions: What is the competitor's basic strategy and how does that strategy threaten our current market position? And what opportunities exist in the market place? Opportunities for any firm not only depend on the size and nature of market demand, but on how well this market demand is being served by other firms. In appraising the extent and quality of the service provided by the competition, a useful starting point is to focus on an industry as a whole, where the industry is made up of a group of directly competing firms. Of principal importance is an assessment of industry trends during the time period covered by the market analysis. Information should summarise industry growth in terms of output, sales, number of firms, and other factors that show how well the industry has been satisfying the potential that exists within a market. An industry analysis should also identify common operating practices which generally distinguish the whole industry. This kind of data serves several purposes. Management is alerted to possible barriers to entering an industry or to staying within the industry. An organisation's management also gains insight into the character of the market through an industry analysis. Industry practices develop over time as the result of the direct experiences of firms so there are often some important market characteristics to be highlighted that have caused particular practices to be used.

Not all firms in an industry will present the same level of competition to a firm. Some may have selected different target markets or may have practically different marketing programmes that are not directly competing with the firm in question. Management may want to assess more fully the strategies and methods of only those firms that are most directly competing for the same customers. For example, DHL Worldwide Express (based in Brussels, with a global presence in 220 countries) will need to carefully evaluate other firms in the industry. This may mean selecting for analysis those operating in the same geographical locations with similar operations and price structures.

The analysis of individual competitors should include an assessment of their financial strengths as well as their operating strengths and weaknesses. Financial information is (still) a clue to the staying power of firms and indicates the level of resources that can be allocated to serving a market. This is illustrated by the competition between different size providers in local areas (DHL operates in 80 000 cities). Smaller niche providers must try to build a market appeal and attract customers even though they are being outspent by larger firms. During boom-bust economic cycles, a financial analysis will show which competitors are likely to have the means to stay in the market and thus to continue to be major competitors.

A market analysis should also determine how well each competitor is meeting the needs of the market. This task should follow a detailed demand and competitor analysis to identify market gaps and needs (see Table 2.7). With this information management can concentrate primarily on operating practices that are specifically designed to serve those needs. The analysis does not have to go into much depth on operating practices that are specifically designed to serve those needs. Nor does the analysis have to go into much depth on operating practices not bound closely to serving particular market needs. If, for example, purchasers are indifferent to the availability of extras such as a one-hour delivery, then a firm does not have to evaluate its competitors in terms of these offerings. Nevertheless, the $30 billion a year package-delivery business would be significantly smaller had Federal Express and UPS not anticipated a surge in worldwide demand for time-guaranteed delivery.

Cleland and King have developed eight basic assumptions which serve as guides for gathering competitor information.[45] These premises are as follows:

1. Competitive business intelligence is essential for ensuring success in competing in a particular market.

2. Markets are changing so dramatically that informal means of maintaining competitive surveillance are inadequate.

3. Reliance on hit-or-miss methods for obtaining such information is ineffective in the long run. A total *system* in the true sense of the word is required for performing the intelligence function.

4. A business-intelligence system can be highly personalised even though it is rigorously organised and operated.

5. Such a system should be action oriented. It should not simply produce reports of aggregated data. Rather, it should also provide managers with exception-oriented information which indicates the need to act and the preferred action to be taken.

6. Business intelligence can be gained from a variety of sources, many of which might superficially seem to be unprofitable.

7. A competitive business-intelligence system should include a security and counterintelligence capability. This capability should rest on the assumption that competitors have a similar system and that they may resort to illegal and/or unethical means to penetrate one's own system.

8. A business-intelligence system can be made most effective without resorting to unethical and/or illegal techniques of data collection.

Table 2.7   Aspects of competitor analysis

Aspect of Analysis	Information Required About Competitors
Marketing Information	Pricing and Discounts Product and Service Specifications Volumes, history, trend, and outlook for a given product or service Market share and trend Marketing policies and plans Relationships with customers Size and deployment of sales and marketing resources Channels, policies, and methods of service distribution Advertising and promotion strategy
Product and Service Information	Evaluation of service quality and performance Breadth of service Processing and product technology Product or service cost Level service capacity Location and size of facilities
Organisational and Financial Information	Identification of key decision makers Philosophies of key decision makers Financial condition and outlook Expansion and acquisition programmes Major problems/opportunities Research and development programmes

According to Cleland and King competitor information must always be examined in terms of the credibility and reliability of its source and content. A simple appraisal system can be developed which considers the view points of the collector and others as to the source and content. Many different guides have been developed to appraise the credibility of information. One such guide, drawn from a military-intelligence context, is shown below. The use of such an appraisal may be the only sensible way for management to judge the information when faced with confirming or contradictory information.

Table 2.8   Information credibility gap

Appraisal of Source	Appraisal of Content
Completely reliable	Confirmed by other means
Usually reliable	Probably true
Fairly reliable	Possibly true
Not usually reliable	Doubtful
Unreliable	Improbable
Reliability cannot be judged	Truth cannot be determined

3 The Development of Strategic Planning

INTRODUCTION

After almost 40 years of development and theory building, the field of strategic management is, today more than ever, characterised by contrasting and sometimes competing paradigms.[1]

The earliest of these paradigms, the classical approach, is characterised by the early work of Ansoff, Chandler, and Sloan. In the 1950s, immediately after the war, the USA had enjoyed an unprecedented period of economic growth, and strategies for the future consisted primarily of extrapolations of the growth levels being enjoyed by the company in the form of budgets and programmes. These plans would be passed down from senior management to the operating units to implement under close financial control.

The classical approach

By the 1960s strategic planning had superseded long-range planning, with the suggestion that the simple extrapolation of trends was fundamentally unsafe and that a more rigorous consideration of the external factors impacting upon the firm was necessary. However, there was still an inherent stability in the economy and it was still a period of growth. Despite the forecasters protestations about turbulence and uncertainty at the time, this was not the problem that it was to become in the 1970s. Despite the publication of books like *Future Shock* by Alvin Toffler which contained the following passage in a section entitled 'The Death of Permanence':[2]

Sir George Thompson, the British physicist and Nobel prize winner, suggests in *The Foreseeable Future* that the nearest historical parallel with today is not the industrial revolution, but rather the 'invention of agriculture in the Neolithic Age'.[3] John Diebold, the American automation expert, warns that 'the effects of the technological revolution we are now living through will be deeper than any social change we have experienced before'.[4] Sir Leon Bagrit, the British computer manufacturer, insists that automation by itself represents 'the greatest change in the history of mankind'.[5]

The postwar economic growth had slowed, some markets were becoming saturated, and demand was being affected. However, Makradakis, an eminent academic, later commented that: 'it is not an exaggeration to say that the 1960s was the most stable period in the history of Western industrialised countries.'[6] Although the rate of growth had slowed, America still experienced 105 months of uninterrupted growth in the economy, longer than ever before. Vancil, in an analysis of the 1964 five-year forecasts of 16 companies, was able to report that they reflected only 84 per cent of the volume actually generated.[7] It is always easier to be a successful forecaster in periods of growth, as the climate is more favourable to business. The rigour of the analysis being used by companies developed dramatically. Business schools were also growing at an unprecedented rate and consultancy firms, such as the Boston Consulting Group, were formed and flourished.

The distinction between levels of management had been made earlier by Anthony in his hierarchy of planning and control, where he introduced the following categories:[8]

Strategic planning	the process of deciding the objectives of the organisation, on changes in these objectives, on the resources used to attain these objectives, and on the policies that are to govern the acquisition, use, and disposition of these resources.
Management control	the process by which managers ensure that resources are obtained and used effectively and efficiently in the accomplishment of the organisation's objectives.
Operational control	the process of ensuring that specific tasks are carried out effectively and efficiently.

These levels closely followed those offered by Ansoff, who described the principal decision classes in the firm as strategic, administrative, and operational.

Table 3.1   Principal decision classes in the firm

	Strategic	Administrative	Op.
Problem	To select product /market mix which optimises ROI	To structure firm and its resources for optimum performance	To realise optimum ROI potential
Nature of problem	Allocation of total resources amongst existing / diversification opportunities	Organisation, acquisition and development of resources	Budgeting, scheduling, supervision and control of resources within principal functional areas
Key decisions	Objectives and goals Diversification strategy Expansion strategy Finance strategy	Structure of information, authority, responsibility flows and resource conversion	Operating levels, pricing and output levels, marketing policy and R&D policy
Nature of decisions	Centralised decisions, incomplete information, decisions non repetitive	Decisions triggered by conflict between strategic and operational priorities and between individual and organisational objectives	Large volumes of decentralised and repetitive decisions

Source: Adapted from H. I. Ansoff, *Corporate Strategy*, Penguin 1987.

Anthony went on to make the point that planning and control did not relate to separable major categories of activities and this was subsequently emphasised by Koontz who wrote that:

Planning and control are so closely interconnected as to be singularly inseparable . . . [and that] there seem to be so many fewer principles of control than principles of planning indicates the extent to which control depends upon planning and how it is largely a technique for assuring that plans are realised.'[9]

we shall see later the emphasis on control by senior management was a significant bone of contention with some of the other, later, schools of thought in strategic management.

Drucker, simplifying the tiers of management to two levels, defined strategic activity as ensuring that the firm *does the right thing* whilst operational activities ensured that the firm *does the thing right*.[10] Ansoff offered a similar distinction, and introduced a time element into the difference, whereby strategic management was concerned with optimising the *potential* return on investment, whilst operational management should concentrate on the *realisation* of the optimum return on investment. He made the further point that whilst distinct, the decisions are interdependent and complementary. The strategic decisions ensure that the products and markets fit a well-chosen path for the firm, based on adequate demand and recognised capabilities. The strategies to be followed would impose operating requirements, such as price-cost decisions, co-ordination of output and demand, and responsiveness to changes in customer needs and process characteristics. The administrative structure of the organisation had to be designed to facilitate the meeting of these changes. In the strategic environment imposed by, for example, Fast Moving Consumer Goods (FMCG), the marketing and production functions would need to be closely coupled organisationally to react rapidly to changes in consumer taste and, in a highly technical environment, the R&D department would need to work very closely with the sales and marketing personnel.

In this sense he confirmed the point made earlier by Chandler in his historical analysis of American business that strategy follows structure.[11] In an investigation of four major US corporations, Chandler had shown that as the economy of the country had developed and companies had taken advantage of alternative growth opportunities that had arisen, they had needed to adopt structures to cope with the operating inadequacies that had occurred. He demonstrated the need for centralised policy making with decentralised operational control – a point which is also made by Sloan in his memoirs of working at General Motors.[12] Whereas General Motors had adapted their structure, separating strategic and operational decision making, Ford had not and had suffered significantly when their founder died.

Drucker made the further point that the senior management of the company needed to pay attention to both operational and strategic management, but that they had no choice but to anticipate the future and attempt to influence and shape it. This again would not be popular with later authors who, firstly, emphasise the short term, but also throw doubt on managers' ability to foresee the future, as will be described later.

For Ansoff, the strategic decision was a deceptively simple one. Would the existing combination of products and markets the firm operated with satisfy the objectives, or was there a need to diversify and/or divest? He proposed a decision process (shown in a very simplified schematic in Figure 4.1) in which the first stage was the setting of objectives for the organisation. This model has remained the cornerstone of formal strategic-planning systems as the following model from Argenti, produced 15 years later shows:

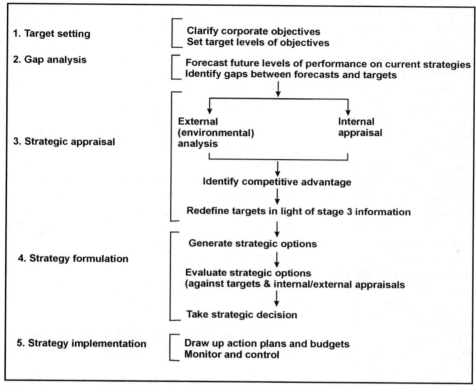

Figure 3.1 Outline strategic-planning process

Source: Adapted from J. Argenti, *Practical Corporate Planning*, Allen and Unwin 1990.

Although we will elaborate in Chapter 4 on the tools and techniques that have been developed for the various stages of the process, it is worth considering the objective-setting process at this stage.

An objective was defined as a measure of efficiency of the resource conversion process and contained three elements. An *attribute* chosen as a measure of efficiency, a *yardstick* or scale by which the attribute would be measured, and a *goal* as the particular level on the scale which the firm sought to attain. Profitability was selected as the main goal of business, rather than simply profit, after a detailed analysis of the then available theories on objectives and objective setting. Recognising that the post World War II influx of technology and the rapidly increasing requirements for capital equipment were putting pressure on short-term profit and focusing attention on the longer-term investment needs, Ansoff rejected microeconomics as having *little relevance to the decision-making process in the real-world firm*. The classical economic statement that the purpose of the firm was to maximise profits was judged invalid by most authors. Steiner made the point that profit maximisation occurs when marginal revenue equals marginal cost, but that firms cannot, in practice, measure either accurately enough to know that profit is being maximised.[13] The concept is fundamentally flawed since it ignores the profit opportunity of introducing a new product or service.

The measures of capital investment appraisal, such as net present value, were similarly rejected since, although superficially attractive, they required complete knowledge of the values of outcomes by assuming that the formulation of alternatives had already taken place. At this time Cyert and March published *A Behavioural Theory of the Firm* which, basically, stated that organisations do not have objectives – only people have objectives,[14] and therefore any objectives established would be the result of a negotiated consensus of the most powerful individuals in the firm. Although Ansoff found the idea of different inputs to the objectives of the firm attractive, in his early work he rejected the ideas of both the behavioural theory and the stakeholder analysis since he felt that neither were suitably developed at the time. The behavioural approach had only demonstrated how objectives could arise in some firms and had not demonstrated how specific strategic objectives were formulated. The stakeholder approach, which attempted to balance the conflicting objectives of the various groups connected with a firm, tended, in Ansoff's view, to confuse responsibilities with objectives which, he felt, were not synonymous. He similarly rejected the concept of survival as the central objective offered by Drucker,[15] survival was inherently unquantifiable and encouraged short termism.

Ansoff considered the time element of objectives by introducing two terms, the time horizon, which would cover the foreseeable future, and the planning horizon, which would cover the period for which the firm could reasonably be expected to forecast with an accuracy of plus or minus 20 per cent. This proximate period was likely to be 3–10 years, but would depend on the nature of the industry, the degree of technological change, susceptibility to fashion, and product life cycles. Within the proximate period, he felt that there would be sufficient data available to be able to forecast profit, and so Return on Investment (ROI) would serve as the objective measure and there would be no need for proxy or subsidiary objectives. The problem of risk was to be dealt with, as it commonly was in practice, by establishing three levels of ROI, using a reference level for 'normal' opportunities and weighted levels for those projects which were deemed to be more, or less, risky.

Argenti subsequently expanded upon this with the concept of performance-risk profiles.[16] This was based on the principle that the company, whilst aiming to satisfy the shareholders' aspirations, should be quite happy to accept projects at declining levels of return so long as the certainty of success was commensurably increased. This can be illustrated graphically:

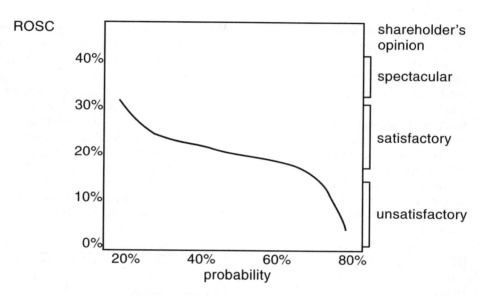

Figure 3.2   A shareholder's performance risk profile

Source: Adapted from J. Angenti, *Systematic Corporate Planning*, Van Norstrand Reinhold 1974.

After the firm had established potentially acceptable levels of achievement in its ROI, there was a need for both an internal and external appraisal. It was at this time that Ansoff introduced the concept of *synergy*. This was the idea that the product-market portfolio of the firm would have a performance greater than the sum of its parts. This concept could, by producing capability profiles, be used as part of the internal appraisal of the firm. Considerations of synergy could also be used to evaluate opportunities for growth or for acquisition. Ansoff went on to define four kinds of potential synergy:

Sales synergy   products use common components of the marketing mix, such as distribution and promotion

Operating synergy   involving higher use of facilities and personnel and the spreading of fixed overheads

Investment synergy arising from joint use of plant and equipment, and other facilities

Management synergy where a new product-market has similar management challenges and requires the same skills and knowledge base as those currently required.

These potential synergistic effects could be recognised as going through two distinct phases; at start up, giving the firm an entry advantage, and another once operating, giving the firm an advantage when starting to build market share. Ansoff proposed measuring the synergistic effects either by estimating the cost economies of joint operations at a particular revenue level, or by estimating the increase in revenue at a particular investment level. He cautioned that there could be negative synergistic effects where there were mismatches, particularly in the sphere of management synergy.

The evaluation of synergistic effects for a particular product market opportunity was to be conducted, using a matrix which compared the contribution of each of the types of synergy to each functional area in terms classified as benefit to parent, benefit to new venture, or joint benefit. Wherever possible these contributions were to be quantified financially.

Functional area	Contribution	Start up synergy		Operating synergy		Expansion of present sales	New product and market areas
		Investment	Operating	Investment	Operating		
General management and finance	to parent to new entry joint opportunities						
R&D	to parent to new entry joint opportunities						
Marketing	to parent to new entry joint opportunities						
Operations	to parent to new entry joint opportunities						

Figure 3.3 Measurement of synergy for product-market opportunities

Source: Adapted from H. I. Ansoff, *Corporate Strategy*, Penguin 1987.

The internal appraisal itself would be constructed as a competence grid which would evaluate the same functional areas of General Management and Finance, R&D, Marketing, and Operations in terms of facilities and equipment, personnel skills, organisational capabilities, and managerial capabilities. This would be compared to the competitive profile, which was essentially the same grid constructed by evaluating the most successful competitors in that product-market segment. For a diversified company, it would be necessary to produce these grids for each product-market segment.

The external appraisal concentrated on industry characteristics, using criteria which included economic potential, cost of entry, synergy potential, competitive characteristics, and competitive profiles. No mention was made of political, societal, and technological factors found in the broader, and now well-known, PEST analysis discussed in Chapter 4. In terms of dealing with these environmental uncertainties, Wheelan and Hunger offered the following advice to mangers: faced with increasing environmental uncertainty managers could either choose to modify their firm or to modify the environment in which they operated.[17]

The sum of Ansoff's analyses resulted in a prescriptive model which offered the following generic strategies:

	Present Products	**New (modified) Products**
Present Markets*	Market penetration	Product development
New (modified) Markets*	Market development	Diversification

Figure 3.4   Ansoff's matrix

Source: Adapted from H. I. Ansoff, *Corporate Strategy*, Penguin 1987.
* Ansoff referred to mission rather than market

This model gave the strategic alternatives for a company. Other models were developed during this period, primarily by the consultancy firms that we have referred to earlier. The fundamental assumption underpinning their use was that market share and large volume was essential for success.

Bruce Henderson, who founded the Boston Consulting Group, propounded, in 1966, the experience-curve theory which was to become central to much of the Group's work, leading to their most famous portfolio model the Boston Box (compare Chapter 4). The early work of the Group has been described by Henderson as an attempt to determine a general theory of competition based on:

1. Observable patterns of cost behaviour,
2. the dynamics of sustainable growth and capital use,
3. the role of capital markets in allowing these effects to be leveraged or discounted, and
4. the relationships between these factors in a system of competition.

Deciding that conventional accounting theory had little to offer as the basis for a model describing this, the conclusion was that cash in and out was all important. From this was to be developed the experience curve which Henderson describes as 'a rule of thumb' and expressed as: 'Costs of value added, net of inflation, will characteristically decline 25–30 per cent each time the total accumulated experience has doubled.' The costs should be computed in cash terms – not accounting terms. Also, volume would be used as a close approximate of experience. Henderson went on to say that the concept had subsequently been misunderstood and over simplified, particularly in the area of product definition, which had to be in terms of perceived value to the customer, since actual products would change. Arguably his most significant comment was that: 'The experience curve cannot be a strategy, or even the foundation of a strategy. It is merely a way to understand why and how competitive costs may shift.'[18]

Shortly after the introduction of the experience curve, the Boston Consulting Group introduced their growth-share matrix, which compared the relative rate of growth of the market to the relative market share of the product – a surrogate for the cost advantage that the product enjoyed. Henderson argued that this substitution was supported by the research conducted by Buzzell and Schoeffler,[19] the founders of PIMS, but Buzzell and Gale go to some lengths to demonstrate that from PIMS' point of view whilst market leadership gives significant advantages market share is a measure not a cause.[20] They argue that market share is a measurement which reflects two very different factors which can affect profitability – scale and quality.

The matrix is shown in Figure 4.5 (see page 131); the logic behind the model was simple:

1. Product market combinations which are growing need more capital (cash).
2. Products which have a competitive advantage generate surplus capital (cash) which can be used to find and support new products.

Henderson subsequently described the matrix as a: 'schematic for focusing attention and providing a useful framework, which was quite useful. Expressing important qualitative relationships but offering serious risks when used as the basis of policy determination.' However it must be remembered that these comments were made in 1984, with the benefit of hindsight, and others have made far more ambitious claims for the use of these, essentially prescriptive, models. The model still features in the majority of undergraduate strategy texts, usually without Henderson's qualifying comments as to its usefulness.

In 1970, McKinsey and Company proposed a modification to the matrix, that was adopted by General Electric, which compared, as before, industry or market attractiveness with the company's position or strength. The difference with this model was that market growth rate and market share were now only factors in the calculation of a composite score for each of the parameters. The model, which again leads to prescriptions for the user, will be described in detail in Chapter 4.

The next significant addition to the classical school involved the work of Michael Porter with the publication of *Competitive Strategy* in 1980 and *Competitive Advantage* in 1985.[21] Three models have been adopted from these works and feature heavily in strategy texts. The five forces contributing to the competitive nature of an industry are described in a model which is shown in Figure 4.4 (see page 121) and described in more detail there. It is worth noting the rigorous language that Porter uses in the description of the factors, which he describes as *forces* and as *structural determinants*. This precise language indicates the strong economic underpinning to Porter's work. Porter's definition of an industry related to where the firm wanted to compete – not necessarily the industry in which it currently operated. This definition, which is much more customer focused, mirrored the work of Abell, who was also on the professorial staff of Harvard Business School at that time. Abell contended that:

> . . . the starting point of strategic planning is the decision to hold, harvest or build market share is not the primary strategic lever. The pivotal act in determining strategy is defining the business in a way that leads to competitive superiority in the customer's eyes.[22]

Considering competitive advantage, Porter states that this can only arise if the company creates value for its buyers. Porter substituted sustainable competitive advantage for profit maximisation as the principal objective of the company. To consider adding value, it is necessary to take a holistic view of the company, as only the successful integration of the various functions of the firm can create competitive advantage. The firm, and its component functions, is considered via a tool called the value chain which is shown in Figure 4.7 (see page 133). Each company will have a value chain, which will be a component of the value system for the industry; the outbound logistics of the lead company interacting with the inbound logistics of the firm that follows it in the industry chain.

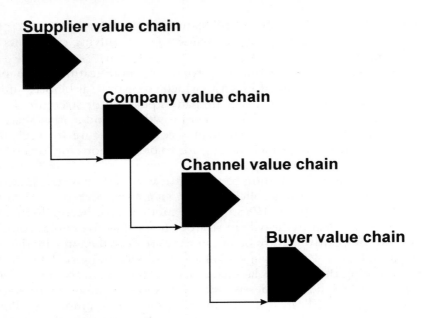

Figure 3.5   Industry value system

Source: Adapted from M. E. Porter, *Competitive Advantage: Creating and Sustaining Superior Performance*, The Free Press 1985.

Somewhat more controversially Porter went on to introduce his three generic competitive strategies: overall cost leadership, differentiation, and focus.

Although the options were not considered to be mutually exclusive by Porter – each required total commitment and organisational arrangements – he considered it rare for a firm to succeed by pursuing more than one strategy at a time and unlikely to be successful. Later, other authors were to describe those firms that chose to ignore Porter's advice pejoratively as 'stuck in the middle'. This term was criticised by some authors since there were perceived to be firms who were successful whilst not fitting into Porter's categories. Additionally, it was felt that some industries did not lend themselves to this form of analysis and that more than one company within an industry could be successful by offering a low-cost product. This dissatisfaction led to other attempts at producing a typology of generic strategies. The work of Mathur was arguably the most complicated.[23]

Mathur felt that the firm should develop its competitive strategy based on the competitive positioning of its outputs, as perceived by the customer when making the purchasing decision. He differentiated these outputs in terms of the merchandise (the physical product) and the support (advice and assistance) – this gave four polar generic strategies:

Support		
Merchandise	Differentiated	Undifferentiated
Differentiated	System	Product
Undifferentiated	Service	Commodity

Figure 3.6   Mathur's polar generic strategies

Mathur then went further by differentiating support in terms of expertise and personalisation:

Personalisation		
Expertise	Differentiated	Undifferentiated
Differentiated	Consultant	Specialist
Undifferentiated	Agent	Trader

Figure 3.7   Mathur's support modes

And merchandise in terms of content and image:

Image		
Content	Differentiated	Undifferentiated
Differentiated	Exclusive	Special
Undifferentiated	Augmented	Standard

Figure 3.8   Mathur's merchandise modes

Together these give a matrix that describes 16 generic strategies – which a firm could choose to adopt:

Support				
Merchandise	Consultant	Specialist	Agent	Trader
Exclusive	System			Product
Special				
Augmented				
Standard	Service			Commodity

Figure 3.9   Mathur's generic strategies
Note: The polar strategies appear in the extreme corners of the matrix.

Although Mathur's work is claimed to offer the benefits of focusing attention on what the customer values – and therefore buys – linking the choice of strategy to consumer behaviour and giving insight into what competencies and skills a company must develop, there are criticisms of this approach. It does not necessarily help the firm to choose a strategy and pays scant attention to the costs associated with the various differentiation approaches offered.

In *The Mind of the Strategist,* Ohmae, the McKinsey consultant, has offered an alternative set of four generic strategies developed on the basis of the type of product offered (old or new) and the method by which competitors are tackled (wisely or head on).[24] His view that achieving a sustainable, competitive advantage is an important objective for the firm is a predominantly Western approach and not necessarily one that would find favour in other cultures, as we shall find later when we consider the work of the systemic school.

In summary the classical school of strategic management gives us a highly formalised and prescriptive system which offers the following claimed advantages:

1. The ability to recognise and reduce risk by providing an early warning system.
2. Provides a complete overview of the company and a rigorous analysis of its environment, there is a better chance that all opportunities are identified and evaluated.
3. Gives a sense of purpose to staff at a number of levels of the organisation.
4. Encourages creativity and innovation in management.
5. Recognises that companies cannot remain static but must move on to cope with an increasingly dynamic environment.
6. Charts the future options of the firm to facilitate choice of the best way forward.
7. Encourages consistency between long, medium and short-term plans.
8. Facilitates control against an agreed plan to facilitate adjustment to strategies as the environment changes.

Thus the classical approach, which has been described as organised entrepreneurship, has the following characteristics:

1. It is highly formalised,
2. involves a sequential and often elaborate planning process, often with many stages,
3. involving rigorous analytical techniques applied to hard data and 'facts',
4. and has an underlying assumption that the future can be quite accurately forecast.

5. It is the prerogative of senior management, particularly the Chief Executive, and involves,
6. separation of the planners from the operational staff.
7. It is inseparably linked with control,
8. leads to prescriptive answers to the decision process,
9. which are fully developed at the end of that process,
10. and can then be implemented by staff planners.
11. The appropriate structure of the organisation could be determined after the strategy had been decided.

The classical approach has not been without its critics and the grouping of the criticisms has lead to alternative schools of thought. Mintzberg has arguably been the most prolific of these critics, making the point, amongst others, that the one thing missing from the approach is the actual *creation* of strategy.[25] In doing so, he draws a distinction between what he describes as the design and the planning schools of thought, quoting Steiner who said that: 'although quite a good bit of progress has been made in developing analytical tools to identify and evaluate strategies, the process is still mainly an art.'[26]

The evolutionary school

The evolutionary school gained prominence during the 1970s when the forecasting techniques common in the previous decade failed to predict the oil-price shocks of 1970 and 1974, and became increasingly popular with the free market movement which flourished in the following years. There was also the feeling that many management teams were unable to make rational decisions since they were unable to grasp the breadth of data necessary to make economically based decisions.

Inability to forecast

The evolutionary school of thought addresses what Mintzberg calls 'the fallacy of predetermination', where he questions the ability of management to forecast the future with any degree of accuracy.[27]

A famous, anonymous Arabic proverb states that: 'Anyone who says that they can forecast the future is a liar, even if they are subsequently proved to be correct.' However, the ability to forecast the future is central to the classical school of strategic planning, and as Allaire and Firsirotu have said: 'Uncertainty is the Achilles' heel of strategic planning ... as it is still practised, [it] is heavily slanted toward the "predict-and-prepare" mode of coping with the future. The strategic plan is a "road map" with a fixed and well-defined target, as well as the steps towards that target.'[28]

As the 1970s dawned and the previously claimed turbulence became a reality, the accuracy of forecasting failed regardless of the complexity of the techniques that were used. Hogarth and Makradakis found that long-range forecasting over two or more years was notoriously inaccurate.[29] They found that the ability to predict in questions of population, economics, energy, technology, and transportation, where there was a wealth of data and considerable experience and expertise, was inadequate. Biases were systematic and errors varied by as much as 'a few hundred per cent'. In an earlier article with Hibon, Makridakis had found that techniques such as simply moving averages and straight extrapolation worked as well as more complicated methods.[30] Pant and Starbuck, in a more recent investigation, have confirmed this view stating that: 'simplicity usually works better than complexity, complex forecasting methods mistake random noise for information.'[31] For Ansoff, the detection of this information in the form of weak signals and its use in causal models rather than extrapolative models was essential if discontinuities were to be forecast.[32] Others doubted the feasibility of recognising weak signals and the ability to forecast discontinuities. Arguing for causal models, Simon said that: 'forecasts are only likely to be reliable when made in the context of a good structural model.'[33] The important issue becomes: How can you build the model even if you can accurately detect the weak signals? As signals are often likely to represent events that have no historical background, how can there be sufficient understanding to model the cause and effect relationships? As we shall see later in Chapters 4 and 6, this is the basis of scenario planning, a technique which can overcome many of the criticisms of extrapolative forecasts.

Inability of rational activity to bring success

Evolutionists also throw doubt on mangers' ability to plan and make decisions in a rational manner, and doubt the effectiveness of the approach. If managers are forward looking, they should prefer discounting techniques such as NPV (net present value) over the more traditional measures, such as ROCE (return on capital employed) or ROI (return on investment), for objective setting. NPV, although arguably subjective, is at least forward looking, whereas ROCE and other profit-based measures are historically based and encourage short-termism. One of the most effective ways to improve ROCE is to limit investment in plant and equipment, thereby enhancing profit by reducing depreciation and reducing the value of the asset base and thus capital employed.

Grant is a strong advocate of long-term, value-maximising financial measures as objectives, claiming that only those strategies offering the highest NPV should be followed.[34] Whilst conceding that discounted cash flows are hard to forecast and that the more recent technique of options pricing are near impossible to value, he claims that the calculations must be attempted. The use of NPV for long-term objectives for extractive companies is encouraged by American accounting rules, which require the annual calculation of the future value of reserves, and a reconciliation with the previous years calculation, to be reported in the annual return to the Stock Exchange.

Despite the difficulty in formulating long-term financially quantified objectives and the problems of persuading managers to concentrate on them, the evolutionary school gained in prominence during the 1980s, as it concentrated analyses at an industry level rather than at an individual company level. Friedman, the eminent promoter of free markets, argued that the behaviour of individual firms is irrelevant, market forces would determine who would survive and who would not.[35] What mattered most would be that the industry – and, by definition, the country – would benefit as a whole. Protectionism was thus a poor idea, and it was better to let weak companies go to the wall and be replaced by new entrants to the industry better able to cope with the changing demands of the market. Using a biological metaphor, Hannan and Freeman used the term 'population ecology' and suggested that *overall efficiency* of an industry is best served by a steady stream of new, innovative companies with the markets rejecting the less fit.[36] Peters, indeed, going so far as to applaud high rates of business failure as indicative of a strong and successful industry, as such evolution has been described as the biological equivalent of cost-benefit analysis.[37]

Faced with this Darwinian selection process, there was debate about the characteristics that would allow a company to be successful. According to some authors, a constant stream of new innovations would lead to success. Sanchez and Sudharshan described the success of Sony Walkman, where the company constantly refreshed the product range, launching 160 different models during the 1980s, but never having more than 20 models on sale at any one point in time.[38] A similar approach can be seen with Swatch and their constantly changing product range. With the traditionally expensive, mechanical, high-precision Swiss watch industry threatened by the Japanese electronic digital watches, the company moved to mass-produced cheaper watches with a totally different 'fun' image. Launched in 1983, the Swatch reached sales of over 70 million units in 1989 having introduced over 450 models over the seven years, including limited editions produced by famous designers.

However, Williamson argues that organisations can only ensure their success by focusing on a perfect fit with the current environment and that economy is the best strategy.[39] The costs associated with flexibility and constant innovation are inefficient, and will invariably lead to failure as more cost-conscious companies undercut. Therefore the conservative organisation that forgoes change and concentrates on overall cost efficiency, one of the strategies advocated by Porter, will ultimately be the most successful.

But with the advent of more efficient markets and faster information flows, others argue that there can be no long-term recipe for success. Whittington quotes McCloskey:'Formal methods will not earn abnormally high profits for long. The formality makes them easy to copy. Going to business school is not a way to acquire immense wealth, because it is too easy to get in.'[40] The market ensures that everyone is aware of the prescriptions for success, and they will not offer competitive advantage once they are generally available. McCloskey, himself, tends to favour the cost-efficiency approach, concentrating particularly on the transactional costs of organising and co-ordinating, claiming that elaborate strategies will quickly be imitated by competitors and any advantage will be eroded.[41]

The point that long-term sustainable advantage is difficult to attain is also made by Miller where he describes the paradox that Icarus's greatest asset leads to his downfall, as he stretches himself too far and flies too close to the sun. Describing the application of the concept to successful corporations, he says:

> . . . that same paradox applies to many outstanding companies; their victories and their strengths often seduce them into the excesses that cause their downfall. Success leads to specialisation and exaggeration, to confidence and complacency, to dogma and ritual.[42]

For evidence, we can look at the number of successful companies described in *In Search of Excellence,* by Peters and Waterman,[43] and see how many have slipped from their previously successful position.

There are two aspects to the paradox. Firstly, that success itself can engender failure with the onset of complacency, but, secondly and more importantly, that the causes of success may become the causes of failure. As organisations become more focused on and efficient at implementing the recipes that have made them so successful, changes in the environment weaken the previously perfect fit that had served them so well. As the needs of the market change, the momentum of the successful formula prevents the organisation adapting to meet the revised challenge. Miller cites examples such as Wang and Polaroid when suggesting that too much success can lead to eventual failure.[44] The argument runs counter to the offered conventional management wisdom that links success with the ability to gain a distinctive competitive advantage. Managers who experience success may develop biases to maintain the *status quo*, only when they encounter problems does the possibility of change arise. Thus, with long-term success, there are few opportunities for managers and organisations to evaluate or change the organisational paradigm.

With this in mind, Miller advocated the use of small independent units within large successful organisations, whose function would be to experiment outside the existing configuration of the firm. Having relatively small budgets, they would be given the freedom to experiment at the boundaries of the business, and get things done quickly and economically. Successful units would be given increasing budgets and grown to significant business units, but the many who would fail would be shut down. Stacey, in his discussion of chaos and self-organisation in business, defines the state of chaos in a system as a function of chance, the precise actions of the system and the environment in which the system operates.[45] Hence the links between cause and effect become confused, and predicting the specific path to achieve long-term success is futile. Only in the short term can successful predictions be made, before the forces of change build up to overcome the negative feedback that the organisation uses to control its performance. According to Stacey, organisations are pulled by powerful forces between a state of stable equilibrium and an explosively unstable state. Success lies at the border between these two states, at a nonequilibrium position between ossification and disintegration. This again suggests that, to be successful, there is a need for organisations to have both an element of bureaucratic, cost-efficient working practices and of organic, risk-taking functions. This has significant implications for the structure of an organisation, where the two extremes would be represented by centralisation and decentralisation, and the degree of autonomy granted to the operating units would also be significantly different.

Cultural differences will also exist in different parts of the organisation and Stacey refers to the need to encourage multiple cultures within an organisation by rotating staff between functions and business units. Both Canon and Honda hire managers from other organisations part way through their careers, when they will have developed particular working patterns. Stacey goes on to advocate getting managers to create chaos by challenging existing perceptions, bringing about the conditions in which spontaneous self-organisation can occur thus making innovation possible. He also argues for the creation of 'organisational slack' to allow the freedom for innovation, which flies in the face of organisational efficiency and the lean approach advocated by Anglo-Saxon management, with such techniques as Business Process Engineering and the current trend for 'downsizing'.

The biological metaphor is carried further by the suggestion that peaceful coexistence is impossible – if two organisations can only be successful by using the same resource, it is impossible for both to survive and grow, one must become dominant and defeat the other. Based on the biological theory of competitive exclusions, this supports the idea that market dominance is all important unless an organisation can differentiate itself sufficiently so that it depends on different resources to those companies which could previously be considered competitors.

Critics who question the relevance of the evolutionary approach have argued that the ability to dominate markets leads to a monopolistic position, and companies are then able both to select the markets they compete in and to minimise any environmental pressures to which they are subjected. Pelikan considered that the turbulent environments organisations competed in should be broadened to include markets for managerial talent, capital funds, and for corporate control.[46] In the latter case, managers who were incompetent would be fired and replaced by those who were more able and better equipped to do the job. This was supported by research by both Slatter and Grinyer et al. into the causes and cures of corporate failure.[47] In the majority of organisations, they found that where a difficult decision had to be made, particularly in those situations where rationalisation and refocusing were necessary with the need to lay off some of the senior management, outsiders had to be brought in to enact the decision. Usually, the company had already made attempts at more moderate strategies, but these had not worked and there was a need to change the organisational paradigm. In these organisations, the arrival of a 'Company Doctor' was called for. A typical example would be the return of Steve Jobs to Apple Computer,[48] where significant changes are forecast, with the cutting of perks, radical changes to the product range, and a build-to-order approach similar to the success story at Dell. The arrival of Jobs has lead to the departure of many of Apple's previous board of directors, which *Business Week* has branded ineffectual.

With the suggestion that a successful formula may become stale, the best approach may not be for the company to look for internal adaptive change, but to break up and reform the company, possibly in smaller units. Adaptation may come from breaking up and thus releasing the human and financial capital to rebuild in completely new forms better able to cope with the new order. According to research done by Ravenscraft and Scherer in their work on acquisitive companies,[49] this is counter to the motivational factors of many boards of directors, most of which are related to empire building, growth to facilitate increased remuneration, and risk diversification. This conflict and resistance to change comes from the differing interest of the owners and the managers, according to agency theorists such as Eisenhardt.[50] Bearing this in mind, there is a need for the clever manipulation of market pressures by owners in order to coerce the desired action from managers, according to Kimberley and Zajac.[51] The argument being that exposure to the pressures of both the market for corporate control and the managerial labour market are enough to make the current management perform optimally. The threat of takeover and subsequent sacking will keep the managers (agents) performing in the interests of the principals (stockholders) for fear that the share price falls and takeover becomes a reality.

This reinforces the argument for a free and open market for information and strikes against anti-takeover measures, which will be in the interests both of the owners, who will enjoy higher prices and dividends, and of the managers, who will build reputation and therefore their own market worth. Shareholders need therefore to promote an active market for managerial labour, where the excellent are headhunted and the weak go to the wall. However, there is evidence that the managerial labour market is not all that efficient – high severance and benefits packages have recently been paid, enraging shareholders who have been powerless to prevent the payments. Ray Irani, at the Occidental Petroleum Corporation, is quoted in *Business Week* as having obtained an obscenely high payout at $95 million.[52] However, other organisations use the market pressure internally to promote good performance. Goold and Campbell, researching models of planning and control, found that in some conglomerates adopting a financial-control approach, many announce their preparedness to sack poor performers and dispose of loss-making subsidiaries, and do so.[53] They report that in one BTR subsidiary, 4 out of 16 divisional managing directors were fired in the space of 3 years. Similarly, Hanson Trust has always maintained that every subsidiary has a permanent 'For Sale' sign over the door and that: 'If anybody thinks they can run it better than us, and is prepared to pay for the opportunity to try, they are welcome.'

The processual school

Like those of the environmental school, advocates of the processual school of strategic planning agree that the future is impossible to forecast, but also believe that the rational process does not happen within the organisation. The markets are felt to be irrational and not the 'natural selector' that environmentalists believe it to be – it is not necessarily the fittest that are selected to survive. Stressing the imperfections of both organisations and markets, proponents of this school feel that luck plays a significantly important part in the process. The prospect of rational decision making in an organisation consisting of different groups of people with different interests and drives is also felt to be unfeasible. They believe that decisions are not made that way in organisations.

The limits of rationality in management teams

The idea that managers act rationally, the concept of 'Rational Economic Man', is rejected and managers are believed to act with 'bounded rationality'. The concept, introduced by Simon and built upon by Cyert and March, refers to a more psychologically acceptable theory of human behaviour, suggesting that the human brain cannot cope with the diversity and volume of information that is suggested by the classical school.[54] Managers are not able to deal with the environmental analysis, internal appraisal, and comparative studies of competitors that are required to go through the rigorous processes suggested. Additionally, the conclusions drawn from the data gathered will be biased, there is always a subjective view taken in any analysis as short cuts are taken based on experience. Trial and error procedures are used to identify what are perceived to be the important, but limited, range of aspects of the search and decisions will be made without fully understanding all of the outcomes of the decisions made.

This is not to say that managers intentionally ignore information and Hrebiniak and Joyce believe that managers have two guiding principles: that of intended rationality and minimum intervention.[55] They contend that within limitations, managers will intend to focus on utilitarian outcomes and create organisational designs which are efficient and effective, whilst encouraging acceptable performance by incentives and control systems. Other factors – both internal to the organisation, such as scarcity of management time, and external to the organisation, such as perception of risk – will determine the intensity with which rationality is pursued. Individual motivations, perceptions, and values will also affect the process of strategy formulation and implementation, and these individual assessments of risk and reward may not necessarily coincide with a superordinate organisational goal. Hence management, for this school, fits the definition of 'the science of making decisions with incomplete information' or as Lindblom describes it, the 'science of muddling through'.[56] Thus, by definition, the decisions made will not always lead to the optimum solution, a satisfying approach has been taken, the best that can be done with the resources available has been.

Since managers are basically averse to risk, the implementation of strategic decisions will be done with the minimum intervention or disruption to the organisation. The actions taken, in order, are likely to be:

1. Tighten up on control procedures,
2. devise new strategies, and
3. change the organisational structure and paradigm.

Only when each stage fails to achieve the desired result will the next, more difficult, and disruptive stage be attempted. At all stages, managers will attempt to solve problems with the minimum of financial and human cost to the organisation. Thus a change of structure, with the consequent disruption to individuals tasks and habits, is only used as a last resort. This is, of course, a rational approach since to address a strategic problem by changing the structure of an organisation when it is possible to achieve sufficient improvement with less fundamental change is inefficient and makes little sense.

Hrebiniak and Joyce go on to categorise the nature of strategic actions designed to address strategic problems in terms of the size of the problem and the implementation horizon, arriving at four strategies. There is an incremental cost structure to these strategies, but basically the size of the problem will have a bigger cost implication than the implementation horizon.

Simple evolutionary change, where the problem is small and the horizon distant, involves not so much change, as modifications to the way things are done. There is usually no explicit implementation plan, but changes to local action and a focus on the latter stages of the implementation model, with modifications to behaviour encouraged by incentives and control. The stages of the change brought about are not always recognised as connected and the result may be heuristic and suboptimal. However, since the costs of the differences are small the cost of suboptimal behaviour is also small.

Managerial implementations describe the situation where the scope of the problem is small, but the time available to adapt is short. Minor shifts in the business environment will necessitate planned action relating to either personnel or to the structure of the organisation. In general, the organisation will not attempt to modify both structure and personnel. Since the change to the environment is relatively small, it is quite likely that organisational slack will be sufficient to absorb the costs of the change.

Sequential implementations will occur when the size of the strategic problem is large, but the planning horizon is sufficiently long to allow components of the model to be modified in turn. In contrast to the previous two modes, it will now be necessary to consider the interdependence of the components. Planning will take explicit account of the relationships between the different facets of structure and personnel.

By contrast, **complex interventions**, which will be necessary when the strategic problem is large and the implementation horizon is very short, are by their very nature difficult to plan for and expensive to carry out. Severe changes to external conditions will bring about this type of situation where rapid action is necessary, involving task forces who will make policy decisions as the situation plays out. This last type of intervention can be typified by the situation described by Stacey when describing the companies that supplied metal paint cans to the paint industry in the 1980s.[57] As the large paint manufacturers shifted their requirements to plastic cans, none of the metal manufacturers were ready for the change. Plastics manufacturers entered the market and took away a large share. In

box continued overleaf

1985, one of the metal-can manufacturers affected, Francis Packaging, was taken over by Suter plc., who installed a new chief executive . The significant uncertainty and the need for rapid action could not be handled using the old organisational paradigm and both personnel and structure had to be changed. The remaining management had to develop, rapidly, new perspectives on the business and how it needed to be fundamentally changed.

There will always be a desire to achieve personal goals and to minimise negative feedback and risk for the individual. And from this point of view, the arrival at the chosen way forward can be considered as the result of a political bargaining process between different coalitions within the organisation. Pettigrew discusses the stages that must be worked through before this kind of intervention can occur.[58] There will most probably be conflict, as well as changes in perspective, to be worked through before those involved will agree on concerted action. Coalitions will develop around individuals or groups who see their career, rewards, or status threatened. Making demands for options which will not only counter threats but will also protect their interests, they will seek to convert others to their chosen path. Building support will involve the exercising of a form of power which is often contrasted to authority. Authority, often described as legitimate power, will come from the structure and 'rules' of the organisation, whereas this kind of power may come from personal characteristics or charisma.

Most writers, including Pettigrew and Pfeffer,[59] see the use of power as inevitable when the conditions for complex interventions are met. The selection of the task-force members and the exclusion of others, the threat to departments and personal fiefdoms, will often lead to further conflict in the organisation which will only be solved by the application of power. Others take the view that the application of power may not necessarily lead to a situation of conflict but may actually lead to co-operation. Kanter sees power as the ability to influence rather than to coerce, using information and foresight that others do not have.[60] The emphasis here is on advocacy and reasoned discussion by a respected leader who skilfully guides the discussion to bring about his chosen course of action.

Once the conflict has been resolved, the choice of action path has been made. For Mintzberg, this emergent strategy is the result of a crafting process where the resultant path and the process of analysis and decision making are mixed together, and inextricably linked as one.[61] The idea that it is a gradual, continuous, and adaptive process is echoed by Quinn, who describes it as 'logical incrementalism'.[62] Contrasting with the idea of the classical school that planners and implementers are separate groups of people, the emphasis here is on intimate involvement with the management of the business, the idea that the routine of running the firm will get in the way of the managers' ability to plan for the future is discounted. Strategy development has become a 'messy' business with the actors heavily involved in the day-to-day running of the organisation. The emphasis here is not on detachment to allow *strategic thinking*, although this is still necessary, but on *strategic acting*, which is the only way the firm can go forward. The idea that thinking and action can be separated is rejected.

For Mintzberg, the distinction between the strategic level and the tactical level blur in the face of reality.[63] He quotes the case of the battle at Paschendale, where the battle was strategically important, but was tactically impossible once the weather had changed to torrential rain and the Allies, unable to advance in the mud, suffered horrendous losses. The detached strategists never saw the conditions all too familiar to the tacticians, that is, the officers in the field, when a quarter of a million troops were killed. Those who were there would be able to interpret the local or immediate conditions and evaluate the strategic impact of what they saw. The importance of detachment as proposed by the classical school is strongly rejected by the processual school who argue that, without involvement, the messages from the environment are unlikely to be picked up, and acted upon, with sufficient speed to capitalise upon the opportunities, or counter the threats, that the company faces. Isolated planners will receive data which will already have been aggregated by the subjective thought processes of those who are nearer to the customers, markets, and competitors. To some extent that interpretation will have suffered, having been subconsciously mediated by a desire to tell senior management what they will want to hear. Additionally, the rich detail, the nuances, and the gossip that will often contain the weak signals necessary for forecasting and foreseeing will have been removed in the production of hard data.

The basic premise of effective data analysis is to present unambiguous data in an objective and quantified way, using quantitative, accounting, or economic measures. However, the fuzzy, societal information is as important, if not more so, and can usually only be obtained by first-hand experience. For this reason, many managers favour face-to-face contact, oral and non-verbal communication being so much richer and more effective than the quantified or written word. Much can be drawn from the look on a customer's face, and from the attitude and posture of the people working in the organisation, and these messages are important to those who are steering the organisation forward. Much of what the managers have thus heard and seen becomes the basis of instinctive or intuitive decisions and actions they will make about the future of the firm. Managers actually know more than they are able to impart to others, but that knowledge will be used by them in their decision making. With that in mind, the idea of the external facilitator having a place in the strategic process has little credibility since the knowledge required is likely to be too complicated and too inbuilt for an outsider to grasp. Similarly, the idea of staff planners, analytically competent as they may be but lacking in operating experience, cannot be expected to make a major contribution. The problem is not just the lack of knowledge of the business, but goes deeper than that as people removed from the day-to-day operations are unlikely to ever be able to contribute fully. It is for this reason that organisations will take people with operational experience into a staff planning position for a limited period, and then transfer them back to operations after a period that rarely exceeds two or three years.

As we have said earlier, this approach is described as 'muddling through', but it is often felt that there is a *strategic intent* which will guide the experimentation and adaptation leading to the emergent strategies that evolve. Mintzberg and Waters have gone so far as to suggest that there will only be an identification of strategic logic after the strategies have been enacted, and that there will be rationalisation of decisions after the event.[64] The consistency of the decisions and the actions will only become apparent and be claimed some time after a number of them have been made.

Although there is generally a criticism of planning and rigorous procedures in most of the processual school's literature, the more managerial authors have acknowledged the usefulness of the rituals of planning as providing comfort for managers faced with uncertainty. The operating manual, reinforcing the idea of 'the way things are done around here', will provide reassurance for those faced with the decision making. Once the political process within an organisation has established a respected leader and a coalition has formed around them, the routine of plans will hold them together and co-ordinate their action. Weick, drawing a comparison between managerial maps and managerial plans, makes the observation that accuracy is not necessarily crucial.[65] He goes on to quote the story of the small detachment of Hungarian soldiers who became lost in a snowstorm in the Alps, and did not return to camp until three days had elapsed. They had pitched their tents and waited until the snow stopped and, on going through their pockets, had found a map which they were able to use to find their way back to the main camp. The officer, who had feared for their lives whilst awaiting their return, was astonished to find that the map was of the Pyrenees. The accuracy of the map was not the important issue, what had been important was that its presence had calmed the soldiers and galvanised them into following standard procedures to look for landmarks and action indicators in order to retrace their steps and reach safety. Similarly, there must be doubt about the accuracy of the maps that the American military used to mount the invasion of Grenada. There was insufficient time for the military cartographers to prepare the large-scale, accurate maps of the area usually deemed necessary for something as important as an invasion, and initially maps from a variety of sources were used. When a common map was found, it was a tourist map prepared in 1895, and none the less adequate to prevent units getting lost. The fact that the military units acted in a co-ordinated manner suggests that it was sufficient for the need.

> The fact that there is an initial map or plan will get people started on an initial course of action and, as the action progresses, they will note the discrepancies between their current experiences and the plan and start to place less reliance upon it, eventually drawing a new map. However, there needs to be that initial plan (or map) as a point of reference against which they can compare their observations about the environment. They activate self-correcting actions and function as starting points which will become redundant as real experience is gained.

Building on Quinn's notion of logical incrementalism, Johnson described his research at Coopers, a clothing retailer, where he investigated the methods by which attempted change was managed.[66] In discussions with managers, he found evidence of the incremental approach, but also found that the results achieved were not particularly good. Johnson deduced that this was due to the way in which the attempted change was managed, and used a model of the beliefs of the organisation to demonstrate an organisational paradigm. He felt that these beliefs could be categorised under six headings and coined the term cultural web to describe this description of the organisational paradigm:

Stories and myths	Typically dealing with heroes, villains, successes, and disasters, they will give insights into the core assumptions about what is important to the organisation.
Symbols	Tangible symbols and symbolic behaviour will give insights into what type of behaviour is rewarded in the organisation.
Rituals and routines	An indication of 'the way we do things around here', as routines will be important to determine what is considered important. The rituals are of a higher order of consideration than routines since they are more deeply embedded.
Organisational structures	The way in which authority and responsibility is distributed within an organisation.
Control systems	An indication of how control is exercised and over what criteria, for instance, stewardship of funds or quality will give an indication of what is important.
Power structures	Will give an indication of which stakeholder groups will influence expectations in the organisation to a greater or lesser extent.

Of the six factors, the easiest to modify when attempting to bring about strategic change tend to be the last three, that is, organisational structures, control systems, and power structures. However, the hardest (and slowest) to modify – the stories and myths, the rituals and routines, and the symbols – are also the strongest influencers of change in the organisation. Where an organisation has been found more likely to adapt to changes in the environment and develop emergent strategies, it has been found to have a more coherent 'ideology', as represented by these three features of the paradigm. After researching the process of strategic change at Hay Management Consultants, Heracleous and Langham proposed that two additional components should be included in the cultural web when considering service organisations:[67]

Communications	The nature of communications and the effectiveness of the methods used are important inputs to the overall paradigm.
Incentives	Normally applied to guide behaviour, how they are perceived, and how well they align with the real motivations of employees is important.

Thus the management of change cannot be a quick fix unless there is a mindset of continuous adaptation and improvement, or as Johnson described it, a 'continuous tension' between the need to preserve the core business and the search for new ideas and their evaluation. This needs to be built into the organisational culture, and echoes to some extent the thoughts of Stacey described earlier. The importance of symbolic actions and mechanisms is strongly argued as providing a reason why divorced analytical and planning functions cannot bring about success within the firm, which must avoid the risk of the strategic issues not being owned. Where they are not, the organisation runs the risk of *strategic drift*, whereby the incremental changes that the organisation makes, which they believe to be driven by environmental changes, do not keep them on track.

For the processual school, the idea that the environment, as well as the organisation, is not the rational feature of the balancing equation – as the classical and environmental schools believe – inhibits the prospect of opportunity-maximising strategies. For them, particularly the 'resource based' theorists, competition is entered into using both the tangible and the intangible resources at their disposal. The intangible resources, particularly the tacit knowledge and skills that take time and learning to evolve, are not easily sold, exchanged, or imitated. These form the core competencies referred to by Grant when he argues that the source of a firm's competitive advantage is the set of resources that are unique to the firm and which are deeply embedded in its patterns of behaviour.[68] Only by continuous effort to build upon and renew these distinct competencies can a firm maintain a long-term competitive advantage over the competition.

Prahalad and Hamel describe these sources of advantage as core competencies, arguing that as standards and expectations are raised by consumers and competitors alike, the only source of long run competitive advantage for a firm will be its superior ability to build – at lower cost and faster than its competitors – the core competencies that develop new and innovative products and services.[69] This will involve the ability to bundle together corporate-wide skills and technologies across the existing organisational boundaries. The idea is that the strategic-business-unit structure, or any other rigid structure that divides the resources of the organisation and creates boundaries between skills and resources, will prevent the establishment of core competencies. This is not to say that building core competencies is about sharing facilities, it is about taking an organisation-wide inventory of key skills and seeing how they can be used together.

> When identifying core competencies, three main tests can be applied. Firstly, a core competence will provide potential access across a wide variety of markets rather than a restricted range. Secondly, a core competence will provide a fundamental part of the perceived benefit in the final offering to the customer. Finally, a core competence will be difficult to copy or imitate by a competitor. For example, many of the laser printers offered by a variety of companies contain an engine manufactured by Canon, their market share of engines is far higher than their market share of end product. These core competencies cannot be built by outsourcing vital components, which may provide a quick route to a winning product, but will provide little of the knowledge enhancing skills necessary.

Similarly, joint ventures with other companies will not build core competencies unless there is a dedicated team of individuals to reverse-engineer the technology, internalise, and disseminate the knowledge acquired. Core competencies can only be built by long-term and consistent investment in improvement and enhancement that may span as much as a decade. To do this, it is necessary to build a *strategic architecture* that transcends the formal organisational structure of the company. This is particularly important for diversified companies where divisional autonomy can dilute the building and effectiveness of core competencies. The strategic architecture is a plan of the future, identifying which competencies will be core, how they should be built, and from which component technologies and skills. Kay similarly describes the firm's distinctive capability as its source of sustainable competitive advantage, arguing that this consists of four components; architecture, reputation, innovation, and strategic assets.[70] He describes architecture as the firm's network of relational contracts with parties both inside and out-side the organisation that add value through the creation of organisational knowledge, co-operation, and the implementation of organisational rou-tines. The choice of architecture will determine whether innovation is fostered or stifled. Reputation is important as a means of communicating informa-tion about the firm's product or service and Kay describes it as: 'the markets method for regulating quality'. Whilst chairman of a consultancy firm, Lon-don Economics, Kay stated that:

> London Economics' distinctive capability is its technical skills in economics, and an established position, particularly in the recruitment market, which makes it quite diffi-cult for others to replicate that stance. That means we should only try to sell work which could only be done by someone with exceptional abilities in economics.[71]

Hamel has criticised the focus on product market positioning and relative short-termism adopted by classical authors such as Porter with their generic strategies, suggesting that these are 'the last few hundred yards of what may be a skill building marathon'.[72] The firm cannot win in the long term by just screening the environment for opportunities without building long-term strength, no matter how attractive those opportunities may be. The build-ing of long-term distinctive capabilities is essential to the health of the organisation. Whilst agreeing that the three central planks of strategy – fit between the firm and its competitive environment, allocation of resources to opportunities, and the investment of 'patient money' – are essential, Hamel and Prahalad contend that the balance in Western companies is often wrong.[73] They argue that leveraging resources is as important as allocation, stretch-ing resources is as important as fit, and that consistency of effort and purpose, the strategic intent, is as important as the amount of financial investment.

The idea of leveraging resources contradicts the downsizing which has been the recent approach to profit improvement. The idea that one can achieve the same performance with less resources has led many Western man-agements to cut staff and investment in the pursuit of 'lean and mean' organisations, with demoralising effects. The increase in acquisitions and mergers has been fuelled by this. Hamel and Prahalad offer five ways that organisations can leverage resources rather than continually reduce them:

1. **Concentrating resources: convergence and focus**
   The need to identify a limited number of key strategic goals, instead of spreading limited resources over a range of medium-term operational goals, will focus the firm on the achievement of long-term sustainable competitive advantage. Having identified those goals, they must outlive any change in leadership and management in the organisation. The resources of the organisation, particularly the intangible resources, must converge on the

attainment of these goals, which may be a ten-year exercise.

2. **Accumulating resources: extracting and borrowing**
    The company must extract experience and knowledge from a variety of sources, both internal and external to the firm. It is not enough to be a learning organisation, there is a need to develop the skills of being a more efficient learning organisation. To borrow resources, companies must become efficient at exploiting the discoveries made by others. The ability to absorb is as important, if not more so, than the ability to innovate. The rapid advance and domination of the electronics industry by the Japanese is, in no small part, due to their ability to copy and even improve upon the inventions of Western organisations.

3. **Complementing resources: blending and balancing**
    The blending and integration of resources will bring about synergistic effects and enhance the value of their contribution to the organisation. The balancing can take three forms, either technological integration, functional integration, or new-product imagination. Balancing resources requires a company to be able to develop, produce, and distribute its products or services with equal skill. It is not enough that they be a good innovator developing excellent new products, the other two features must be there or be available to an equal extent.

4. **Conserving resources: recycling, co-opting, and shielding**
    To recycle resources, a company must look for additional uses for a particular technology or corporate brand. The use of an umbrella brand name for products, rather than individual brand names for each product, has worked well for some companies. The management of corporate reputation is important for although an esteemed brand name will not rescue an inferior product, it will boost the performance of a good one which will, in turn, boost the value of the brand. Co-option involves the somewhat Machiavellian approach of either playing one competitor off against another, so that they both waste resources, or joining forces with one to jointly combat another. Invariably, this is built around the control of a critical resource or component and the Japanese domination of the television market, having first become the largest producer of cathode-ray tubes, is a point in case. To shield resources, it is necessary to not reveal too early one's true intentions by not attacking the market leader in their home market, but in as yet undefended territories or in a slightly different market segment thus allowing the building of a defendable position before a full confrontation becomes inevitable.

5. **Recovering resources, expediting success**
    The ability to compete on time by shortening lead times at all stages of the

process from innovation to delivery will offer a two-fold advantage. Firstly, the company will recover its financial and human investment that much more quickly; and secondly, the opportunity to avoid imitation by competition before market domination has been achieved.

The concept of the learning organisation had been propounded by Senge, who proposed the five essential disciplines of systems thinking, personal mastery, working with mental models, building shared vision, and team learning.[74] For Senge, the compelling reasons for the development of learning organisations were the evolution of industrial society and the fact that the capabilities of such organisations were only just being understood. For Ayas, the essential design components of a learning organisation were the relationships between culture, structure, strategy, and systems, and by incorporating these features the innovative capability and learning capacity was likely to be maximised.[75] He further stressed the importance of career development paths to enhance team working and learning, training in leadership, team building, systems thinking, and job rotation and recommended that rewards should be team oriented.

Stalk has claimed that the ability to compete on time was a major source of competitive advantage for many Japanese companies allowing them to dominate the market segments in which they competed.[76] By reducing the time consumed in every aspect of the business, companies such as Sony and Honda have been able to reduce costs, improve quality, and stay close to their customers.

Hamel and Prahalad, in describing the concept of stretch, compare the approaches of a market leader and a smaller competitor in the same market. The market leader, with a satisfactory return from its efforts, is likely to have the aspiration of maintaining the *status quo* and effectively to have limited ambitions. The smaller player on the other hand, with the ambition of achieving the position of market leader, has more to play for and is likely to have a greater gap between ambition and resource base. A large player is likely to compete by bringing its considerable resources to bear in an approach which the authors liken to the First World War approach of 'whoever runs out of ammunition first, loses', but the smaller player, to be successful, is likely to adopt the tactics of the guerrilla. By exploiting the strength of the market leader in a judo like approach, the small player will look for undefended niches rather than head-on confrontation. It is not that the smaller player is inherently more nimble by virtue of size, but that there is a great deal of stretch in aspirations. The size of the challenge will bring out the best in the company, and the unreasonableness of the ambitions will encourage innovative strategies and creativity in getting the most from their limited resources.

The authors make the further point that, whilst the resource reduction route is demoralising, when the concept of leveraging and stretch are applied to the organisation, the workforce are more likely to be highly motivated as they see growth in performance being achieved without asset disposal.

In contrast to others in the processual school, Hamel and Prahalad claim that industry foresight, although limited, is possible to achieve.[77] Although involving the investment of significant amounts of intellectual effort on the part of management, it is a necessary component of developing the strategic focus referred to earlier.

The systemic school

The basic belief of the systemic school is that all of the previously described approaches have their merits when put into the relevant sociological and cultural context. All can be equally valid, depending on the cultural and historical context in which they are considered.

Anglo-Saxon management systems

The concepts of both rational economic man, as proposed by the authors of the classical school, and of the managers of the efficient organisation, as proposed by the environmentalists, have been brought about by the social conditioning that the managers of the organisations concerned have undergone. Their behaviour has developed over time from the inputs received from their families, education, the state, and even their religious upbringing. For the systemic school, the cultural and political situation outside the organisation is just as influential as the internal one which the processualists discuss. It is possibly worth remembering that Weber's original work was an investigation of the 'Protestant work ethic', which led on to his description of bureaucracy.[78] Subsequent to this, Mead has considered the different forms of bureaucracy, adherence to it, and the rules that have developed in different cultures.[79] Although culture is not the only driver, those cultures that most need the rules that are associated with bureaucracy tend to adopt a more ideal model.

Bureaucratic procedures are, in general, adopted by an organisation to ensure that members' behaviour is predictable and to reduce uncertainties, in much the same way that formal planning systems would be adopted. Where the full bureaucratic model is adopted, there is a high degree of regulation and members respect the unequal distribution of power and a superior's right to exercise it. Amongst other countries, including Japan, Mexico, and other Latin American countries, he quotes France as being an adopter of the full bureaucratic model. He goes on to quote the work of Aiken and Bacharch who investigated differences between Belgian local authorities.[80] In those areas dominated by the Walloons (French culture) the full model was adopted, whilst in the Flemish (Dutch) areas a market model of bureaucracy was followed. The market bureaucracy is typified by a greater reliance on interpersonal mechanisms for social control, with less reliance on impersonal rules and more short circuiting of officials.

The market bureaucracy model, typified by the United Kingdom, America, and other Anglo countries, places more reliance on the formation of coalitions within firms and a more negotiated approach to power and influence, tying in with the processual school of thought. The other types of bureaucracy described are workflow bureaucracies, where the emphasis is on regulating activities rather than relationships, and the personnel bureaucracies, which tend to occur in collectivist cultures, where power is typically centred on the individual rather than their rank. Typically in the personnel bureaucracy, managers need to exhibit a higher level of expertise than those that report to them. Germany, Switzerland, and Israel are described as workflow bureaucracies, whilst personnel bureaucracies are typified by the countries of East and West Africa, and South East Asia. Hofstede, in fact, considers the personnel bureaucracy to be like an oriental family.[81] However, there are distinct differences between the Chinese and Japanese management systems, and Fukuda claims that Hong Kong Chinese companies depend less on informal channels of communication than Japanese companies, the Chinese manager being less likely to pass on information to others unless (s)he can see its distinct relevance to them.[82] Thus Chinese management systems cannot be truly regarded as collective.

The attitude to employment of family members also shows distinct differences across cultural boundaries, and this has implications for the use of experts from outside the firm and the relationship between the owners and managers of an organisation. In Anglo cultures, nepotism (the employment of family members) is viewed with suspicion and is often considered a recipe for disaster. Bork, writing of American firms, says that family members should only be employed when they can offer exceptional expertise significantly superior to outside candidates.[83] Other American writers, such as Brandt,[84] caution that family firms must supplement the board of directors with respected professionals who owe no allegiance to any family member. We can contrast the Chinese model of the family business where family members are actively preferred over outsiders, where a priority is placed on family loyalty and Confucian values. The business will depend upon worldwide family connections for information and the transfer of capital. The senior management of a Chinese company is unlikely to include other than family members and this tends to lead to rapid decision making.

These cultural differences, upon which we have only touched here, have significant implications for the growth of multinationals and how they plan and control strategically. Whether there can be truly stateless corporations operating in a borderless world is open to debate. Many Anglo multinationals may have a large proportion of their employees abroad, but many of them are expatriates with much of their asset base in the home territory. Most Swiss multinationals remain solidly nationalistic by virtue of articles of association that limit foreign ownership of their voting shares, and similarly, most Japanese boards of directors are dominated by nationals. Bartlett and Ghoshal distinguish between four different types of multinational companies:[85]

---

multinational
Headquarters decides financial policy, but otherwise allows a high degree of autonomy to subsidiaries who are allowed to decide upon management style, and to respond to local product and market differences. Phillips and Unilever are considered typical.

global
Headquarters are responsible for strategic, marketing, and managerial policies, which are centralised. The need to capitalise upon the economies of scale available from global operations means that the products developed ignore specific local needs.

international
Here the headquarters will retain control over the same features as the global company, but to a lesser extent. Products and services developed for the home market will be extended to other markets with similar characteristics, and then allowed to diffuse into other markets. The passage to other markets will be managed on the basis of efficiently managing the development of the product life cycle.

transnational
The company will combine the features of the other three models and is designed to respond to the simultaneous demands of global efficiency, national responsiveness, and worldwide learning. Although some resources will be managed from the centre, managerial expertise will be spread around the divisions and developed by strong interdependencies. Products and services are designed to be globally acceptable, but with local adaptation.

For the systemic school, the objectives that companies set for themselves are also driven by the national culture in which they operate. In Anglo economies, where there is a ready market for shares and well-established stockmarkets, objectives tend to be set around the profit motive and the need to satisfy the owners with regular dividends. Shareholders need to be satisfied in the short term or they will sell shares and acquisitions resulting in a deposed board of directors. The hostile takeover is a phenomenon which is, to a larger extent, unfamiliar to other economies, and national priorities will often supersede the profit motive. When Nixdorf Computers of Germany needed to be taken over, the comment was made in the local press that it did not matter who took over the company, as long as the acquirer was another German company. In Germany, takeover bids for public companies, particularly hostile ones, are very rare. Contrast the acquisition in America of Honeywell, another computer company, which was made, without comment, by Bull, a state owned French company. With a different pattern of share ownership in Japan, where there is cross ownership of shares between companies and large shareholdings by banks, there tends to be a longer-term view. Objectives are more likely to deal with market penetration and innovation.

The whole concept of strategy and the ability to affect the future is alien to some cultures, where the belief is that everything is dependent upon luck and fate or in the hands of the Gods. Pascale states that the Japanese do not have an expression for 'corporate strategy', and that it seems to be an Anglo concept.[86]

Summary

Having described the four different approaches to strategy as defined by Whittington, we can see that they differ widely in their methodologies and prescriptions for management. The classical school is thoroughly prescriptive, both in its analysis and in its treatment of the results of that analysis. With its tools, techniques, and prescriptions so frequently described, Whittington quotes 37 books in print,[87] it is very familiar to most readers. For the evolutionists, there is no need for a rational approach to analysis, particularly of future markets which they firmly believe cannot be foreseen. Far better, according to them, to make the organisation as efficient as possible to survive whatever the market may throw at them. They will still allow that there can be a rational process and profit seeking within the organisation, but that it must be geared towards short-term survival. For the processualists, the prospect of deliberate strategy making is unfeasible since the organisation and the environment are irrational, and cannot be credited with the ability to determine the best course of action or the best player in the field. By contrast with the others, the systemic school of thought suggested that the most important consideration is the cultural and societal situation in which the organisation must operate. Where a society deems that formal planning is important, then that is what should be done, not only must the right thing be done, it must be seen to be done. In Chapter 6 we will endeavour to pull together the most appropriate of each of the approaches and to identify the issues which will face companies in the future.

4 Strategic Management Models, Tools, and Techniques

INTRODUCTION

Descriptive models of strategic management

In Chapter 3, we discussed the emergence of strategic management and its role in modern-day business management. In this chapter, we focus on contributions to the field of strategic management. There are three levels of strategy in a multibusiness firm: corporate strategy, business strategy (also termed competitive strategy), and functional strategy. A *corporate strategy* is a strategy for a portfolio of business units. This strategy specifies where, that is, in which industries and in which countries, a multibusiness firm competes. A *business strategy* is a strategy for a single business unit. This strategy classifies how the business unit's managers compete in a given industry. A *functional strategy* is a strategy for maximising resource productivity within the constraints of the other two strategies. Research would suggest that in the domain of strategic management, both normative and descriptive models are used. Normative models deal with what the firms should do. Descriptive models deal with what firms actually do. The literature on strategy may be further divided into contributions that focus on the *process* and on the *content* of strategic management.

The origin of the present vocabulary can be traced back to the early 1960s, when strategy was largely equated with corporate planning. One of the early influential writers was Alfred D. Chandler of Harvard Business School. His studies of US corporations and their historical development, published as *Strategy and Structure* in 1962,[1] demonstrated persuasively that the structure of an organisation was determined by its strategic goals, and the actions and resources employed to achieve them. The organisation's function, he argued, was to implement strategy, and all its varied management structures and hierarchies developed from that objective. This declaration has remained a foundation stone of strategy studies and thinkers over the last 35 years.

The Chandler model described how four large, multidivisional US corporations (General Motors, due Pont, Exxon, and Sears Roebuck) changed from a functional structure to a divisional structure. The work undertaken by Chandler was important because it was the initial description of the emergence of the divisional structure, and because it explains why a divisional structure proved to be more effective for these companies. Chandler begins by summarising the centre's role in a functionally organised company. Here the centre's role is critical: it sets overall direction, co-ordinates between functions, provides central services, allocates resources, and estimates performance. As the functional departments grow larger, this role becomes increasingly complex. Traditionally, such firms had decentralised functionally, for example, to accounts, marketing, R&D. The multidivisional firm decentralised by type of business activity, so that each operating business unit would have its own accounts and its own marketers.

The 1960s saw the output of management theory devoted to the strategy subject. The most influential academic of his day was Igor Ansoff. His book, *Corporate Strategy*, set out to be a practical formula for strategic decision making within a business firm. According to Ansoff:

> strategic problems are harder to pinpoint, they require special attention. Unless specific provisions are made for concern with strategy, the firm may misplace its effort in pursuit of operating efficiency at times when attention to strategic opportunities (and threats) can produce a more radical and immediate improvement in a firm's performance.

Ansoff goes on to say:

> A proper balance of managerial attention requires three kinds of provisions. One is to provide management with a method of analysis which can help to formulate the firm's future strategy. The second provision is to provide a method by which management can determine the administrative structure which will be needed to manage under the new strategy. The third provision is to provide a method for guiding the transformation from present to the future strategy and from the present to the future administrative structure.[2]

The Ansoff model (shown in Figure 4.1)suggests that most strategic decisions are made within a restricting environment of resources and are therefore limited to a choice of alternatives. In essence strategic decisions are concerned with:

- The scope of the firm's activities
- The matching of the firm's activities to its environment

- The matching of the activities of a firm to its resource capability
- The allocation of major resources in a firm
- The values, expectations, and goals of those influencing strategy
- The direction a firm will take in the long term
- The ramifications for change throughout the firm

The object is to produce a resource allocation pattern which will offer the best possibility for meeting the firm's objectives. Interestingly, Ansoff did not argue the process of strategic planning in broad terms; rather he focused his model on the more narrow issue of corporate expansion and diversification. Ansoff later decided that his original writings had been too prescriptive, and spent the next 20 years refining his concepts and building more flexibility into the planning process to serve the increasing upheaval and unpredictable pace of business change. By the late 1960s, most US business firms had started to absorb Ansoff's teachings into their business vocabulary. Early definitions of strategic management focused attention to the long-run performance of a corporation through the component known as *strategic planning*.

Strategic planning

This is the part of strategic management which aims at the formulation of a firm's strategy. An important issue in this material is how the process of strategic planning should be arranged. It is argued that the process of strategic planning should consist of a logical sequence of steps. Planning as programme activity needs to have a systematic element to it to produce a well-defined result. The process requires a high degree of co-ordinated decision making provoked by the dictates of strategy. A strategic plan can have the following components:

1. A definition of the desired future scope of the company, including a statement of identity: 'What business is the company in or should it be in and what kind of company is it or should be?'[3]
2. A classification of the competitive advantage of the firm, including its particular competencies in relation to its competitors and the market niche it intends to occupy.
3. A declaration of the purpose, mission, goals, and objectives of the company and the measures used to judge performance.
4. A declaration of how to allocate the resources needed to implement and accomplish the programme.

Early adopters of strategic planning (models and techniques) encountered three serious problems:

1. Paralysis by analysis – which occurred when a series of plans produced little by way of results in the marketplace.
2. Organisational resistance to the introduction of strategic planning into the firm.
3. Ejection of strategic planning from the firm as soon as erstwhile forceful support of planning by top management was withdrawn or relaxed.

According to Ansoff, one reaction to these experiences, expressed by both managers and academics, was to argue that strategic planning was an unproductive invention, and that it did not produce the intended results.[4] In response to this reaction, several research studies have been carried out during the past 20 years, addressing the question: Does systematic strategic planning improve financial performance of the firm? The first of these studies, performed by Ansoff and his colleagues, reached the statistically significant conclusion that when properly used, strategic planning does produce significant improvements in the firm's performance.

In one of his more recent books, *Implanting Strategic Management*, Ansoff proposes a link between decision-making behaviour and the environment imperatives.[5] Ansoff concludes, very much in the contingency theory tradition, that the nature of the business and, in particular, the strategic challenge facing management should be determining factors in the choice of decision-making behaviour. He points out that under some circumstances, a company needs to operate highly sophisticated decision-making processes, whereas under other circumstances, it is more cost effective for the company to rely on *ad hoc* decision making.[6]

The typical large multibusiness firm has three levels of strategy: corporate, business, and functional. These components of strategy form a hierarchy within most large corporations. They interact closely with each other and must be well integrated if the total corporation is to be successful. The model presented in Figure 4.2 reflects the strategic management process (at all levels) within the organisation and is the author's adaptation from Churchman's four-factor model.[7]

At the centre of the model is embedded Churchman's first important message: identify the organisation's values. Without knowledge of its values, an organisation cannot develop its mission, goals, and objectives. Churchman's remaining imperatives can be found within the four boxes. They are: strategic planning, organisational structure, strategic control, and resource requirements. Outside the boxes are forces and constraints that affect the other factors. The whole model shows how the organisation's strategy must equalise the demands imposed by external and internal forces, suit the overall functioning of the organisation, and use resources in a manner that meets goals and satisfies values. The arrows show significant interdependencies among the four factors of strategic management. Each of these factors joins strategic management to the existence of the organisation's internal or external environment, and each factor directly or indirectly affects the other three.

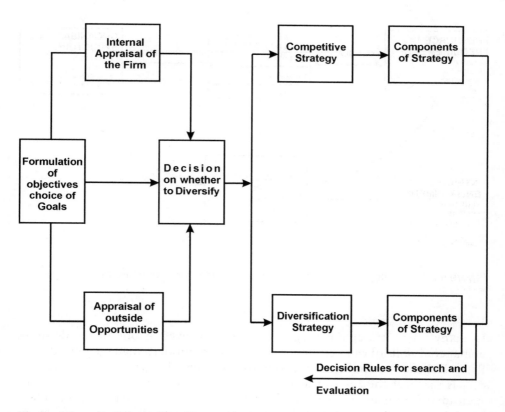

Figure 4.1   Decision schematic in strategy formulation

Source: Reproduced with the kind permission of the publisher from Igor Ansoff, *Corporate Strategy*, Penguin Business rev. edn, London 1987, p. 196.

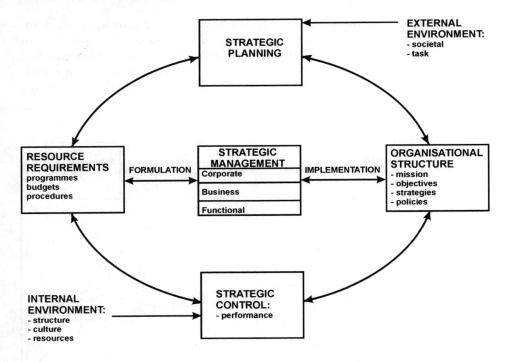

Figure 4.2   Strategic management model (adapted from Churchman)

In many ways, strategic management can be viewed as one of the defining managerial skills of this century. As the father of modern management theory Peter Drucker has pointed out, one of the ways of characterising this century is that it is the age of the large institution.[8] The one unifying aspect of such institutions is the need to imagine the future in a changing and challenging environment. A firm needs both corporate objectives (i.e., what business should we be in?) and business unit objectives (i.e., how should the firm position itself relative to its competitors' markets?). In essence, strategic management seeks to resolve the central strategic questions in a range of ways. It seeks to:

● Define organisation character, mission, and objectives (what kind of organisation are we and do we want to be?).
● Define strategic capability and distinctive competence (where can we best add value to society; where can we compete?).

- Assess environmental opportunities and threats (what's the current and future shape of the playing field on which we have to operate?).
- Match capabilities with opportunities (the crucial task – search for best fit).
- Develop organisational focus (the provision of a consistent, long-run direction which unifies effort).
- Construct appropriate structures (without which strategy will not be delivered).
- Communicate purpose (both internally and externally).[9]

Other management theorists, such as Kotler and Tilles, share this descriptive point of view. Kotler points out that the development of strategies has two main benefits: they facilitate the achievement of objectives *and* they require people to come together.[10] This aids better understanding and focus, and a shared sense of opportunity, direction, significance, and achievement. The importance of shared objectives is also identified by Tilles, who states that the need for an explicit strategy stems from two key attributes of an organisation: that success hinges on people working together, thus mutually reinforcing corporate inputs *and* that these efforts have to be done in rapidly changing conditions.[11]

Establishing concise objectives is, clearly, the foundation step. Objectives should be carefully designed so that an effective plan develops. To facilitate efforts, objectives should be stated in specific terms related to the fundamental philosophies and policies of a firm. Obscure or unspecified objectives lead to vague, undefined, and unco-ordinated plans, and to decisions taken under the pressure of particular situations, leading to actions which are often incompatible. The supposition of strategic planning seems to be that objectives are decided upon by the top management for the entire organisation and, having been decided, they arouse the process of formulating strategy and then rush down the hierarchy, themselves functioning as devices of control by which to measure performance.

The external environment

Change has been a dominant characteristic of the twentieth century, and its pace and composition have also increased. In the UK, for example, the period between 1948 and 1971, while still going through change, was relatively stable and predictable. The economic growth was continuous throughout the 1950s and 1960s. Unemployment and inflation were low and steady, and a high degree of social agreement prevailed. Political parties had similar agendas, and both technological and market changes were manageable. What replaced this relative calm was the oil crisis of 1973. In the UK, this crisis exposed previously dormant markets to considerable threats since familiarity with previous established conditions had led to complacency.

In Chapter 1, we discussed briefly the significance of *external* and *internal* triggers, and their resulting influence within the competitive global environment. Strategic planning is considered the key pathway between strategic management and the organisation's external environment. Before firms can begin devising strategies, they must scan the *external* and *internal environments* to identify possible opportunities, threats, strengths, and weaknesses. The framework demonstrated in Figure 4.3 can be used to analyse these environments.

Environmental scanning is the first step in finding and analysing external threats and opportunities. At this early stage in the process, managers need to identify all general events and trends that could be applicable to the firm's performance in the future. The notion of the environment encapsulates very many different influences, and the difficulty is understanding this diversity in a way which can contribute to strategic decision making. Experience would seem to suggest that this approach is productive when practised in a group-dynamics situation. Group sessions often result in an enhanced awareness of reasons for strategic revisions or insights about future development. During the scanning session, managers undertake to identify factors relevant to PEST environment (see Table 4.1 and Chapter 1, pages 1–26).

Scanning each of the PEST factors should reveal most of the environmental aspects that need to be considered. Strategists, however, sometimes add two more factors to complete the analysis. They are:

Competition: factors that involve actions taken by current and potential competitors, market share, and concentration of competitors.

Geography: factors related to location, space, topography, climate, and natural resources.

In the book *Exploring Corporate Strategy*, Johnson and Scholes give warning of the danger of using the 'balance sheet' approach to environmental scanning, which consists of listing all possible environmental influences in an endeavour to identify opportunities and threats. They say:

> . . . it is relatively easy to see that an organisation might have a whole range of things going for it and a range going against it: long lists can be generated for most organisations. However, if environmental analysis consists of this alone the limitations are significant. No overall picture emerges of what are really important influences on the organisation. What is more, there is the danger that attempts will be made to deal with environmental influences in a piecemeal way rather than make more fundamental strategic responses.[12]

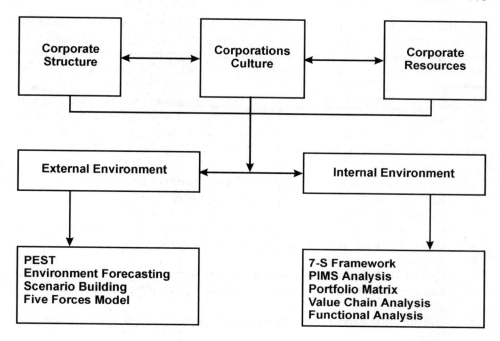

Figure 4.3   Framework for analysing external and internal environments

Table 4.1   Key generic environmental factors

Political	Economic
● Tax laws	● Money supply
● Stability of Government	● Wage controls
● Environmental legislation	● Interest rates
● Government incentives	● Energy costs
● Union laws	● GNP\GDP trends
● Foreign trade regulations	● Crime (law and order) trends
Societal	**Technological**
● Changes in population demographics	● Spending on Research and Development
● Lifestyles	● Developments in technological transfer
● Attitudes to work and leisure	● Rates of technology obsolescence
● Job expectations	● Productivity improvement trends
● Birth and Death expectancies	

An alternative to the PEST model is to use Vulnerability Analysis. Research by Hurd would suggest that many managers play down the threats and weaknesses in favour of the firm's strengths and opportunities.[13] Vulnerability analysis can assist in strategy formulation by forcing managers to critique the organisation's strategic plans. The process starts by asking one very simple question: What supportive elements, if suddenly taken away, might seriously damage or even destroy the business? These supportive elements are the foundations upon which the organisation depends for its lasting existence. The following 12 categories have been identified by Hurd:

1. Customer needs and wants served by the product or service.
2. Resources and assets: people, capital, facilities, raw materials, technological know-how.
3. Cost position relative to competition, by major cost components.
4. Consumer base: its size, demographics, trends.
5. Technologies required.
6. Special skills, systems, procedures, organisation.
7. Corporate identity: logo, image, products, corporate culture, role models.
8. Institutional barriers to competition: regulations, codes, patent laws, licensing.
9. Social values, life styles, common norms, ideals.
10. Sanctions, supports, and incentives to do business, particularly in such fields as medicine, nuclear materials, restaurants, securities, import-export.
11. Customer goodwill: product safety, product quality, company reputation.
12. Complementary products or services in the stakeholder system.

The complete process of undertaking vulnerability analysis involves seven steps. They are:

1. Identify supportive elements.
2. State how the removal of a supportive element would threaten the business.
3. State the most conservative consequences of each threat.
4. Rank the impact of worst consequences of each threat.
5. Estimate the probability of each threat materialising.
6. Rank the company's ability to deal with each threat, should it materialise.
7. Determine whether the company's vulnerability to each threat is extreme or negligible.

Environmental forecasting

Few organisations and their managers would deny that PEST factors are a crucial aspect in strategic decision making. Given this truth, the obvious question is how these factors can be forecast with any degree of exactness. Several studies have examined the impact of environmental forecasting on organisational performance and profitability. For example, Georgoff and Murdick describe how managers at Compaq Computer Corporation chose the best combination of techniques to deal with difficult problems, such as when IBM, Hewlett-Packard, and other companies would enter the portable computer market, and how IBM's change in price would affect its potential profitability.[14] The author's examined the problem of forecasting by taking into account the following considerations:

- Time horizons (reasonable future period of time).
- Technical sophistication (experience needed to forecast future events).
- Cost (the expense of updating forecasts).
- Data availability (currency, accuracy, and representativeness of data).
- Variability and consistency of data (relationships assumed among variables).

They went on to examine four basic approaches that could be used for forecasting. These were:

1. Judgement methods, including the Delphi method and *scenario writing*.
2. Data-oriented methods, including market research, consumer surveys, and industrial and market surveys.
3. Time-series approaches, including moving averages, exponential smoothing, and time-series extrapolation.
4. Causal models, including correlation or regression models, leading-indicator forecasting, and econometric models.

Georgoff and Murdick found that by combining forecasts, they were able to achieve results that were significantly more accurate than those yielded by any individual forecasting technique.

Scenario building

Back in the 1950s, Herman Kahn developed a methodology for scenario writing.[15] It was not, however, until the mid 1970s that scenario building started to emerge as a forecasting tool.[16] Scenarios are written narratives describing the future and seeking to answer two questions:

1. What are the precise steps that might cause some hypothetical situation to develop?
2. What alternatives exist for preventing or facilitating the occurrence of the hypothetical situation?

It is normal practice to write scenarios using experts and managers and these scenarios are then used in examining contingencies that may face the organisation in the future. Linneman and Klein have argued that the best time to include top managers is at the beginning of the scenario process.[17] The process starts with the decision and the selection of the scenario builder. It requires in this individual a sensitivity to the PEST environments in which the organisation finds itself. Some individuals are very skilful at discerning trends and forces at work within society or the international community; this skill will usually be supported by wide reasoning and thinking in order to monitor the external environment. According to Wack, identifying predetermined elements is fundamental to serious planning.[18] You must be careful however, Paul Valery, the twentieth-century French philosopher, said: *'Un fait mal observe est plus pernicieux qu'un mauvais raisonnement.'* ['A fact poorly observed is more treacherous than faulty reasoning.']. Errors in futures studies usually result from poor observation rather than poor reasoning.

There are certain base criteria that can be brought to bear in the selection process. The starting point must be the perceived disadvantages or risk to the organisation. This is where the various micromodels and linkages are useful, since they embody those macroeconomic influences that systematically affect the markets and trading environments of the firm. For example, a service business may be exposed to the whims of consumer spending or interest rates. Although an assumed change of any economic significance to the base-case will eventually influence most sectors of the economy, it may affect one sector first and to a far greater extent than others.

One of the first companies to utilise scenarios in a big way was Shell Oil. Shell Oil's use of scenario building was a key factor in them surviving the 1973 energy crisis. Shell continue to use scenarios as a planning technique that teaches managers how to think about unknown future possibilities. They separate what is predetermined from what is known or certain, and they separate what will happen from what cannot happen. The managers at Royal Dutch Shell have come to accept this technique to cope with the necessity to constantly adapt and innovate in today's competitive environment.[19] The steps in scenario building are well chronicled in Schwartz,[20] and the eight steps suggested are given in Table 4.2 below. The benefit of scenario building is that there is more commitment by management, which leads to greater agreement of the actions needed to carry out the strategy that is chosen. The variety of approaches for writing scenarios offer versatility and ensure managers will find one with which they feel content.

Table 4.2   Steps in developing scenarios

Step	Description
1	Identify Focal Issue or Decision
2	Key Forces in the Local Environment
3	Driving Forces
4	Rank by Importance and Uncertainty
5	Selecting Scenario Logics
6	Fleshing Out the Scenarios
7	Implications
8	Selection of Leading Indicators and Signposts

Lit review

Porter's five forces model

Michael Porter has argued that the competitive environment within an industry depends on five forces: the manoeuvring for position among the current competitors within an industry; the threat of new entrants into the industry; the threat of substitute products or services being introduced into the industry; the bargaining power of buyers; and the bargaining power of suppliers.[21] Figure 4.4 diagrams these competitive forces. One approach to competitive analysis is to use these five forces as a conceptual framework for identifying the organisation's competitive strengths and weaknesses, along with threats to and opportunities for the organisation from its competitive environment.

Competitive rivalry

Rivalry among existing competitors takes the familiar form of jockeying for position – using tactics like price competition, advertising contests, product introductions, and increased customer service or warranties. Rivalry occurs because one or more competitors either feels the pressure or sees the opportunity to improve position. This pattern of action and reaction may or may not leave the initiating firm, and the industry as a whole, better off. Some forms of competition, notably price competition, are highly unstable and quite likely to leave the entire industry worse off from the standpoint of profitability. Price cuts are quickly and easily matched by rivals. Rivalry in some industries is characterised by such phrases as 'cut-throat' or 'warlike', whereas in other industries it is termed 'polite' or 'gentlemanly'. Intense rivalry is the result of a number of interacting structural factors:

- numerous or equally balanced competitors
- slow industry growth
- high fixed or storage costs
- lack of differentiation or switching costs
- capacity augmented in large increments
- diverse competitors

In general, the more intense the competition in an industry, the more arduous it is for new firms to enter and for existing firms to survive.

Threat of entry

New entrants to an industry bring new capacity, the desire to gain market share, and often substantial resources. For example, prices can be bid down or incumbents' costs inflated as a result, reducing profitability. The threat of entry into an industry depends on the barriers to entry that are present, coupled with the reaction from existing competitors that the entrant can expect. If barriers are high and/or the newcomer can expect sharp retaliation from new competitors, the threat of entry is low. The most common barriers to entry are:

1. Economies of scale.
2. Product differentiation.
3. Capital requirements.
4. Switching costs.
5. Access to distribution channels.
6. Cost disadvantages independent of scale.
7. Government policy.

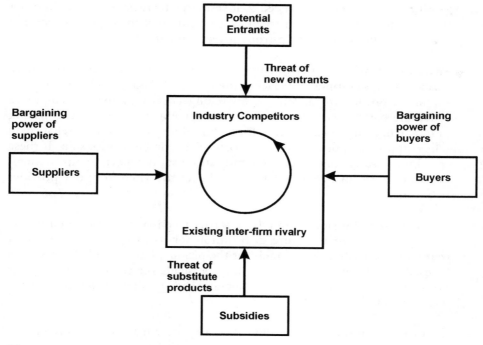

Figure 4.4 Forces driving industry competition

Source: M. E. Porter, *Competitive Strategies*, Macmillan, New York 1980.

1. **Economies of Scale**: refers to reductions in unit costs of a product as the absolute-volume period increases. Scale economies can be present in nearly every function of a business, including marketing, purchasing, and distribution. For example, in the banking industry economies are large in the management of current accounts, but they are less significant in mortgage lending. It is important to examine each component of costs separately for its particular relationship between unit cost and scale.

2. **Product differentiation**: means that established firms have brand identification and customer loyalties, which stem from past advertising, customer service, product differences, or simply being first into the industry. Differentiation creates a barrier to entry by focusing entrants on spending heavily to overcome existing customer loyalties. Such investments in building a brand name are particularly risky since they have no extricating value if entry fails. Product differentiation is perhaps the most important entry barrier in health-care products, over-the-counter medicines, cosmetics, investment banking, and public accounting services.

3. **Capital requirements**: the need to invest large financial resources in order to compete creates a barrier to entry, particularly if the capital is required for risky or unrecoverable up-front advertisement.

4. **Switching costs**: a barrier to entry is created by the presence of switching costs, that is, one-time costs facing the buyer through switching from one supplier's product to another's. Switching costs may include employee retraining costs, cost of new ancillary equipment, cost and time in testing or qualifying a new source, need for technical help as a result of reliance on seller support aid, or even psychic costs of severing a relationship. If these switching costs are high, then new entrants must offer a major improvement in cost or performance in order for the buyer to switch from one provider to another.

5. **Access to distribution channels**: a barrier to entry can be created by the new entrant's need to secure distribution for its product. To the extent that logical distribution channels for the product have already been served by established firms, the new firm must persuade the channels to accept its product through price breaks, co-operative advertising allowance, and the like, which reduce profits.

6. **Cost disadvantages independent of scale**: these may be attributed to:

   ● proprietary product technology,
   ● favourable access to raw materials,
   ● favourable locations,
   ● government subsidies,
   ● and learning or experience curve.

7. **Government policy**: the last major source of entry barriers is government policy. Government can limit or even foreclose entry into industries with such controls as licensing requirements and limits on access to raw materials. More subtle government restrictions on entry can stem from controls such as air and water pollution standards, and product safety and efficiency regulations. For example, pollution control can increase the capital needed for entry, as well as the required technological sophistication, and even the optimal scale of facilities. Standards for product testing, common in industries like food and other health-related products, can impose substantial lead times.

Threat of substitutes

All firms in an industry are competing, in a broad sense, with industries producing substitute products. Substitutes limit the potential returns of an industry by placing a ceiling on the prices firms in the industry can profitably charge. Substitutes not only limit profits in normal times, but they also reduce the bonus an industry can reap in boom times. Identifying substitute products is a matter of searching for other products that can perform the same function as the product of the industry. Substitute products that deserve the most attention are those that are subject to trends improving their price-performance trade-off with the industry's product, or are produced by industries earning high profits. In the latter case, substitutes often come rapidly into play if some development increases competition in their industries and causes price reduction or performance improvement. In general, the greater the pressure from substitute products or services, the less attractive the industry.

Power of buyers

Buyers compete with the industry by forcing down prices, bargaining for higher quality or more services, and playing competitors off against each other – all at the expense of industry profitability. A buyer group is powerful if the following circumstances hold true:

1. It is concentrated or purchases large volumes relative to seller's sales. Large volume buyers are particularly potent forces if heavy fixed costs characterise the industry – as they do in the pharmaceutical industry.
2. The products it purchases from the industry represents a significant fraction of the buyer's costs of purchases.
3. It faces few switching costs.
4. It earns low profits.
5. Buyers pose a real threat of backward integration.
6. The buyer has full information.

A critique of the bargaining power of the buyers of an industry's products enables strategic managers to measure the firm's market power. The greater the bargaining power of buyers, the less advantage the sellers have.

Power of suppliers

Suppliers can exert bargaining power over participants in an industry by threatening to raise or reduce the quality of purchased goods and services. Powerful suppliers can thereby squeeze profitability out of an industry unable to recover cost increases in its own prices. The conditions making suppliers powerful tend to mirror those making buyers powerful. A supplier group is powerful if the following apply:

1. It is dominated by a few companies and is more concentrated than the industry it sells to.
2. It is not obliged to contend with other substitute products for sale to the industry.
3. The industry is not an important customer of the supplier group.
4. The suppliers product is an important input to the buyer's business.
5. The suppliers group's products are differentiated or it has built up switching costs.
6. The supplier group poses a credible threat of forward integration.

In general, the greater the bargaining power of the supplier, the less advantage the firm has. A process known as backward vertical integration is frequently used to acquire suppliers with which the firm has weak bargaining power.

It is worth noting that within an industry there may be distinct strategic groups present who, by virtue of their different strategic postures, will enjoy the competitive forces, as defined by Porter, to a different extent to other players. Cool and Dierickx describe the strategic groups present in the pharmaceutical industry and delineate the players on the basis of prices charged and level of R&D expenditure.[22] Two distinct strategic groups emerge. Those companies with a high R&D spend, who can be classified as the proprietary group, are able to charge premium prices for blockbuster drugs. They are, of course, pursuing a high-risk, high-reward strategy since they are dependent upon a regular supply of successful innovative products to replace those where the patent has expired. When patents do expire, the second strategic group, the generic group, are able to step in and manufacture cheaper copies, eating into the margins that the proprietary group are able to charge. The generic group follow a safer, lower risk strategy and enjoy consequently reduced rewards. An analysis of the five competitive forces will be different for these two groups. Barriers to entry will be significantly higher for the proprietary group, and buyer power lower. Similarly, the nature of the competition will be different. For the generic group, competition will be much more price oriented, but for the proprietary firms competition will be based on superior R&D performance. There will be mobility barriers preventing firms transferring from one strategic group to another, but invariably those companies which have 'lost their way' and are following an isolated path rather than a recognised strategy will founder.

If we take Porter's model showing factors affecting the competitive position of any organisation and list the changes 2001 could bring (Table 4.3), it is clear that action is needed now to prepare for the most likely of these. Firms should also be trying to *outwit* the strategies of their known competitors and attempting to see where new entrants are going to come from. Although these five competitive forces are at work in any industry, the balance of power between the different countries in an industry can vary. For example, an industry might be populated by a number of small-scale competitors. An example in the UK is hairdressing: there are few large chains of hairdressers; most hairdressing salons are independent. Alternatively, an industry might be dominated by a small number of large competitors. In the UK, the electricity utility is dominated by National Power and Powergen. There may also be a combination: few leading companies may dominate the market, but smaller ones might exist. Again, here in the UK, there is a small number of booksellers (such as W. H. Smith) with a substantial country-wide presence, but there is a large number of independent book shops. Similarly, the fast food industry in the UK features major chains such as McDonald's, as well as independent providers. The largest concentration of British competitive advantage is in consumer packaged goods, including alcoholic beverages, food such as confectionery products and biscuits, personal products such as cigarettes, cosmetics, and perfume, and household products such as toothpaste, soaps, and cleaning preparations.

The UK sustains competitive advantage in industries that draw advantages from pure science. The fact that Britain has an upper tier of highly educated people, whose wages are relatively low in world terms, points to a long tradition that has created early mover advantages, a well-established infrastructure in finance, trading, and the arts, and unusual or high-end demand. Such industries – for luxury consumer goods and services, finance, information, general business services, and others – many of them concentrated around London, vividly illustrate the self-reinforcing effects of geographical concentration. The problem is that they do not create enough well-paying jobs to employ all of Britain's citizens, and lack of success elsewhere in the UK has meant that regional disparities have become greater and greater.[23]

Table 4.3 **Factors affecting competitive advantage in the year 2000**

Industry Competitors (Existing Firms)
Entrants ● Foreign National Companies ● International Companies ● Global Companies ● New liaisons
Substitutes ● New European culture, new tastes and requirements in existing foreign products and services replacing existing offerings ● Competitiveness of single market results in more R&D by firms producing new, better substitutes to existing product/service perhaps at lower prices
Buyers ● Changes in demand patterns ● Greater choice ● National loyalties lessen ● Bargaining power changes ● Lower costs
Suppliers ● Wider market opportunities mean suppliers can find new contracts elsewhere. Consequently firm's existing business is less important ● Costs increase/decrease ● Standards improve/worsen

The internal environment

The internal environment was very briefly described in Chapter 1, you will recall that the internal environment consists of factors (or variables), strengths, and weaknesses that are within the organisation itself and are not usually within the short-term control of management. Organisations should attempt to identify those factors within their firm that may be important strengths and weaknesses. A *strength* is a resource or capacity the organisation can use effectively to achieve its objectives. A *weakness* is a limitation, frailty in the organisation that will keep it from achieving its objectives. In broad terms, an effective strategy is one that takes advantage of the firm's opportunities by employing its strengths and that wards off threats by avoiding them, or by correcting or compensating for weaknesses.

One specific method used in performing an internal organisational analysis is through the application of a combination of six distinct approaches:

1. 7-S Framework
2. PIMS Analysis
3. Portfolio Analysis
4. Value Chain Analysis
5. Functional Analysis
6. Financial Analysis

The seven Ss framework

The seven Ss framework is attributed to McKinsey consultants, Pascale, Athos, Peters, and Waterman.[24] This approach to internal scanning and analysis involves gathering information on seven organisation variables. The seven variables, shown in Table 4.4, form a pattern that managers must somehow balance to be successful. The framework states that organisations can be managed only by identifying the full matrix of factors that make up a working, functioning organisation.

Table 4.4   The seven Ss framework developed by McKinsey et al.

Structure	The lines and boxes of the organisation chart as well as the committees, project teams, and task forces
Strategy	Plan of course of action leading to the allocation of a firm's scarce resources, over time, to reach identified goals
Staff	The people within the organisation
Style	Characterisation of how key managers behave in achieving the organisation's goals; also the cultural style of the organisation
Systems	Proceduralised reports and routine processes, such as meeting formats
Skills	Distinctive capabilities of key personnel or the firm as a whole
Shared Values	The significant meanings or guiding concepts that an organisation invests in its members

A key factor to remember about the framework is that the seven Ss can not be treated in isolation from one another. The assumption that if you get the structure right the people will fit is plainly wrong, as is the notion that if you get the right people then success is guaranteed. Structure and staff are important but so are the other five factors. It is also important to consider the soft variables: style, systems, skills, and shared values very seriously since they are just as important. Advice from Peters and Waterman is that you need to think of the seven S's as seven compass points. It is only when they are all aligned and pointing in the same direction that you can truly call yourself well organised.

PIMS analysis

PIMS, the *Profit Impact of Market Strategy* research, was organised in 1973 by the Marketing Science Institute and the Harvard Business School, who researched 57 major North American corporations involving 600 individual business for the three-year period 1970-72. The research focused primarily on ROI because this is the performance measure most often used in strategic planning. It was recognised, however, that ROI results are often not entirely compatible between businesses because of variations between depreciation policies.[25] The PIMS model was designed to answer the following questions:

- What factors influence profitability in a business, and how much influence does each one have?
- How does ROI change in response to changes in strategy and in market conditions?

The independent variables in the model were assembled under four headings:

1. Competitive position of the business (relative market share, product quality, price, promotion, new-product development).

2. The business environment (growth in industry, rate of inflation, customers, replacement cycle).

3. Structure of the production process (capital intensity, degree of vertical integration, productivity).

4. Discretionary budget allocation (R&D budgets, marketing budgets).

To date, PIMS research has identified nine major strategic factors that account for 80 per cent of the variation in profitability across the businesses in the database.[26] In working with these factors, the Strategic Planning Institute has prepared profiles of high ROI firms as contrasted with low ROI firms. They found that the firms with high rates of return had the following characteristics:

- Low investment intensity (the amount of fixed capital and working capital required to produce $ of sales).
- High market share.
- High product quality.
- High capacity utilisation.
- High operating effectiveness (the ratio of actual or expected employee productivity).
- Low direct costs per unit, relative to competition.

Some firms consider the PIMS findings controversial. It is observed that PIMS research has consistently reported that a large market share should lead to greater profitability. George Day has noted, however, that the influence of market share is most apparent with high value-added products, where there are significant barriers to entry and the competition consists of a few large, diversified firms with the attendant large overheads, for example, plastics, major appliances, automobiles, and semiconductors. In Day's opinion there are many situations where the relationship between profitability and market share is very tenuous.[27] From a manager's perspective, many of the contributing factors of poor profitability and market share have tended to be those outside their short-term control. In the assessment of a firm's internal strengths and weaknesses, the PIMS framework is still a powerful tool in measuring and comparing their relative position. To perform a PIMS analysis, the firm can use a proprietary checklist of variables. After rating each variable in the checklist, the firm consults results of the PIMS study to determine which strategy will have the best chance of success.

Portfolio analysis

The portfolio analysis model (some times referred to as the product portfolio matrix or growth share matrix) was developed by the Boston Consulting Group (BCG) in 1973. The model is based on a close association between market share and cash generation. What characterises portfolio analysis from PIMS is its focus on the specific role of each product in the overall strategy in the firm. The model is based on the generation of cash flow as a measure of success and the allocation of particular product groups. It uses market growth (vertical axis) and relative market share (horizontal axis) as the two decisive parameters. Based on its cash flow characteristics and relative market share, each product can be positioned in the matrix (see Figure 4.5). The concept behind the model is that the firm with the largest cumulative volume gains the benefits of the experience curve first, so market share is crucial. The BCG noted that as a function of accumulated experience, a process of learning takes place over time. According to the BCG, value-added costs tend to decrease by up to one third each time accumulated production doubles. The four strategies portrayed in the model: Stars, Cash Cows, Dogs and Question Marks are briefly described below:

1. A **star** is a product which has a high market share (or leader) in a growing market. As such, it needs substantial amounts of cash to maintain its position. However, the experience-curve benefits will help reduce costs, hopefully at a faster rate than competition in the market.

2. The **cash cow** is a product or business with high market share, low market growth. Such products bring in far more money than is required to maintain their market share. As these products move along the decline stage of their life cycle, they are harvested for cash that will be invested in alternative products.

3. **Dogs** have low share in static or declining markets. Their poor competitive position results in poor profits. They often drain cash and will invariably use up a disproportionate amount of company time and resources.

4. The **question mark** (sometimes referred to as the problem child in some texts) have low market share and high market growth. These tend to be new products with high potential for success, but require substantial amounts of cash to turn them into stars.

Research by Hambrick et al. into the BCG model generally supports its assumptions and recommendations, except for the advice that dogs should be promptly harvested or liquidated.[28] A product with a low share in a declining industry can be very profitable if the product has a niche in which market demand remains stable and predictable. If sufficient competition abandons the industry, a product's market share can increase by default until the dog becomes the market leader and thus a cash cow.

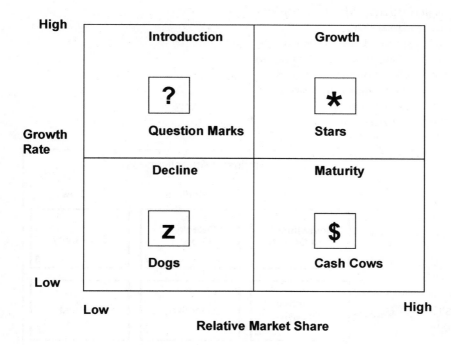

Figure 4.5   Portfolio matrix

The BCG model has been extended and developed to incorporate more re-finement. One such model is the General Electric/McKinsey model (Figure 4.6) which includes nine cells and is based on long-term industry attractive-ness, business strengths, and competitive position. The cells are divided into three groupings: investment and growth (1, 2, and 4), selectivity/earnings (3, 5, and 7), and harvest/divest (6, 8, and 9). In the nine cell model the two axes are:

Industry attractiveness, which includes:

- market size and growth rates
- industry profit margins (historic and projected)
- competitive intensity
- economies of scale
- technology and capital requirements
- social environment
- emerging opportunities and threats
- barriers to entry and exit

Business strengths, which include:

- relative market share
- profit margins relative to competitors
- ability to compete on price and quality
- knowledge of customers and market
- competitive strengths and weaknesses
- technological capability
- calibre of management

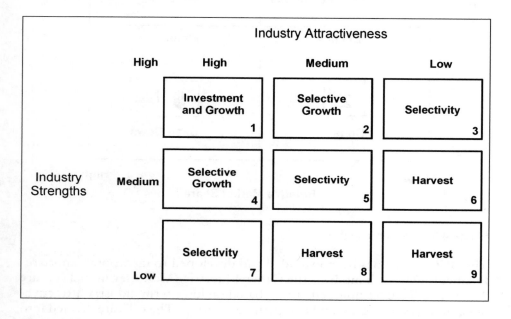

Figure 4.6   Nine-cell matrix

Value chains

The value chain is a way of examining the character and limit of the synergies that do or do not exist between internal activities of a firm. The methodical examination of individual value activities can lead to a better understanding of an organisation's strengths and weaknesses.[29]

In his book *Competitive Advantage*, Michael Porter defines value as:

> the amount buyers are willing to pay for what a firm provides them. Value is measured by the total revenue, a reflection of the price a firm's product commands exceeds the costs involved in creating the product. Creating value for buyers that exceeds the cost

of doing so is the goal of any generic strategy. Value, instead of cost, must be used in analysing competitive position since firms often deliberately raise their cost in order to command a premium price via differentiation.[30]

Figure 4.7 is a schematic representation of the value chain showing its component parts. Most organisations undertake hundreds of activities in the course of converting inputs to outputs (products and services). Such activities can be classified as either the primary or support activities that all businesses must undertake in some form.

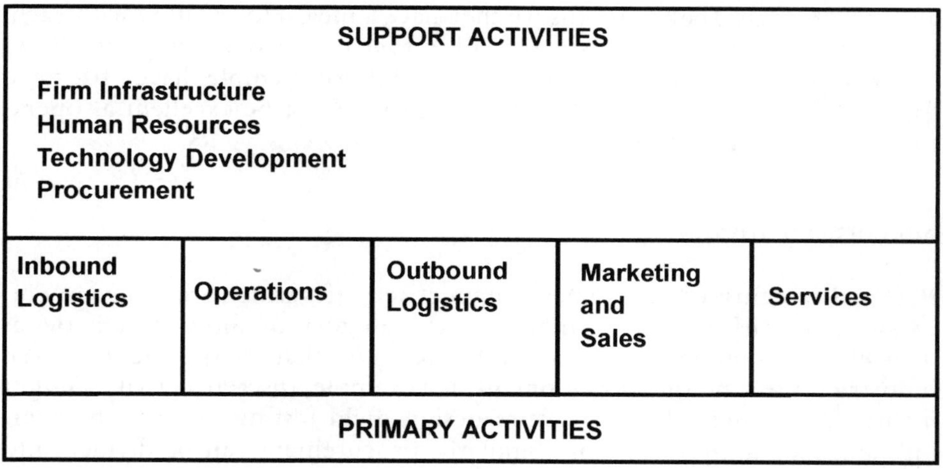

SUPPORT ACTIVITIES				
Firm Infrastructure Human Resources Technology Development Procurement				
Inbound Logistics	Operations	Outbound Logistics	Marketing and Sales	Services
PRIMARY ACTIVITIES				

Figure 4.7   Porter's value chain

Primary activities

Primary activities can be divided into the following five categories:

1. **Inbound logistics**: activities associated with supplies and which include receiving, storing, and dissemination of inputs (includes warehousing, inventory management, vehicle scheduling).
2. **Operations**: activities associated with transforming inputs into outputs (products and services). Machining, packaging, assembling, maintaining, and testing are examples of operations.
3. **Outbound logistics**: include all the activities required to collect, store, and distribute output. These activities focus primarily on the delivery of outputs to buyers (and includes warehousing, materials handling, delivery operations, shipping, order processing, and scheduling).

4. **Marketing and sales**: activities associated with providing a means by which buyers can purchase the product or service, and inducing them to do so (advertising, selling, channel selection, pricing, and promotion are examples of such activities).

5. **Service**: includes all the activities required to keep the product or service working effectively for the buyer after it is sold and delivered. Training, consultancy, installing, repairing, supplying parts, and fine tuning are examples of service.

To some extent every organisation performs all these five primary activities and, accordingly, they must ensure they have a means for dealing with each. Which are important, however, depends on the nature of the business. Service providers like McDonald's and Disneyland, for example, have little need for proficiency in outbound logistics, but each must be excellent at operations and marketing and sales.

Support activities

Porter also identified four generic support activities which are shown in Figure 4.7. As with primary activities, each category of support activities is divisible into a number of distinct value activities that are specific to a given industry. In technology development, for example, discrete activities might include component design, feature design, field-testing process engineering, and technology selection. Similarly, procurement can be divided into activities such as qualifying new suppliers, procurement of different groups of purchased inputs, and ongoing monitoring of supplier performance.[31] The four support activities are:

1. **Procurement**: this is the function of acquisition of inputs or resources for the firm. It includes all the procedures for dealing with suppliers.

2. **Technology and development**: concerns the hardware, software, procedures, and technical knowledge brought to bear in the transformation of the firm's inputs to outputs. Its most important component is knowledge. Some forms of technological knowledge are scientific. Other forms are more of an art, for example, recipes used by restaurants.

3. **Human resource management**: this consists of all the activities involved in the recruitment, training, development, and remuneration of staff.

4. **Firm infrastructure**: consists of a number of activities including general management, planning, finance, accounting, legal, government affairs, and

quality management. Infrastructure, unlike other support activities, usually supports the entire chain and not merely individual activities. The infrastructure can help or impede the achievement of competitive advantage. If the infrastructure is working well, the firm can gain a substantial competitive advantage. If it is not working well, an otherwise effective firm can lose its competitive edge.

The four support activities described above interfuse the entire organisation. When evaluating the support activities of a firm, its managers must look at how each activity is performed throughout the firm, not just by its designated unit (Table 4.5).

Table 4.5   Summary of value chain activities

Support Activities	Primary Activities				
	Inbound Logistics	*Operations*	*Outbound Logistics*	*Marketing and Sales*	*Service*
Procurement	Warehousing and transportation	Machining Packaging	Warehousing and transportation	Promotion, selling and channel selection	Financing and other financial facilities
Technical Development	Knowledge and technology transfer	Process development	Shipments	Information gathering	Repair and maintenance
Human Resource Management	Recruitment, remuneration and training	Subcontractors	Subcontractors	Distributors	Employees' goodwill
Firm Infrastructure	Materials handling and procurement systems	Inventory management Quality assurance Production Planning	Delivery and scheduling	Order processing	Customer service

Support activities are not always undertaken by the organisational unit responsible for them. The need for cohesion among organisational units is a indication of value-chain linkages. There are often many linkages within the value chain, and organisational structure often fails to provide instruments to co-ordinate them. The information necessary for co-ordinating or optimising linkages is also rarely collected throughout the chain. Managers of support activities, such as human resource management and technology development, often do not have a clear view of how they relate to the firm's overall competitive position, something the value chain highlights.

Functional analysis

One of the simplest ways to scan and analyse the internal environment of a co-operation is through functional analysis.[32] Ansoff proposes that an organisation's skills and resources can be organised into a *competence profile* according to the typical business functions of marketing, finance research and development, and operations.[33] Functional structure in organisations is logical and traditional, and accommodates the division of work into specialist areas. Ansoff proposes that strategic managers conduct internal scanning and analysis by examining the corporations current structure, culture, and resources.

Financial analysis

There are a number of ways in which the financial performance of an organisation should be considered and these include:

- value chain analysis
- financial ratio analysis

Value chain analysis

Whereas conventional management accounting focuses on the internal cost structure of the organisation in an attempt to maximise the *value added* (that is, the difference between the revenues generated and costs incurred), value chain analysis adopts an external focus considering the whole industry and firms at every stage within it. Management accounting therefore only considers part of the picture and ignores the opportunities which may be offered by reconfiguring the value chain.

Stemming from the work of Porter, a more quantified approach can be

Lit review

taken to the analysis of the value creating processes within an organisation and the costs associated with those activities. Additionally, the analysis should look outside the firm to the whole industry chain, considering the costs and value created within all of the industry's stages. There are three stages which need to be followed:

1. Identify the industry's value chain and assign costs, revenues, and assets to value creating activities.
2. Diagnose the cost drivers regulating each value activity.
3. Develop sustainable competitive advantage, either by superior cost control or by modifying the value chain to the company's advantage.

It is impossible to consider a whole industry in sufficient detail without segmentation into its various stages, and it is necessary to identify the distinct activities of which it is made up. If we consider the television industry, for instance, the following sequential stages can be identified:

1. Film libraries, programme makers, and live events.
2. Programme commissioners.
3. Programme schedulers.
4. Broadcasters.
5. Transmitters.

Similarly, the oil industry can be subdivided into:

1. Exploration and production.
2. Refining.
3. Marketing of refined products.

For both of these industries, there are companies which are fully vertically integrated (the BBC in television and Shell in oil, for instance) and who operate in all stages, while others focus on fewer stages, choosing to specialise in those areas where they have a particular advantage. With a detailed analysis, the identification of further subdivisions is possible.

To be recognised as a separate significant activity, stages should exhibit the following characteristics:

- be material in terms of operating costs
- show different cost behaviour, and have different cost drivers to the adjacent stages
- be capable of being performed in different ways by competitors
- have a relative high potential for creating competitive advantage by differentiation.

Return on assets calculations should be performed for each identified stage by identifying the incurred costs, the assets utilised, and the revenues generated. It may be necessary to use internal transfer prices where no arms-length sale occurs, and this may prove to be one of the most difficult parts of this stage of the process.

The next stage is the identification of cost drivers. This involves more depth than the conventional management accounting approach, which invariably relates cost to throughput or output volume. There are many more factors than volume driving the costs of a firm. Newman's analysis of the post-deregulation airline industry demonstrates, amongst other factors, the problems that carriers caused themselves by concentrating on volume and blaming overcapacity.[34] The problem was not one of owning overcapacity, but of operating overcapacity. Had airlines been prepared to reduce flights, rather than cut whole routes, their losses would have been reduced.

Riley offers two categories of cost drivers, structural and executional.[35] The concept of structural cost drivers draws on industrial organisational literature and identifies the cost implications of strategic choices that the firm makes in respect of:

Scale	The degree of horizontal integration. What size of investment has the company made in the various functional areas necessary for its operations?
Scope	The degree of vertical integration. Within how many of the identified stages of the industry has the firm chosen to operate?
Experience	How long has the organisation been doing this particular activity?
Technology	What processes are being used at each stage of the firm's value chain?
Complexity	What is the breadth of the service or product offering?

For each of these, it has been demonstrated that there are both economies and diseconomies of scale and scope. Similarly, a more complete and complex service range is not necessarily better. Extensive experience is not necessarily a good thing, as Shank and Govindrajan show in their description of Texas Instruments,[36] whose overemphasis on being the lowest cost producer of outdated microchips caused them severe problems.

The executional cost drivers relate to a firm's ability to perform its component functions and, invariably, more is usually better – although there can, again, be diseconomies. Although no list of cost drivers can be exhaustive, there are fundamental factors which are likely to be present in all organisations. Amongst such a basic list would be included:

Participation	The involvement and commitment of the workforce to continual improvement.
TQM	Achievements regarding process and product quality.
Utilisation	The level of capacity used.
Efficiency	The efficiency of the plant layout.
Design	The effectiveness of the service or product as seen from the consumer's perspective.
Linkages	The effectiveness of the linkages with suppliers and customers, both internal and external.

As can be seen from the list, considerations of quality and its implications for cost within an organisation play a significant part in the analysis. Despite Deming's contention that the measurement of cost of quality is a waste of time,[37] many other authors, particularly Juran,[38] consider it essential. Simpson and Muthler describe the situation at Ford in the early 1980s, when the concentration on efficiency of plant operation, rather than a policy of defect reduction, virtually brought the company to bankruptcy.[39] By shifting to a consideration of a broader set of cost drivers, the company was able to rescue itself and has modified its management accounting system accordingly. This and many other examples of the importance of quality have led to a greater emphasis on total quality management (TQM), which we will return to in Chapter 5.

It is a mistake to take the direct costs from the management accounts and to assume that they relate to the primary activities in the value chain, whilst assuming that overheads should be tied to the support activities. At this point, a technique such as activity based costing (ABC) can be used to clarify the analysis. Overheads have no divine right to exist and have been described as: 'Costs that are in the too hard box – too hard to work out what is causing them.' Very few costs are truly fixed, but are often treated as such for convenience. The identification of cost drivers is a difficult process – however, the insight gained by the firm in doing so will pay significant dividends in the quality of their future decision making. With a clearer picture of the cost drivers in the firm, it is easier to identify the best approach to developing a sustainable competitive advantage, either by better control of those cost drivers or by reconfiguring the value chain.

Whilst better cost control may be a primarily, but not exclusively, internal consideration, the modification of the value chain is unlikely to be successful without thorough consideration of both suppliers' and buyers' value chains. Once a firm starts to make modifications to its processes, the impact on those around them must be assessed. If a company intends to move to a just in time (JIT) system of inbound logistics, what will be the impact on their suppliers? Will they require significantly higher margins to be able to fund their internal reorganisation and investment? The introduction of electronic data interchange (EDI) will most probably benefit both ends of the changed process, but it should be discussed rather than imposed, and other potential benefits should be explored.

FINANCIAL RATIO ANALYSIS

The analysis of the financial performance of the firm is an essential part of both the functional analysis and the competitive analysis, which follows this section, since it will highlight areas where the company can improve its profitability and often reveal useful information about other industry players. Any financial analysis must be done on a comparative basis and be conducted over a sufficient length of time to iron out the effect of any one-off events. This process of analysis will often be made easier by a process of 'normalising' or 'common sizing' the accounts. Consider an extract from the consolidated profit and loss of BAA for the years 1987 and 1988:

	1997	Percentage of turnover	1998	Percentage of turnover	Change over time 1997–98
Revenue					
Continuing operations	1,373		1,442		5%
Acquisitions			237		
Total turnover	1,373		1,679		22%
Operating costs					
Wages and salaries	220	16%	272	16.2%	23.6%
Social security costs	18	1.3%	17	1%	<6%>
Pension costs	8		8		0%
Retail expenditure	176	12.8%	321	19.1%	82.4%
Depreciation	110	8%	123	7.3%	11%
Amortisation			11		
Maintenance expenditure	72	5.2%	90	5.3%	25%
Rent and rates	68	4.9%	87	5.2%	27.9%
Cost of trading property sales	20	1.5%	4		
Utility costs	77	5.6%	76	4.5%	0%
Police costs	38	2.8%	38	2.3%	0%
General expenses	75	5.5%	111	6.6%	48%
Operating profit	491	35.8%	521	31%	6.1%

Source: Extracted from BAA Annual Report for year ended March 31, 1988.

Vertical analysis, by a comparison with competitors or industry standards, is made easier by considering every cost line as a percentage of the turnover for the year. Similarly, horizontal analysis, or time series analysis, is made easier by considering percentage growth rates over time. Over a longer period of time than we have used here, the figures would be adjusted for changing prices to investigate the presence of real growth as opposed to price inflation. The choice of inflation rates would depend on the industry being considered, but for consumer services the retail price index will usually suffice. Although we have only taken an extract of the profit and loss account here and considered only two years, the effect of the calculations on simplifying the analysis can be seen. We can identify more easily that the effects of the acquisitions on revenue have been significant, but since they have been part of the company for less than a year, BAA management have not, as yet, had an opportunity to fully apply their core competence of retail management to have a full effect on the operating profit. This is further reflected in the fact that retail expenditure has risen as a percentage of turnover, caused by the acquisition of Duty Free International Inc.

With access to sufficient information, vertical analysis would be done for each of the business segments in which a firm operated. With vertical analysis, the choice of suitable comparators is often difficult since identification of companies that are sufficiently similar in terms of their business portfolio and operating characteristics may be hard. By virtue of their degree of vertical integration within an industry, we would expect their operating ratios to be different, and for this reason, it is often better to apply logic to the result of the calculation rather than any prescribed ideal value. Similarly, the rise of multinational conglomerates with diverse interests has made selection of comparable firms more difficult.

Figure 4.10, at the end of this chapter, shows the pyramid of financial ratios often described as Dupont Analysis. The pyramid demonstrates how improvement in each performance ratio contributes to the primary ratio Return on Capital Employed, defined here as:

$$\text{Return on Capital Employed} = \frac{\text{Operating Profit}}{\text{Net Capital Employed}}$$

This in turn is a result of multiplying the Asset Utilisation Ratio (or Asset Turnover) by the net profit margin:

$$\text{Asset Utilisation} = \frac{\text{Net Turnover}}{\text{Net Capital Employed}}$$

and:

$$\text{Net Profit Margin} = \frac{\text{Operating Profit}}{\text{Net Turnover}}$$

If we consider different retail companies such as Sainsbury and Aldi, we would expect to see both making a respectable ROCE, but doing so in a different way. Sainsbury sells a mixture of own-brand products and branded goods from expensively outfitted, out of town, superstores, whereas Aldi operate a no-frills service leaving the customer to unpack the goods from the outer cartons in sparsely furnished, relatively cheap rented outlets. Aldi's net profit margin will naturally be lower than that of Sainsbury, and its asset turnover will be significantly higher since its capital invested would be markedly lower. The strategic positioning of the two stores, and the perceived quality of the shopping experience, are thus reflected in the ratios.

By using the next cluster of ratios we can gather further information about the performance and strategy of the companies. Net turnover is a combination of average selling price and sales volume, net capital employed consists of the fixed assets and net working capital whilst the operating result is arrived at by deducting cost of sales and other costs from the net turnover.

The average selling prices for Sainsbury and Aldi will reflect the margins they are trying to achieve and Sainsbury's will be higher. However, both will work hard to maximise their sales volume and there are thus no fundamental differences there. As regards the Net Capital Employed (NCE), we have, to some extent, already described the difference between the two companies in their investment in fixed assets. However, whilst Sainsbury invest heavily in information technology and bar code all of their stock so that control is easier and the passage past the checkout quicker, Aldi take a different approach. The rate of pay for Aldi checkout staff is significantly higher at more than double that of Sainsbury's, but Aldi's till operators are required to memorise the cost of all items of stock, none of which are individually priced. Aldi thus do not invest in bar-coding equipment, and do not have to unpack and stack stock on shelves. Their investment in fixed assets is thus lower, but the higher staff costs eat into their margin, again reflecting their chosen positioning within the industry.

Working capital can be broken down further into stock, debtors, and creditors, and both stores will work hard to minimise the investment in working capital, turning stock over as many times as possible, whilst taking as much credit as their suppliers will allow. We would normally expect the current ratio,

$$\text{Current ratio} \quad = \quad \frac{\text{Current assets}}{\text{Current liabilities}}$$

to be significantly less than one for an efficient supermarket.

Over the last few years, Sainsbury has been surpassed by Tesco as the premier supermarket group within the UK, and the ratios we have described can be used to demonstrate why if we consider the following figures:

J. Sainsbury plc

Year ended Feb. 28	1995	1996	1997
Key figures (£M)			
Turnover	11 357	12 627	13 395
Capital employed	3 996	4 235	4 482
Operating profit	868	756	695
NPAT	539	478	401
Earnings per share (pence)	29.8	26.8	22.0
Growth (%)			
Turnover		11	6
Capital employed		6	6
Operating profit		<10>	<8>
NPAT		<11>	<16>
Earnings per share (pence)		<10>	<18>

Tesco plc

Year ended Feb. 28	1995	1996	1997
Key figures (£M)			
Turnover	10 101	12 094	13 887
Capital employed	4 127	4 214	4 521
Operating profit	578	724	774
NPAT	381	466	520
Earnings per share (pence)	18.9	22.2	24.1
Growth (%)			
Turnover		20	15
Capital employed		2	7
Operating profit		25	7
NPAT		22	12
Earnings per share (pence)		17	9

Year ended Feb. 28	1995	1996	1997
J. Sainsbury plc			
ROCE %	20.96	17.82	15.46
Profit margin %	7.38	5.98	5.19
Asset turnover (times)	2.84	2.98	2.98
Tesco plc			
ROCE %	3.97	17.16	17.1
Profit margin %	5.72	5.98	5.57
Asset turnover (times)	2.44	2.87	3.07

We can see that the ROCE for Tesco's has improved sufficiently to rise above that of Sainsbury, which has been declining. This has mainly been due to Tesco achieving higher margins than Sainsbury whose margins have reduced, but also because Tesco have been able to improve their asset-turnover ratio considerably. This must in part be due to the fact that Sainsbury have increased their capital employed by 12 per cent over the three years, whilst Tesco have only increased theirs by 9.5 per cent and have shown a significantly larger increase in turnover.

By looking at the relative sales densities of the two firms, we see that whilst Sainsbury have shown a marginal improvement, Tesco's has been quite significant, underlining their better use of assets:

Year ended Feb. 28	1995	1996	1997
Relative sales density £psf/week			
J. Sainsbury plc	20.25	20.42	20.47
Tesco plc	17.11	18.26	19.78

Similarly, consideration of the stock turnover for the two companies gives a notable difference in performance:

Year ended Feb. 28	1995	1996	1997
Stock turnover (times)			
J. Sainsbury plc	13.62	15.14	16.61
Tesco plc	22.40	19.93	23.35

Again, whilst Sainsbury has shown an improvement in the rate at which it is able to work its current assets, Tesco is significantly more efficient. This reflects itself in the current ratio for the two companies:

Year ended Feb. 28	1995	1996	1997
Current ratio			
J. Sainsbury plc	0.48	0.47	0.44
Tesco plc	0.39	0.36	0.37

As mentioned earlier, there can be no prescriptive values for ratios and it is often better to apply logic to the result of the calculation. Similarly, there is no hard and fast list of which ratios should be used. Operating ratios can be created to investigate a particular performance characteristic and, as long as they are calculated consistently, will be effective. This can be done by comparing performance to a particular limiting factor. For a supermarket, display space is a premium and so relative sales densities are an important measure, but for a take-away restaurant, such as McDonald's or Burger King, the limiting factor is operator time. Anything that can be done to increase the value of a transaction without increasing the time taken will show operating improvements for the outlet.

Competitive analysis

In the Porter model, the unit of analysis is the competitive forces within the industry. In this model, industry structure determines the firm's behaviour, which in turn decides the firm's performance. If industry structure completely decided a firm's conduct, there could be no difference between the conduct of the firms in the same industry. For example, if industry structure determines a firm's pricing strategy, all firms in the industry should, in essence, follow the same pricing strategy. Alternatively, if all firms in the industry have the same unit cost profitability, differences between firms in the same industry would be ascribed to random events. In the real world, however, firms are clearly not alike. In fact, they differ in substance, structure, and dimension. Such dimensions include: marketing practices, financial condition, operating conditions, and breadth of operating techniques. Such differences may be due to differences in market intelligence. For example, firm ABC may decide to advertise a high-quality brand product and firm XYZ to pursue a high-volume line because they do not have access to the same information and are thus committed to a strategy.

Most firms think they know who their major competitors are, and most operating managers would advocate that they know quite a lot about them. Knowing your key competitors and their strategies is absolutely fundamental. Environmental scanning and environmental forecasting are key inputs in competitor analysis. The purpose of undertaking competitive analysis is to give the management of an organisation a comprehensive understanding of its competitive environment. This understanding should enable management to further assess its strengths and weaknesses, and to partially ascertain threats and opportunities to the organisation from its industry environment.

Competitive audits

The literature for undertaking competitive analysis is rich in approaches and techniques. Most strategic-planning models advocate the use of checklist questions. Key areas examined include: future goals, current strategy, capabilities, and assumptions, with respect to organisational structure, market position, financial structure, research and development capabilities, past objectives, and strategies. Typical questions to ask include:

- Is the competitor satisfied with its current position?
- What likely moves or strategy shifts will the competitor make?
- Where is the competitor vulnerable?
- What will provoke the greatest and most effective retaliation by the competitor?

Information on competitors can be obtained from many different sources and Table 4.6 gives some useful sources of competitive information. Information on competitors should be compiled, catalogued, analysed, and communicated to all key managers.

Table 4.6   Sources of competitive information

Advertising Agencies	IRS financial summaries (USA)
Company Accounts	Legal Institutions
Companies House	Lloyds of London (UK)
Confederation of British Industry (UK)	Management and Business Periodicals
Employees	Monopolies and Mergers (UK)
ERISA Filings (USA)	Newspapers (e.g., UK, *Financial Times*)
Freedom of Information Act (USA)	Suppliers to the industry
Government Agencies	Stock Markets
Government Reports	Trade Unions
Industry Analysts	Trade Journals
Investment Banks	Uniform commercial code filings (USA)

Recent thrusts

A paper by Ghoshal and Westney presented the results of a detailed study of three large organisations. In their study, they examined the techniques and models applied when undertaking competitor analysis. Ghoshal and Westney identified six distinct functions served by competitor analysis in organisations:[40]

1. **Sensitisation**: in order to *shake up the troops* by challenging the organisation's existing assumptions about particular competitors and including, in some cases, changing the definition of the most significant competitor or of the most crucial dimensions of competition.
2. **Benchmarking**: which provides a set of specific measures comparing the firm with its competitors.
3. **Legitimisation**: which means to justify certain proposals and to persuade members of the organisation of the feasibility and desirability of a chosen course of action.
4. **Inspiration**: which gives people new ideas about how to solve problems in the process of identifying what other firms did in similar circumstances.
5. **Planning**: namely the use of competitor analysis to assist the formal planning process, much more dependent, interestingly enough, on information from the formal (competitor analysis) function than any of the other uses.

6. **Decision making**: meaning contribution to operational and tactical decision making by managers, which provides the second largest number of examples cited (after planning).

Managing the competitive environment

Firms can waste precious resources responding to other firms in the same industry, with whom they are not really competing. To be a true competitor, the firm has to be selling to the same set of customers or market segment, and serving some of the same functions. For example, if the company is selling to a totally different segment, their actions may not affect one's sales, share, or profit. The question of to whom to respond must also be coupled with the question of whether it is necessary to respond at all. Some competitors' actions may not affect one's own market, even when they are selling into the same customer set. Further, some industries learn how to coexist peacefully. This is generally neither black nor white, but lies along some continuum. Some industries will appear attractive, depending on the level of competitive intensity. Whether to respond to competition depends on whether the competitive action has an impact in the marketplace that affects the firm's performance, either in the short or the long term. Whether to initiate an action and how depends, in part, on your competitors' ability to respond by negating the impact of your firm's actions. Clearly, one needs to assess the competitive advantages and how sustainable they are before deciding how to respond. The next step is an assessment of the competitors' strategies and intentions. Can we learn from some of their actions or commitments (capacity, annual report proclamations, available resources, etc.) about their capabilities? One must also be cautious of who else might be entering the market – the likelihood of new competitors. All of this is intended to give us a better ability to anticipate our competitors' actions or reactions.[41]

Strategic mission, objectives, and structure

Strategic mission

Inertia is the enemy of progress. Past insights ossify into clichés, processes lapse into routines, and commitments become ties that bind companies to the same course of action. Perhaps the most vital and fulfilling element of a strategist's job is to prevent burdens of the past. A manager's role is not to toil long and hard to make the inevitable happen. His or her job is to make happen what otherwise would not happen. Although somewhat a cliché, but still highly relevant is the axiom: If you don't know where you are going, any road will take you there. A strategy, in a comparable sense, is just a means to achieve an objective or goal. Therefore, before a strategy can be proposed or implemented, the firm must develop a clear idea of where it is going and, more importantly, why. Management or leader values and expectations play a significant part in strategy formulation. In some respects, strategy can be thought of as a reflection of the attitudes and beliefs of the leaders in the organisation. An expression used to describe attitudes and expectations is 'mission'.

The notion that an organisation needs a guiding mission is strong in the literature on strategic management. For example, Selznick suggested that the key function of leadership is to identify the *distinctive competencies* of the organisation, and to build on them: 'leadership goes beyond efficiency when it sets the basic mission of the organisation and when it creates a social organism capable of fulfilling that mission.'[42] A well-instituted mission statement defines the fundamental, unique purpose (or *raison d'être*) that sets a business apart from other competing firms, and identifies the scope of the corporation's operations in terms of the products and services offered and the markets served.

Research undertaken by Pearce and David found that 68 per cent of all North American corporations have formal, written mission statements.[43] Harvard Professors Donaldson and Lorsch have also argued the importance of mission through competency-based strategies.[44] In his book Bennis describes the essential role that mission plays in strategic leadership.[45] To gain the support of *stakeholders*, managers need a challenging vision that translates what is essentially an act of imagination into terms that describe possible future courses of action for the organisation.

The concept of mission implies that, throughout a corporation's many activities, there should be a shared theme and that those corporations with such a common theme are better able to direct and administer their activities. For example, when Jack Welch took over as chief executive officer (CEO) of General Electric (GE) in 1981, his shared theme was to make GE number one or number two in their respective markets. You will recall from our seven Ss framework (Table 4.4) that shared values play a significant part in shaping the organisation's culture. IBM has been one of America's most successful corporations for the last 50 years. It is known for its outstanding development of strategy, structure, systems, style, skill, and staff, and the fit between them, and for its equally advanced development of shared values. Writing in *The Art of Japanese Management*, Pascale and Athos describe IBM's basic beliefs and the underlying mission which underpins the business.[46] These beliefs are:

- To give intelligent, responsible, and capable direction to the business.
- To serve our customers as efficiently and as effectively as we can.
- To advance our technology, improve our products, and develop new ones.

- To enlarge the capabilities of our people through job development and give them the opportunity to find satisfaction in their tasks.
- To provide equal opportunity to all IBM employees.
- To recognise our obligation to stockholders by providing adequate return on their investment.
- To do our part in furthering the well being of those communities in which our facilities are located.
- To accept our responsibilities as a corporate citizen of the US and in all countries in which we operate throughout the world.

Campbell and Yeung stress that the process of developing a mission statement should create an 'emotional bond and sense of mission' between the organisation and its employees.[47] Commitment to a company's strategy and intellectual understanding on the strategies to be pursued do not necessarily translate into an ardent bond; hence strategies that have been formulated may not be implemented. Campbell and Yeung stress that an emotional bond comes when an individual personally identifies with the underlying values and conduct of a firm, thus turning intellectual agreement and commitment to strategy into a sense of mission. Campbell and Yeung also differentiate between the terms 'vision' and 'mission', saying vision is 'a possible and desirable future state of an organisation' that includes specific goals, whereas mission is more associated with behaviour and with the present.

Strategic objectives (the decision process)

Managers and employees throughout the organisation should participate early and directly in setting strategic objectives and decision making. Strategic objectives (and decisions) deal with the mission of the firm and its relationship with the outside world. A strategic objective will influence the organisation's performance for a long period of time. In setting strategic objectives, many models focus on factors peculiar to the individual strategist. The dominant approach is to set objectives within a rational decision framework. According to Steiner et al.: 'a decision is rational when it effectively and efficiently assures the achievement of aims for which the means are selected.'[48] More appropriate is that rational decisions maximise net value achievement, where the sacrifice in one value necessitated by a decision is more than offset by an increase in the achievement of another value.[49] Although there are many models of the process of rational objective setting, the literature tends to agree with the following steps:

1. Establish a complete set of strategic objectives with potential outcomes.
2. Prepare a complete inventory of values and resources.

3. Generate a complete set of alternative strategies or solutions.
4. Prepare a complete set of predicted benefits and costs of each strategy or solution choice.
5. Compute the expected value of each choice.
6. Select the choice that has the highest expected value.

If the strategist could perform each of these steps completely, then a decision that maximises net value achievement would result. The definition of rational objective outcomes can change from manager to manager, or even from situation to situation. For strategic decisions, some of the objectives that have been used to define rational decisions are return on capital employed, high net worth ratios and profit growth in addition to profit maximisation. Some of the other areas in which organisations may set objectives are:

- Higher stock prices
- Increased market share
- Streamlining the value chain
- Improvement of social image or reputation
- Increasing employee stakeholder ownership
- Lower tax liability
- Increase technological leadership

The literature would suggest that objectives are not strategic unless they can be measured (e.g., in quality, quantity, cost, and time) and achieved, that is, unless they are closed. Johnson and Scholes, however, do not share this view. They argue that *open statements* may, in fact, be just as helpful as closed statements. They state: 'there may be some objectives which are important, but are difficult to quantify or express in measurable terms.' And go on to say: 'An objective such as to be a 'leader in technology' may be highly relevant in today's technological environment, but may become absurd if it has to be expressed in some measurable way.[50] This view seems to be shared by Goold and Campbell, who site Cadbury and UB. The objective-setting process in Cadbury and UB involves agreement on strategic direction for a business, but with objectives set mainly in terms of broad financial aggregates to allow business-unit managers flexibility in the detail of implementation, that is to set non-measurable activities such as those associated with organisational structure and style.[51]

Objectives are needed at corporate, business, and functional levels in the organisation. They should be deep-rooted measures of managerial performance. Hamel and Prahalad stress the need for organisations to develop a competitor focus at all corporate, business, and functional levels by gathering and widely distributing competitive intelligence; every employee (from

CEO to front-line worker) should be able to benchmark their efforts against best-of-breed competitors so that the challenge becomes personnel.[52] This is a challenge for strategists of the organisation. Organisations should provide training for all employees to guarantee they have and maintain the skills necessary to be world-class competitors.

Many researchers, CEO, and professional managers attribute a significant part of the recent US competitive decline to the lack of long-term objective strategy orientation. Many top business managers – like Jack Welch (GE), Michael Elsner (Disney), and Bill Gates (Microsoft) – argue that bonuses, share options, and merit increases need to be based on strategic long-term objectives.

Structure and structuring

Organisation structure is usually understood to imply a permanent arrangement of tasks and activities. Within this general definition, organisation structure has been defined to include two dimensions. One dimension of structure is the formal configuration of roles and procedures, and this is the framework of the organisation. The framework aspect of organisation structure includes rules, prescriptions of authority, division of labour, and hierarchy of authority. The concept of formal structure was influenced by the ideas of Max Weber in 1949, and by subsequent work on the formal, impersonal aspects of bureaucracy (see Hall and Child[53]). According to Daft and Macintosh, additional elements of the organisational structure include the subsystems that allocate resources and reinforce central control.[54] In addition to the corporate body of rule books, procedures, and policies, these systems include budgets, management information systems, technical training systems, and operational controls and reports that provide for resource allocation and vertical control.

One metaphor of organisation structure is the organisation as a stage play. Actors play assigned parts in a script written by management. From this view, senior managers implement strategic decisions by changing the rules, revising the organisational blueprint, or rewriting the script.[55] In order to translate a decision into action, managers may redefine duties and roles, reallocate budget resources, enact new operational performance criteria, or change the division of labour and task specialisation. Top managers change the formal structure to implement the new behaviours appropriate to a new strategy. Referring back to Chandler's *Strategy and Structure,* with which this chapter began, Chandler concluded that changes in strategy lead to changes in organisational structure.[56] Structure, he claims, should be designed to facilitate the strategic pursuit of a firm and therefore follows strategy. Without a strategy or reasons for being (mission), structure is not important. He found a particular structure sequence to be often repeated, as organisations grow and change strategy over time, (see Figure 4.8). For example, in the early years corporations tend to have a centralised functional organisational structure that is well suited to their producing and selling a limited range of products or services. As they add new products and services, purchase their own sources of supply, and generate their own distribution networks, they become too complex for highly centralised structures. In order to remain successful, this type of organisation needs to shift to a decentralised structure with several semi-autonomous divisions (also known as the divisional structure). This type of structure is also called the *M-form* (for multidivisional structure) by Williamson, the noted economist.[57]

Researchers in strategic management have stressed that structure is not the only organisational variable that is important in strategic analysis.[58] Structure and 'structuring', a broader term that covers the organisational-structure issue and how it blends with the overall management process, are nevertheless still of great importance. Structure and structuring are particularly important as firms grow, and they become of crucial strategic concern when firms compete on international grounds. Changes in strategy often require shifts in the way an organisation is structured. Structure largely directs how objectives and policies will be established. For example, the format for objectives and policies established under a business-unit structure is couched in business-unit terms. Objectives and policies are stated largely in terms of products in an organisation whose structure is based on product groups. The structural format for developing objectives and policies can significantly impact all other strategy activities.

Mintzberg, in 1979, developed a taxonomy of organisational structures, which included Entrepreneurial, Bureaucratic, Divisional, and Matrix structures (see Table 4.7).[59] In addition to these four categories developed by Mintzberg, an intermediate structure, the strategic business unit (SBU), is often used as the basis for developing strategic plans. Research, undertaken by Davidson and Haspselagh in 1980, into 180 USA-based organisations showed that the most common structure was the global-product structure followed by the international-divisional structure.[60] There is, however, no one correct organisation design or structure for a given strategy or type of organisation. What is right for one organisation may not be appropriate for a similar firm, although successful firms in a given industry do tend to organise themselves in a similar way. Take, for example, consumer-goods companies – these companies tend to emulate the divisional structure by product form organisation. Small firms tend to be functionally structured. Medium-sized firms tend to be divisionally structured (i.e., decentralised). Large firms tend to use a strategic business-unit or matrix structure. As organisations grow, their structures generally change from simple to complex as a result of linking together several basic strategies.

Table 4.7   Taxonomy of organisational structures

	Some Advantages	Some Disadvantages
Entrepreneurial	Opportunity for flexibility Innovation and initiative Informality	Owner dependent Staff must take on risk Little specialisation
Bureaucratic	Central control/procedures Specialised knowledge Increased planning analysis	Functional co-ordination Over specialisation Too much tight control
Divisional	Shared authority Rapid response to changing conditions Direct performance Shared authority	Duplication of effort Many staff needed Too independent
Matrix	Projects within functional structure Focuses on market needs Decentralised decision making	Dual command structures Relationships change Conflict of authority Poor reward systems

It is suggested that the more complex the organisation structure, the more the simple structures may become hidden and forgotten.[61] The original components or *experience* may become lost because of employee changes, because of aversion to the topic, or because the direct relationships have become unclear. More complex structures allow more diverse information to be recognised and processed. On the other hand, a simple structure may cause strategists to ignore many environmental signals and to reject them because they are not recognised.

The term 'experience' refers to an organisations contact with the environment which forms the basis for knowledge structures. The notion of complexity is based on the assumption that as a firm gains more experience and learns from it, it will become more expert at what (see learning curve) it is doing. As it becomes more expert, the knowledge structure builds on the base established by past experiences. As the knowledge structure becomes more complex, it is able to encompass a greater number of new institutions and problems.

Future structures

All types of managers need to be aware of the environmental and techno-logical developments which have produced fundamental changes in the ways in which firms have been organised in the 1990s and will continue to be in the year 2000. Organisations are evolving from pyramid to fishnet (organic) structures as hierarchies collapse and broad, interwoven, flexible structures emerge. The trend where firms are less preoccupied with outcomes, and more focused on process, will continue. For example, the principle of re-engineering has been widely adopted by Pan-European firms, and most large corporations now invest (and will continue to do so) in understanding and improving their business processes. According to Johansen and Swigart, the move towards re-engineering, redesign, or similar reinventions of business processes, is being fuelled by a number of different interests.[62] Financiers and investors hope for greater profits through increased productivity. Man-agers envision work that flows with more efficiency if workers are *empowered* to solve problems themselves.

Electronic networks are replacing office buildings as the focal point of business transactions. Employees of the future are less likely to work for large corporations, and those that do will participate in business teams and *ad hoc* alliances. The organic organisation calls for changing rolls, attitudes, expectations, and cultures at a moment's notice. Such shifts are creating enormous ambiguity for many managers and employees in the organisation. While many of the shifts are mediated by twentieth-century technology, the force behind these changes is people and their cultures.

The significance of these developments to managers in their capacity as strategists is that they must be prepared to:

- Help employees to succeed in the agile, flatter, and more flexible organisations of the future.
- Design organisations which can operate within different time zones.
- Create an environment in which decision making is speeded up by shortening lines of global communication, delegating authority as close as possible to the point of action, and making the best use of information technology.
- Create and design work in which employees learn useful skills from which a high level of motivation can be gained.

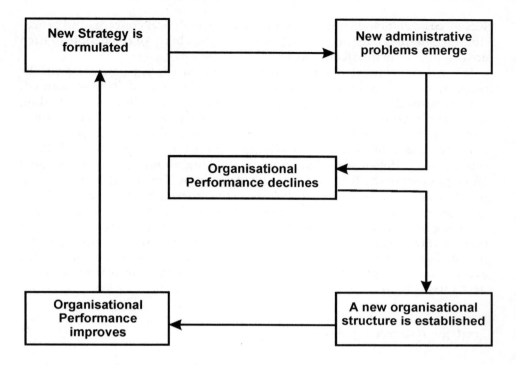

Figure 4.8   Chandler's strategy-structure relationship

Analysis and allocation of strategic resources

All organisations have at least four types of resources at their disposal and they are: people, financial, physical, and technological resources. Strategic management allows these resources to be allocated according to priorities established by the objectives of the firm. According to Ansoff: resource analysis should single out the particular resources which may become *limiting factors* in the firm's strategic activities. Such factors might include limited capital for investment, access to cheap or highly skilled labour, and technological know-how.

Various methods of analysis are used to assess resources and plan their allocation. Because resources have functional significance in a firm's activities, strategists tend to analyse resource requirements under the commonly accepted functional headings of finance, marketing, operations, human resources, and information technology (see Figure 4.9). Managers who have responsibility for resource allocation should be aware of the contributions each functional area can make to the organisations overall performance.

Resources will include both the knowledge of analytical concepts and procedural techniques common to each area, and the ability of the people in each area to utilise them effectively.

It is widely acknowledged that allocating resources to particular divisions or department does not mean that strategies will be successfully implemented. A number of factors tend to prevent effective resource allocation including an overprotection of resources, too great an emphasis on short-term objectives, organisational politics, vague strategy objectives, a reluctance to take risks, and a lack of sufficient knowledge. Beneath the corporate level, there often exists a deficiency of methodical thinking about resources allocated and strategies of the firm. This point is debated by Yavitz and Newman who point out that managers normally have many more tasks than they do. Managers must allocate time and resources among these tasks. Pressure builds up. Expenses are too high. The CEO wants a good financial report for third quarter. Strategy formulation and implementation activities often get deferred. Today's problems soak up available energies and resources. Scrambled accounts and budgets fail to reveal the shift in allocation away from strategic needs to currently squeaking wheels.

Strategic resource capability

An organisation's resources are not confined to those which it *owns*. Strategic capability is strongly influenced by resources outside the organisation which are an integral part of the chain between the product or service design, through production and marketing, to the use of the product, or service consumers. The most successful organisations have a consistent resource *theme* running through the (Porter) value chain. For example, if an organisation chooses to compete largely through cost leadership – this should be found in many aspects from procurement, to targeting markets, and customer support. Importantly, this cost competition will also be sustained by the special *linkages* which are developed within the value chain or with suppliers, channels, or customers. A full understanding of a company's use of resources also requires an analysis of the *effectiveness* with which resources have been used. The effectiveness of an organisation can be critically influenced by the ability to get all parts of the value chain working in harmony – including those key activities which are within the value chains of suppliers, channels, or customers. This is a key task of management and is largely concerned with developing and sustaining common attitudes and values amongst all of those in the value chain so that people see the purpose of the product/ services in similar ways and *agree* on which activities are critical to success.[63]

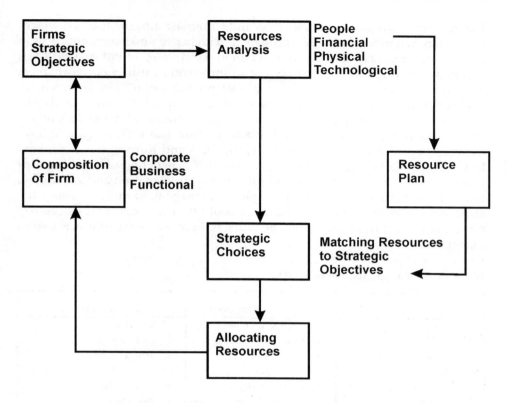

Figure 4.9   Resource allocation process

Resource analysis techniques
Some of the most valuable and well-known concepts and techniques used in the process of defining resource requirements for strategic decisions are listed below:

- Market segmentation
- Product life cycle
- Capital budgeting
- Shareholder value
- Core competence
- Value chain analysis
- Experience curve
- Decision support systems

Research by strategy consultants Bain and Company into the use of management resource tools tested 25 of the most widely used management tools in today's market.[64] The aim was to offer an objective assessment of what tools are in use and how effective they are in improving business performance. The use of management tools is a global phenomenon. The research revealed that organisations around the word use roughly the same number of tools and, more interestingly, the same type of tools. This would suggest that – despite clear differences in business culture that exist at a micro level between organisations in the Far East, the USA and Europe – at the macro level, global markets create the same competitive challenges. Increasing global competitiveness creates demand for the same information and knowledge and would seem to be generating a global management culture, using the same structures assembled by the same tool kit. Table 4.8, reveals the top ten management tools that, over the years, have seen the greatest use among managers.

Table 4.8   Global managers' tool kit

Asia	United Kingdom	North America
1. Groupware	1. Self directed teams	1. Groupware
2. Core competencies	2. Customer satisfaction	2. Cycle time reduction
3. Pay for performance	3. Core competencies	3. Strategic alliances
4. Micromarketing	4. Service guarantees	4. Shareholder value analysis
5. Re-engineering	5. Horizontal organisations	5. Micromarketing
6. Self-directed teams	6. Total Quality Management	6. Benchmarking
7. Shareholder value analysis	7. Cycle time reduction	7. Competitor profiling
8. Benchmarking	8. Strategic alliances	8. Customer retention
9. Cycle time reduction	9. Benchmarking	9. Self-directed teams
10. Technology forecasting	10. Customer retention	10. Customer satisfaction

According to UK managers, the best tools are those which deliver improved financial performance – a greater profit growth, improved cash flow, and higher share price. The best contributors are perceived to be self-directed teams, customer satisfaction measures, and core competencies, whilst the least benefit is from competitor profiling, groupware, and value chain analysis.

Short-term financial results remain the prime focus of the majority of UK managers (57 per cent) – compare this with Japan, where only 27 per cent of managers say this is the most important focus and 45 per cent believe that building new capabilities is more important.

Areas of Primary Focus	Respondents
Financial results	57%
Long-term performance	21%
Building customer relationships	12%
Competitive positioning	6%
Organisation integration	3%

Resource allocation

Most organisations in the UK still have a central unit which plays a key role in the allocation of resources. The ultimate and most powerful way in which the centre can influence strategy is through resource allocation. By supporting one investment project rather than another, the centre can affect the whole shape of the portfolio. All of the companies exert influence of this type, although in difference ways. Some link resource allocation closely to long-term business plans; others adopt a more project-by-project approach. Some give considerable freedom to division managers – others wish to sanction even the smallest expenditures. Some largely react to divisional proposals – others take the lead in sponsoring changes in the portfolio, including acquisitions and divestment. The way the centre allocates resources is therefore a critical part of the influence process.[65] The real value of any resource allocation programme lies in the resulting accomplishment of an organisation's objectives. Effective resource allocation does not guarantee successful strategy implementation because programmes, personnel, controls, and commitment must breathe life into the resources provided. Strategic management itself is sometimes referred to as a resource allocation process.

Core competencies

The notion of core competencies, particularly technological competencies, has long been part of strategic thinking. As long ago as 1957, Selznick used the term distinctive competence to denote what a particular business was uniquely good at by comparison with its close competitors. Selznick suggested how distinctive competencies and what he called *organisational character* – what we would now call culture – could be combined to fulfil an organisation's basic mission – at least analogous to strategic intent. Selznick's idea of distinctive competence pinpointed the competitive element which differentiates one business from another. Such differentiation is no longer enough because the current speed of technological development means that competitive advantage based on singular competence is unlikely to be sustainable for long.

Prehalad and Hamel argued that core competencies are the bases on which to build strategies.[66] Their argument resulted from studies examining the way in which successful firms, mainly Japanese, appeared to systematically acquire, develop, and exploit combinations of fundamental technologies, in order to develop generic or core products with which to dominate global markets. Multiple core competencies can thus give business a sustainable competitive advantage. By identifying its distinctive competencies and relating them to its core products, a firm can be specific with its plans to develop those capabilities and acquire new ones where necessary, and so maximise the utility of its limited resources to achieve the greatest sustainable advantage. The inability of a firm to identify core competencies correctly will result in the firm overlooking attractive opportunities and pursuing poor ones. Core competencies are the basis for producing a competitive advantage.

The achievement of a transformational strategic intent will almost inevitably demand competencies which may, at first, appear far beyond the capacity of the relevant firm. Competencies have therefore to be leveraged up as far as possible. The acquisition and nurturing of competencies which are not core is wasteful of resources and effort, and only serves to dissipate concentration on the core. It is therefore preferable to buy in non-core competencies and focus all internal efforts on the acquisition and development of core competencies.[67] Core competencies which are lacking can be developed internally through focused investment and R&D, or acquired externally through various forms of collaborative arrangements. It should be noted, however, that internal development is increasingly expensive and beyond the means of all but the largest organisations. Moreover, in an era when diffusion of technology is rapid, the resultant competitive advantage may be short lived.

Prehalad and Hamel provide several such examples of the use of core competencies. The success of NEC, for example, systematically exploited the convergence of core competencies in computing and communications. A committee oversaw the development of these core competencies and resulting core products. This was supported by other co-ordination groups and teams which cut across the traditional organisational structure, and ensured that each member of the organisation knew and understood the strategic intent. They developed competencies internally and also through over 100 purposive collaborations and alliances with other organisations. Between 1980 and 1988 sales grew from $3.8 billion to $21.9 billion and the company became the world's number one in semiconductors, and a leading player in telecommunications and computers.[68] The organisational implications of this approach to strategy formulation in the face of rapidly developing technology are clearly recognised in the growing literature on the deconstruction of organisational monoliths to forms based around more or less loosely coupled teams and alliances.[69]

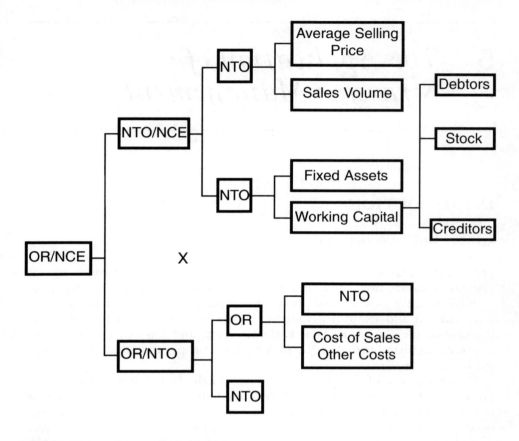

Figure 4.10   The Dupont Analysis

5 *The Application of Strategic Management*

INTRODUCTION

Global business drivers

From our discussion in Chapters 1 and 2, it is evident that more service organisations are now operating across national borders. For an organisation to be truly global, it needs to undertake business (at a minimum) in both eastern and western hemispheres. It could be argued that with the increase of non-Japanese Asia; Latin America, and Eastern Europe firms, operating in just the triad of North America, Europe, and Japan is no longer sufficient.

The emergence of the global economy and the fact that national and regional economies no longer exist as independent structures offer several new opportunities and threats for service businesses. This global economy has now resulted in more competitors, some of which are very effective. More and more US organisations are being bought by foreigners. For example, Japan spent close on $6 billion in 1990 to purchase American companies using the strong yen and their immense export earnings. Foreign acquisitions represent a future trend in the US. Daniel Schwartz (managing director of Ulmer Brothers, a New York investment bank), was quoted as saying: 'the former Rust Belt of the Midwest could quickly become the "Sushi Belt"; we're facing more competitors worldwide, many of whom are very aggressive.'[1]

Not only does a global economy mean more competitors, it also creates greater opportunity. For example, many large computer-service providers in the US earn significant revenues from overseas operations. On a wider perspective, the global economy introduces greater complexities with which firms have to deal. Technological advances made in the last decade have added to these complexities and opportunities. The western hemisphere is now in direct competition with the eastern hemisphere, and firms are fighting for economic survival, future markets, and profits. In this global economy firms are also up against the complexity of dealing with different cultures and commitments. Operating in a global economy has been a very painful experience for many European and US firms, it demands continuous innovation and significant changes in the way organisations operate and manage themselves, specifically, in the way they manage to increase quality and productivity.

Despite the reality of the global market place, there are indications that US managers, unlike their European counterparts, do not recognise the global challenge confronting them. A survey of 1500 managers undertaken by Solomon found that only 35 per cent of Americans thought 'experience outside the HQ country' was very important, compared with 74 per cent of their foreign counterparts.[2] Only 18 per cent of American managers called the 1992 unification of Europe substantial, compared with 34 per cent of Latins, 52 per cent of Japanese, and 55 per cent of Europeans.

Firms in the next century will have little choice but to innovate, change more, and change more frequently than in the last century. This represents a formidable challenge for those with management and profit and loss accountabilities. Among the responses that firms (and their competitors) are assembling in order to cope with this changing environment are global business drivers, such as those described below.[3]

Produce global or semi-global products: Coca-Cola and Pepsi-Cola are globally standardised products sold almost everywhere. McDonald's hamburgers and french fries are becoming global products. Gucci bags are too. Some successful semi-global products establish primary markets in selected countries and bolster these sales with lucrative secondary markets in other countries.

Supply the needs of global customers: for example, it is possible to design a car for select, perhaps top-of-the-line, customers around the globe. Dr Ohmae (1990) cites Rolls-Royce and Mercedes-Benz as examples.

Serve global corporate customers: General Electric, General Motors, Royal Dutch/Shell, Toyota, British Petroleum, Daimler-Benz, Fiat, and Samsung are among the large corporations that have global operations. They answer a worldwide need for many products and services.

Buy from global supplies: a domestic firm serving domestic customers may well find that its best source of raw materials and components or financing lies outside its home nation. As more nations strive to trade on their comparative economic advantages, global sources of inputs will become more attractive.

Defend against global competitors: a global competitor can use cash flow, profits, and economies of scale secured in one country or business intelligence gained from operating in that country to improve its competitive position in another country. A company may have to go global to mitigate this advantage.

Disperse the firm's value-added chain globally: companies, such as Lewis Galoob Toys, act like global strategic brokers and place their operations wherever best in the world to execute any business function in their value-adding chain. As more countries specialise for comparative economic advantage, and as the workforces of the world compete for jobs, this driver will become more attractive. It is important to note that quality considerations as well as cost considerations can influence the decision to disperse a firm's value-adding chain globally. Some spots in the world are world-class performers or best-of-class performers in executing certain aspects of the value adding chain.

Disperse globally to minimise risk: due to increased uncertainty in the global environment, it may be necessary for a firm to spread its activities over several countries in order to reduce its exposure to political, economic, and social changes in any one country or location.

If we compare the categories of services identified in Chapter 2, it transpires that most industry globalisation drivers apply to services, but their impact varies by service type and industry. For example, government (expressed in terms of economic policy, regulation, and protectionism) drivers are often industry specific. This highlights the importance of conducting a systematic evaluation of globalisation drivers for individual industries, rather than taking generalised views that service businesses can be more or less easily globalised than manufacturing businesses. In the final analysis, the profitable survivor will be the firm which manages to argument its global operations successfully, whilst constantly introducing changes in response to its market segments and pursuing opportunities inherent in the global economy.

Value chains and a firm's strategic core

The need to evaluate strategic alternatives is a paramount prerequisite to understanding the global opposition. Many of the strategic tools and concepts discussed in Chapter 4 can be applied to all types of strategic problems. Indeed, organisations can develop effective global strategies by systematically analysing both the specific global business drivers affecting their industries and the distinctive characteristics of their service businesses. A major aspect in international business is the increasing use of strategy formulation. One key theme is that strategy formulation is dependent, to some degree, on industry characteristics and on those specific business drivers. A second key aspect is the use of global strategy – it should be remembered that the use of global strategy differs by dimension for each element of the value chain. As a mechanism for analysing the competitive position of a firm's internal operations, Porter introduced the value-chain concept, by which every single activity within a firm's cycle of production, marketing, delivery, and support can be broken down to reveal the potential for improving both cost and differentiation at an early stage. A firm gains competitive advantage by performing these strategically important activities more cheaply or better than its competitors. The value chain links into those of its suppliers upstream and its buyers downstream, and each needs to be understood as part of the competitive process, as do the value chains of competitors. Differences among competitor value chains are a key source of competitive advantage.

In its generic form the value chain is the flow from inbound logistics, marketing, and service, with an overlaying infrastructure of procurement, technological development, human resource development, and organisation and management. When the value chain of a business unit is linked to the value chains of its suppliers and customers, a value system is defined, which is similar to the total vertical marketing system. Adding competitors to the value chain will allow for the analysis of horizontal relations within the industry. Some organisations have used the concept of value chains to define the efficient boundary of a firm and as an analytical means of defining the firm's strategic core. The strategic core of a firm is represented by assets of high specifity which are necessary to attain the firm's strategic goals. Such assets should be governed internally, making the full range of organisational incentives available for their control. The strategic core should be close to the firm's business idea, which sets it apart relative to other competing firms (see Itami[4]). For example, IBM uses the slogan 'IBM means service' – they see their service system as a core asset which puts them in the lead over other mainframe computer manufactures. Strategic core is not a static concept which, once established, can be exploited until retirement. In a changing world, a strategic core which secured a competitive advantage last year may be of little economic value this year.

One method of defining a firm's strategic core is to realise that time is often the critical variable in competitive success. For example, Norsk Data saw its strategic core as its ability to cut short the development phase in the medium computer market. Given this situation, Norsk decided there was little need to protect the technology in their new products – the critical issue was to maintain flexibility so that the next computer model could be developed in a shorter period of time than its competitors.

Though a firm can have innumerable strengths and weaknesses *vis-à-vis* its competitors, there are two basic types of competitive advantage a firm can possess: low cost or differentiation. The significance of any strength or weakness a firm possesses is ultimately a function of its impact on relative cost or differentiation. Cost advantage and differentiation in turn stem from industry structure. They result from a firm's ability to cope with the five forces better than its rivals (see Figure 4.4, p. 121). Michael Porter in his book, *Competitive Advantage,* spells out three alternative generic strategies (Figure 5.1) which a firm can follow: cost leadership, differentiation, and focus.

Porter's generic competitive strategies

Cost leadership: is a low-cost competitive strategy which aims at the broad mass market and requires offensive building of efficient scale facilities, vigorous pursuit of cost reductions from experience, tight cost overhead control, avoidance of marginal customer accounts, and cost minimisation in areas such as R&D, service sales force, and advertising. According to Michael Porter, cost leadership is perhaps the clearest of the three generic strategies.[5] If organisations are to sustain cost leadership prosperity across their range of activities, they must be clear about how this is to be accomplished through various elements of the value chain.

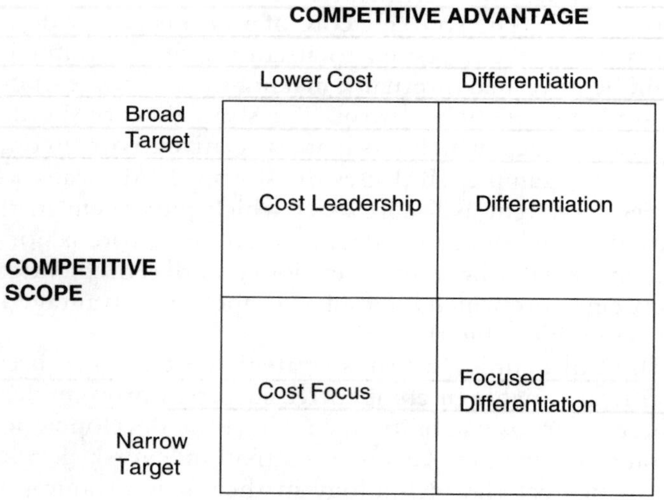

COMPETITIVE ADVANTAGE

	Lower Cost	Differentiation
Broad Target	Cost Leadership	Differentiation
Narrow Target	Cost Focus	Focused Differentiation

COMPETITIVE SCOPE

Figure 5.1   Generic competitive strategies – after Porter

Being a low-cost leader should help defend the firm against each of the five forces discussed in Chapter 4. Low-cost providers are in a better position to survive a price war, and an awareness of this may block higher-cost competitors from competing on price. Demands from buyers to lower price are likely to be weak, as customers are unlikely to be able consistently to get a better deal from a cost leader's rivals. If suppliers raise prices, the low-cost producer will not be forced as much as other, higher-cost competitors. The firm's low-cost position may well deter entry, especially if the potential entrant hopes to compete on price.

A cost leader must achieve parity or proximity in the bases of differentiation relative to its competitors to be an above-average performer, even though it relies on cost leadership for its competitive advantage. Parity in the bases of differentiation allows a cost leader to translate its cost advantage directly into higher profits than competitors. Proximity in differentiation means that the price discount necessary to achieve an acceptable market share does not offset a cost leader's cost advantage, and hence the cost leader earns above average returns.[6]

There are a number of drawbacks to implementing a cost-leader strategy. These include:

- The risk of technological change that may increase the need for large sums of capital investment to retain position, this may cancel out all cost advantages achieved.
- The threat of competition from other countries like India, where costs are even lower than Taiwan and South Korea.
- The threat by competitors to portion the market, or build up a high-price, high-quality brand image. An overall low-cost service provider would then have to compete on cost in each market segment it operated in and hope that cheaper prices can compete successfully against brand image.
- In the last decade, we have seen a cost-inflation yo-yo – this is always a danger, especially when competitors in other countries do not have the same rising labour costs.

Differentiation: the second of Porter's generic strategies is aimed at the broad mass market and involves the creation of a product or service that is perceived throughout its industry as unique. It selects one or more attributes that buyers in an industry perceive as significant, and uniquely positions itself to meet those needs. It is rewarded for its uniqueness with a premium price. In shipbuilding, for example, Japanese firms follow a differentiation strategy, offering a wide array of high-quality vessels at premium prices.[7] An organisation which has successfully pursued the use of differentiation strategy is the US WordPerfect Corporation. Started in 1980, WordPerfect Corporation chose to compete against Wordstar for the MS-DOS, IBM-compatible word-processing market. To differentiate its software from the competition, WordPerfect became the only company to offer its customers a toll-free help line. At first, the company spent very little on advertising, and sales grew largely through word of mouth. By 1989, WordPerfect had gathered a 60 per cent market share of word-processing programmes and had grown to take third position in personal-computer software. When the company introduced WordPerfect 5.0 in May 1988, monthly sales tripled to 133 000 units and the company received so many calls that the 800 lines into Utah were jammed, cutting off Delta Air Lines and the Church of Jesus Christ of Latterday Saints.[8]

With a successful differentiation strategy, loyalty to the firm's products will increase and, assuming that customers are not too price sensitive, the firm can charge premium prices for its products and services that are higher than those which could be charged by the least-cost producer in the market. It is likely that a firm which uses a strategy of differentiation will not be the market leader in terms of market share. The principal risk with a differentiation strategy is that *customers will not want to pay premium prices* for the different product or service. Some further implications for differentiation strategy are as follows:

- The firm must provide some distinguishing characteristic such as superior quality.
- The firm must continually seek to innovate and to stay ahead of its rivals in quality and other differentiating attributes. For example, if rivals innovate, the firm should try to imitate them quickly. Consequently, a differentiating firm will need to have a large budget to support R&D and advertising.

According to Mathur it is worth noting that *price* does not always need to faithfully track differentiation; it also plays an independent role in fine tuning a competitive strategy. A positively differentiated offering can be sold at a premium price, however, the seller is not obliged to charge the whole or any of that premium. In some cases, it may be advantageous to charge less than the full premium, and thereby invest in extra market share by sacrificing near-term profits. Such gains in share may lead to scale economies and consequently longer term advantages. The investment in market share by keener pricing is less often available in the limiting case of commodity-buy strategy. Like all investment, the one in market share incurs competitive risks: competitors may respond by price cuts of their own or with innovations that leapfrog and displace the seller's offering, thereby devaluing its investment.[9]

Focus: the focus strategy involves the selection of a market segment, or group of segments, in the industry and meeting the needs of that preferred segment (or niche) better than the other market competitors. Focus strategies as portrayed in Figure 5.1 can be either cost or differentiation focused. Both variants of the focus strategy rest on differences between target segments. *Cost focus* takes advantage of differences in the cost behaviour in some segments, (a cost-focus strategy does necessitate that a trade-off between profitability and overall market share be made) while *differentiation focus* exploits the special needs of buyers in certain segments, such as luxury goods. For example, A. T. Cross niched itself in the high-price pen-and-pencil market with its famous gold writing instruments that most executives, managers, and professionals own. Instead of branding all types of writing instruments, A. T. Cross has stuck to the high-price niche and enjoyed great sales growth and profit.[10]

Dwight L. Gertz, a vice president at Mercer Management Consulting Inc., Lexington, Massachusetts, suggests that US companies should walk away from the broad marketplace and zero in on a narrow market. For example, USA, the insurance and financial-services firm deals only with military officers and their families: 'What they demonstrate is that it's better to serve a small group, even a shrinking group, perfectly than it is to chase after the world as a whole.' Gertz says the principle of selective focus, which he dubs 'customer franchise management', is also being applied with success in distribution, airlines (Southwest Air-Lines and British Airways), gasoline retailing, and drug retailing.[11]

Like the other two generic strategies, there are a few risks to adopting the focus strategy. These are:

- The market segment may not be large enough to provide profits for the firm and its shareholders.
- The segment's needs may eventually become less distinct from the main market.
- Competition may move in and take over the chosen market segment.

Although there are risks associated with each of the three generic competitive strategies, Porter argues that a firm must pursue one of them. A *stuck-in-the-middle* strategy is almost certain to make only low profits. This firm lacks the market share, capital investment, and resolve to play the low-cost game position, or the focus to create differentiation or a low-cost position in a more limited sphere. To counter this *stuck-in-the-middle position,* Verdin and Williamson provide a classification of five groupings on which exploitation of Porter's cost and differentiation drivers depend. These are:

1. **Input assets**: input access, loyalty of suppliers, financial capacity.
2. **Process assets**: proprietary technology, functional experience, and organisational systems.
3. **Channel assets**: channel access, distributor loyalty, and pipeline stock.
4. **Customer assets**: customer loyalty, brand recognition, and installed base.
5. **Market knowledge assets**: accumulated information and the systems and

processes to access new information, on the goals and behaviour of competitors, the reactions of customers, suppliers, and competitors to different phases of the business cycle, and so on.

Explicit recognition of the portfolio of assets which underpins any cost or differentiation driver helps in pinpointing where potential, long-term competitive advantage lies. If all competitors have equal access to the assets necessary to reap the benefits of a driver, then it will cease to be a source of competitive advantage. It is only when it is slow and costly for a rival to gain access to some of the necessary, underlying assets (rendering these assets strategic) that a particular driver will offer scope for sustained competitive advantage. The processes by which the services of particular assets are accessed therefore play a critical role.[12]

Once a firm has chosen to pursue one of Porter's generic strategies, it is likely to continue along that path for some time. This is illustrated by Gilbert and Strebel,[13] who offer a strategic map of the PC industry. The map outlines the evolution of a company's strategy by an arrowed time line. As the map shows, a firm pursuing a cost-leadership strategy may, at a latter stage, have to consider some development towards product differentiation. Users of PCs will compare standard, low-cost products with the differentiated products. They may increasingly demand a number of the differentiating features, forcing the low-cost producers to incorporate these in their product offerings. Buyers do not simply (it would seem) seek value for money. Hence care should be taken not to overemphasise Porter's useful distinction in generic competitive strategies (Figure 5.2).

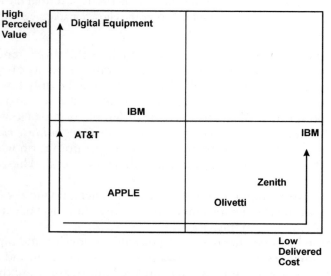

Figure 5.2   Strategic groups in the PC industry

Aligning cost leadership and differentiation

It is sometimes difficult to distinguish in practice between those organisations who pursue cost-leadership strategies and those who pursue differentiation. The risks of pursuing either cost leadership on its own or differentiation seem to be of pushing into the middle ground. Advances in technology mean that increased differentiation need not be achieved at the expense of substantial increases in cost. The two are not mutually exclusive. Fulmer and Goodwin point out: 'all firms, in essence, follow a differentiation strategy. Only one company can differentiate itself with the lowest cost; the remaining firms in the industry must find other ways to differentiate their products and services.'[14] Likewise, going for a low-cost/low-price strategy does not prohibit differentiation. Examples are given by Fulmer and Goodwin of where differentiation and cost reduction go hand in hand. Thus, in banking, the automatic cash dispenser leads both an improved customer service (i.e., level of access) and to cost savings (reduction in administration and labour intensity).

Another case is Benetton: Benetton operates its stores with no back-room storage: what is on the shelves is the only stock on hand. Through a highly responsive service and manufacturing network, through a highly responsive communication and information system, Benetton can respond very quickly to consumer demand for products and keep its costs below the competition. Benetton derives its strength from simultaneous pursuit of two contradictory objectives – economies of scale and manufacturing flexibility – through negotiated strategy. Aldo Palmeri, Benetton's former CEO, describes the company as 'vertically deintegrated'. That means that upstream, the company subcontracts 90–95 per cent of its activities in manufacturing to independent or partially owned indotto. In this way, Benetton can still respond flexibly to changes in market mood. But, by centralising the purchases of raw materials, Benetton – the worlds largest purchaser of wool – also obtains considerable cost advantages.

Reymond Miles and Charles Snow argued that competing firms within a single industry can be classified on the basis of their strategic orientation into one of four basic types:[15]

Defenders: businesses that concentrate on optimising their performance in existing product markets.

Prospectors: businesses that are constantly seeking market opportunities for new products.

Reactors: businesses that lack a consistent strategy-structure-culture relationship.

Analysers: businesses that analyse the changing competitive environment to determine whether and when to match competitors' new product or optimisation moves.

Each of these types has its own preferred strategy for responding to the environment, and has its own combination of structure, culture, and processes incorporated within that strategy (Table 5.1). Research by Segev, comparing Porter's, and Miles and Snow's respective strategic models, exposes that the two concepts are in the main compatible.[16] A *defender* tends to follow a cost-leadership or cost-focus strategy, whereas a *prospector* tends to follow a differentiation or differentiation-focus strategy. A *reactor* follows no consistent strategy and is thus in Porter's terminology 'stuck in the middle'. Since the *analyser* refers to an organisation using different strategies in different industries in which it competes, no one business-level competitive strategy will fit this type of firm.

Table 5.1   Miles and Snow: defender, prospector, and analyser model

	Defenders	Prospectors	Analysers
Objectives	Stable market niches.	Exploitation of new products via market opportunities.	New ventures mapped to existing organisation.
Strategies	Cost efficient with emphasis on price and service to defend position in market place.	Growth attained by product development Monitoring marketing opportunities.	Steady growth via market penetration. Followers in the market place.
Control Systems	Centralised control emphasis on cost efficiency, extensive use of formal planning.	Emphasis on flexibility, decentralised control, use of *ad hoc* measurement.	Intensive planning, complicated roles between business processes.

Beyond Michael Porter

Looking back at Porter's contributions to strategic management over the last 25 years – from his Ph.D. dissertation (1973) to his recent work on the role of national competition (1994) – indicates that substantial changes have taken place in his thinking. Evidence would suggest that this is not just a matter of Porter progressively directing his attention to different analytical theories. It is also a matter of his scholastic approach significantly changing, to a large extent under the impact of the attempt to approach different phenomena. Some would argue that it is far from clear what the relationships are between, for example, Porter's five-forces framework, the value-chain analysis, and the Diamond framework.

In the last 15 years, there have been several challenges to Porter's theory of generic strategies (see, for example, both Miller and Hill[17]). Problems with generic strategy concepts have surfaced and there is some evidence that organisations and their managers have varying interpretations of Porter's ideas. The most common criticism has been that, while low-cost and differentiation strategies are empirically identifiable and are linked with above average profitability, Porter's dichotomy of cost differentiation cannot be maintained. Several academics (including Miller) have found evidence of the successful combination of low-cost and differentiation strategies. Hill argues that joint low-cost and differentiation strategies should not only exist, but also be necessary for competitive success in a variety of circumstances. These conclusions appear at first sight to contradict Porter's model, and several writers, among them Miller again and also Murry,[18] have interpreted them in this sense.

Porter does, however, allow for exceptions to his rule that cost leadership and differentiation are incompatible. He also states clearly that all competitors, including differentiators, should seek to minimise their costs – providing this does not threaten their source of differentiation – and that a successful differentiation must at least maintain a cost base near the industry average. The cost leadership is about lowest cost, not low cost. This distinction is, however, absent from empirical investigations which are carried out as part of a strategic profile and, at best, identify a mere intention to lower costs. In these circumstances, a correlation between cost and differentiation strategies is scarcely inconsistent with Porter's model, and even a correlation between successful differentiation and below-average costs may say more about the inefficient or the stuck-in-the-middle firms – someone in the industry has to make below-average profits – than about the correctness, or otherwise, of Porter's model.

Critical capabilities

As indicated at the start of this chapter, the competitive environment has become more hostile. For example, Bowman and Carter write lucidly in their paper,[19] referring to increasing competition from rapidly developing nations, globalisation of markets, and the more recent effects of recession, which have all combined to make life more difficult for most firms. Instability in many markets, due to political, economic, and social upheaval (e.g., Eastern Europe), coupled with the pace of change and shortening product life cycles, has increased uncertainty and dynamism in the environment. Niches that were once safely protected by brand or other entry barriers are being increasingly penetrated. Now, no firm seems to be immune from price competition, so that being *customer focused* and delivering excellent value is becoming an order-qualifying rather than an order-winning capability. These developments can be expressed as changes in two of the contingency variables facing firms. Specifically:

1.   **The environment**: has become more hostile, more unpredictable, and more dynamic.

2.   **Tasks**: the need for fast-paced innovation, coupled with the need to offer high value at low cost (not necessarily low prices), has increased the task complexity of the firm.

A firm's particular chosen competitive position and the product and services it sells are important, but only at a given point in time. In a rapidly changing competitive environment, products quickly become obsolete and static competitive positions are rapidly overtaken. This places new demands on organisations to be able to respond consistently to changing markets with new products and ever-mproving competitiveness. A firm can achieve this ongoing renewal by identifying, developing, and maintaining its *critical capabilities*. Capabilities are a company's proficiency in combining people, process, and technology to allow it to continually distinguish itself along the dimensions that are important to customers. For example, in a high technology industry, the ability to quickly develop new state-of-the-art products with features and performance that deliver value to customers creates an enduring advantage. In a commodity industry, it may be the ability to constantly reduce costs through innovative actions that creates lasting competitive advantage.[20]

Professor Gary Hamel – one of the new breed of strategic thinkers – focuses on what he terms competition for competence. Hamel suggests that competence has three different dimensions, functionality, market access, and product integrity, plus the understanding that a core competence can be contained in any one of these dimensions. The emergence of *competency based strategies* (CBS), which offer a different perspective on business, have emerged in the last five years. Edwards and Peppard argue that sustainable advantage derives from unique, inimitable *strategic competencies* possessed by firms.[21] For example, they site Grand Metropolitan's (GrandMet) use of CBS, which they distinguish from the traditional generic strategies, followed by many of their competitors, that address issues such as the composition of the product portfolio, market selection, acquisitions, and divestments. GrandMet claim that such strategic decisions are easily copied by competitors.

Their CBS deals with establishing excellence in the core competencies necessary to operate effectively in its chosen marketplace in the future. For GrandMet, such critical competencies include things such as managing individual brands, product launching, market penetration, and manufacturing and operational excellence. They are not readily recognised by competitors as key strengths and they are they are neither easily nor quickly copied. But it is these CBS that enable the firm to react, adapt, and prosper in such a volatile and competitive environment.

One way of identifying a *strategic competence* is that it provides a gateway to new opportunities. It is necessary to distinguish between competencies that allow a firm merely to be in business and competencies that really are strategic to its capacity to generate future growth and profits. Secondly, a strategic competence has to be a skill that represents some reasonably complex synthesis of hard and soft technology, tacit and explicit knowledge, and so on, that is, it is not easily imitated. IDV, the UK spirits company that owns Smirnoff and Bailey's, provides an example. The brand Bailey's is not a core competence of IDV, but the ability to take the brand from nowhere, invest it with heritage and culture, and then to position it in peoples' minds is a core competence. It is this capability which is complex and difficult to imitate. In this sense, a strategic competence is a complex skill, not an individual asset or brand.

From time to time maverick competitors will try to change the 'rules of the game' in a market. These are often small or relatively young firms who lack the large accumulated asset bases of entrenched competitors. Because they face impediments to competing on the basis of rapid cost expansion of existing types of assets, they seek to prosper by satisfying customer needs on the basis of new sets of assets, unfamiliar to existing competitors. A classic example is the challenge which was presented to the traditional, large-scale film-processing laboratories by networks of one-hour film processing stations. The established film processors had perfected the assets and knowledge bases (competencies) to collect exposed film from retailers, transport it to centralised processing facilities, and develop films cost effectively in complex, large-scale plants without misplacing individual customer's photos.

The maverick one-hour film-processing networks served the customer on the basis of a very different bundle of assets. The competencies required to put these in place were equally different to those that had been important in the past. Competencies in franchising, miniaturisation of equipment, materials distribution and de-skilling of the operation were critical in successfully underpinning this new way of better satisfying an existing market.

Disney uses the concept of core competencies to organise its Magic Kingdom and other amusement-park operations. A core process for Disney is close and friendly customer contact. All activities within Disney's amusement parks are organised and positioned in such a way that guests are treated exceptionally well. Almost every possible guest need, or considerations of human comfort and convenience, and information booths, and kiosks that sell ice cream, camera film, souvenirs, and first-aid kits are located throughout the parks. Disney is customer service at its ultimate. Although every Disney amusement park contains vital functions (engineering, operations, maintenance and repair, sales), Disney's approach to customer service blends all functions into defining core process. The over-riding priority placed on fast and friendly customer service transcends each of the individual functions. In fact, a growing number of firms from other service industries are studying the Disney approach to organising its core activities around the customer. By making friendly customer service its core process, Disney lays the foundation for its distinctive competence – providing memorable emotional experiences, or the special Disney Magic.[22]

STRATEGIC VISION

Inventing a strategy

Whether one is looking at strategy locally or globally, it is extremist to think in broad terms about the service sector, or service industries, as though all organisations face more or less the same strategic problems or have the same strategic goals. One of the critical concerns in the area of business strategy is that of strategic vision. This imperative is commonly associated with the head of the firm, who is expected to define a vision for the firm, and communicate it in a way that generates contagious enthusiasm. Hamel and Prahalad argue that the vision of the firm should carry with it an *obsession* that they refer to as 'strategic intent'.[23] It implies a sizeable stretch for the organisation that requires leveraging resources to reach seemingly unattainable goals. For example, using the case of Jack Welch again – his vision for General Electric (GE) was to make GE *number one or number two* in its chosen business operations. Welch's *vision* spearheaded a revolution that has seen sales increase from $27 billion in 1980 to approximately $70 billion in 1995, accompanied by a profit growth from $1.5 billion to $5 billion and a six fold increase in stock value to $90 billion, making GE the second largest company in the US, behind only Exxon, up from eleventh position in 1980.

History records that when Jack Welch became CEO of GE in 1981, he dispensed with all GE's short- to medium-term strategic-planning mechanisms, and mandated that all GE businesses be first or second in an industry – or else get out. From a manager perspective, this mandate was easy to understand. Although Welch disbanded most of GE's strategic-planning infrastructure at the corporate level, he dispensed with neither long-term planning at the business-unit level nor the necessity for business-unit managers to undertake analyses in order to justify their plans. Eileen Shapiro tells the story of one former GE Executive after Welch had downsized the corporate strategic-planning staff:

> Jack and his peanut gallery (other corporate officers and staff) would line up on one side of the room. We'd come in with our team, ready to give a succinct summary of our strategy and any changes we were proposing. Then Jack and the peanut gallery would engage in a toe-to-toe and belly-to-belly debate with us about the business's merits and what it would take to win. Did we do analysis and planning before we went in? Oh man! You'd get your head handed to you if you hadn't! If you couldn't defend your strategy and didn't know the facts and figures, you'd be dead meat.[24]

The concept behind Welch's thinking was to *democratise strategy* down to the coalface. Strategy, however, is not only created by people at the top of a company or in its planning department. Strategy needs the wealth of information and knowledge possessed by people to make it happen, by people who are continually dealing with customers, competitors, technologies, and suppliers. To quote C. D. Tam, General Manager of Motorola's Asia Pacific Marketing Operations: 'You can't run a semiconductor business as a one-man show, you can't know it all. You may have a very high IQ, but you can't be equal to 2000 employees in brain power.'[25] Gary Hamel, writing in the *Harvard Business Review* says:

> The capacity to think creatively about strategy is distributed widely in an enterprise. It is impossible to predict exactly where a revolutionary idea is forming; thus the net must be cast wide. In many of the companies I work with, hundreds and sometimes thousands of people get involved in crafting strategy. They are asked to look deeply into potential discontinuities, help define and elaborate the company's core competencies, ferret out corporate orthodoxies, and search for unconventional strategic options. In one company, the idea for a multimillion-dollar opportunity came from a twenty-something secretary. In another company, some of the best ideas about the organisation's core competencies came from a forklift operator.
>
> To help revolutionary strategies emerge, senior managers must supplement the hierarchy of experience with a hierarchy of imagination. This can be done by dramatically extending the strategy franchise. Three constituencies that are usually under represented in the strategy-making process must have a disproportionate say. The first constituency is young people – or, more accurately, people with a youthful perspective. Of course, some thirty-year olds are 'young fogies,' but most young people live closer to the future than people with gray hair. It is ironic that the group with the biggest stake in the future is the most disenfranchised from the process of strategy creation.[26]

According to Hamel and Prahalad, democratising strategy creates a new way of thinking about a process for pooling collective knowledge and commitment in an organisation, and channelling it. Many people say there is no natural constituency for change in a large company. Hamel and Prahalad argue the contrary, that there is a natural desire for change in all companies, but there are no forums for mobilising that desire for change. They say that (mobilising and directing) the desire for change should be seen as an integral part of the strategy process involving both substantive and organisational issues. To emphasis this, Ghoshal and Bartlett offer an example of a large American computer company.[27] Confronted with the challenge of rapidly changing customer demands, and the constraints of a traditional matrix organisation that impeded the company's ability to marshal its own formidable technological resources to help its customers solve evermore complex problems, the company decided to restructure itself – to create a network of entrepreneurs (*visionaries*) in a global corporation. Muzyka et al. view this entrepreneurial process in the following way:[28]

- Create (or recognise) and develop an opportunity.
- Evaluate its desirability – its economic potential and the personal and financial risks involved.
- Marshal the resources needed to exploit it, including but not limited to the financial, managerial, technical, and physical resources.
- Possess the will or tenacity to see the innovation through and for the leadership to develop a following.
- Manage the launch, including competitive and co-operative relationships and networks.
- Manage the downstream realisation of the value of the opportunity, including creation of value.
- As the organisation grows, ensure that individuals throughout the organisation are able to repeat the process of realising opportunities by providing appropriate organisational structures, processes and behaviours, and by acting as a facilitator and role model.

As described by the company's top management, the objective was to create a management approach which starts with opportunity and capitalises on the innovation, creativity, and excellence of people to secure the future of the company. This objective was enshrined in the vision statement: to build a global IT service company based on people who are enthusiastic about coming to work every day, knowing that they are highly valued, encouraged to grow, and increase their knowledge, and are individually motivated to make a positive difference. To achieve this vision, the company restructured itself into a large number of relatively small units, each headed by a person formally designated as an entrepreneur. There were different kinds of entrepreneurial units corresponding to different tasks, such as product creation, field sales and support, or industry marketing. All shared a common mandate, however, to think and act as heads of companies in a network holding: pursuit of opportunities was defined as their key challenge. Each entrepreneur was assured significant support, and the top management collectively declared that everyone in the company worked for the entrepreneurs. At the same time, it was emphasised that no one could afford to own or control all the expertise, resources, or services necessary for achieving his or her objectives, and that independent judgement and action had to reflect this pervasive interdependence, so as to effectively leverage the network of organisational resources available in a global operation (Figure 5.3).

Once a specific vision has been accomplished another must be created or momentum can be lost. For this reason, some organisations have also expressed their goals in terms of broad purpose, which represents a more basic statement of why the company exists, what it stands for, and what it hopes to accomplish. Examples of mottoes include: British Airways, 'To Fly To Serve'; or Komatsu, 'Work for the world. Care for the community. Making tools for a better life in response to social needs.' Whereas the vision represents an intermediate destination, the purpose expresses the objectives behind the journey.[29] Creating a vision clearly requires a different mindset to that associated with conventional strategic analysis. It is about creating possibilities that will stretch the organisation rather than about identifying empirical probabilities. It is about creating competitive advantage by standing in the firm's future rather than its past. That is not to say that it can be unrelated to reality – the subsequent stages of the strategic-action process provide a good check on this – merely that it should be based on future competitive aspirations instead of the limitations of immediate circumstances.

Figure 5.3   The network organisation

The role of leadership in strategy formulation

A study undertaken some 25 years ago by Eastlack and McDonald studied the leadership characteristics of CEOs of 211 companies, 105 of whom were listed in the US *Fortune 500,* and found that those CEOs who involved themselves in strategic planning also headed the fastest growing companies.[30] This does not prove that strategy formulation produced faster growth, but it does indicate that the CEOs of high-growth companies felt formal strategic planning produced enough benefits in their firms to devote a substantial proportion of one of their most limited resources, namely senior management.

Asked what has shaped their firm's values and beliefs, many managers cite the influence of the firm's founder or CEO. In many multinational organisations, the leader has had a lasting impact on the firm's strategic formulation and direction. An important ingredient in the process of strategy formulation is the commitment and leadership of senior management, especially the CEO. Clearly, the chief executive can (and will) affect the clarity and outcome of the firm's strategy, as well as the resources committed to its implementation. For example, Harold Geneen, CEO of ITT, had an important impact on the company's management processes. While his successors have refocused the company's strategy and reshaped its organisation, Geneen's influence is still felt in the discipline he instilled through his, now famous, management systems and review meetings.

From our discussion on *vision*, the CEO's commitment to strategic success should be infectious, positively affecting the commitment of managers, and increasing the probability of agreement on the chosen plan of action. Increasingly, the challenge facing many CEOs is to:

1. Define the opportunities in the external business environment.
2. Ensure that the firm has access to adequate people, technology, and capital.
3. Ensure that the firm has effective management processes for ensuring that its resources are applied to the profitable exploitation of those opportunities.

In the last decade, CEO (and boardroom) competencies related to the facilitation of strategic learning and change have become increasingly important. In the 1980s, too many managers felt constrained by the history and organisation of their company. Research would suggest that, in many cases, when deciding a strategy such as organisational structure, the existing organisation has been regarded as a point of departure. In the new, more flexible world that is emerging, every effort needs to be made to leave open the question of the nature of the organisation required until the board has first determined, or caused a determination of, what needs to be done, by whom, and how their contribution might best be facilitated. As a greater number of CEOs focus on the need to create more flexible and adaptable business units, we can anticipate many more managers in the next millennium playing an increasing role in strategy formulation, with longer-term responsibilities relating to reshaping the organisation to meet their firm's strategic business development opportunities.

To emphasis this point – recognising the importance of interfacing, and bringing on board those managers that need to make strategy work, was uppermost in the mind of Dennis Malamatinas, CEO of Smirnoff Vodka, a subsidiary of International Distillers and Vinters (IDV). Malamatinas had championed *(visioned)* Smirnoff to become the world's leading Vodka brand, outselling the number two brand by 3.5 times. With the twin objectives of driving Smirnoff to the leading position in the spirits industry and of dislodging Bacardi, the campaign captured the essence of the brand in the words 'pure thrill'. The pure-thrill campaign has set new standards for advertising in the spirits industry, receiving 26 awards. What was the toughest part of the campaign? Implementing it – because it was not invented here! Malamatinas comments: 'If you were to ask me some of the key ingredients, I'd say vision, persistence, commitment, passion, patience, risk taking – a blend of all these.' By focusing on the key managers and involving them both at the IDV corporate centre and in the businesses, by listening to their concerns, by emphasising the quality of the brand, and by making himself visible, Malamatinas's push to make Smirnoff a global brand was achieved.[31]

Strategy formulation

The European environment with its affluent millions provides firms with many markets and profit opportunities. A key factor of these markets is that customers increasingly expect products or services that perform as specified; they expect the best possible value at reasonable cost; they demand the service needed to maintain products; and assurance that products will perform as specified. We have argued that in the 1990s competitive world, an appreciation of the importance of time often spells the difference for winning competitors and companies. In the service industry timeliness is often the difference between winning a customer or losing one. Gummesson offers the following lessons on the service quality, and considers it to be the most important factor for successful firms.[32] At the time of writing, 1989, he considered that the field of quality in service industries lagged behind manufacturing industries, and that there was considerable dissatisfaction from consumers. This was particularly true of the public sector – which has to be the largest part of the service economy. His lessons are as follows:

1. Select the relevant approaches and techniques from manufacturing quality management, but beware – not all are appropriate. Not all techniques are universally applicable – they may need customisation since people, the service providers, are not the same as machines.
2. Service quality must be considered in two stages, process quality and outcome quality. This is one of the fundamental differences between products and services, the consumer is involved in the 'manufacture' of the service, and the consumer may suffer a bad experience during this encounter – even if the end result and future benefits are acceptable.
3. There is a need for service designers. There is no tradition of service design, and as Gummesson says, in public service the design is often left to someone with a background in law, with customer utility treated as a legal matter rather than a satisfaction of established need. By definition, the relationship between the front-line service provider and the customer will tend to be confrontational. He quotes Deming that 94 per cent of faults in manufacturing are common-cause faults, that is, designed-in rather than the fault of an operative – is it likely then that the percentage will be significantly less for services?
4. Pursue both a zero strategy and a junk-yard strategy: when errors occur, be prepared to solve them quickly and smoothly. Always aim for zero defects, but recognising that problems can arise empower front-line staff to deal

with them effectively and quickly. A well-designed service will have a standard operating procedure, but will recognise the existence of the unexpected.

5. When service organisations hide behind outdated values of authority and monopoly, quality will never develop. The cure for this is more than 'Smile Courses', it is the profession's established code of ethics that serve to keep the client in place rather than protect them or ensure their satisfaction.

6. Convert administrative routines into internal services. Use the techniques of process management to recognise that there are internal customers as well as external customers. As with manufacturing – the earlier a defect is spotted, the less expensive it is to fix.

7. Quality of computer software is crucial for quality of services. Approximately 70–80 per cent of investment in information technology goes to service industries. As we have described elsewhere, software development has its own quality routines, but in the hands of the service provider, it can be a significant weapon for competitive advantage (see the Airlines case study, Chapter 7) or a cause of disaster, viz the recent opening of Hong Kong's new airport with the attendant problems of lost luggage and delay.

8. Combine the management aspects of product quality, service quality, and computer software quality with customer perceived quality to develop a holistic quality strategy. The customer is not buying product quality or service quality, they are buying utility and needs' satisfaction. Each of the forms of quality mentioned has generic traits and drivers which must be learned and mastered, but which must be taken together and combined into an holistic approach to both internal and external customers.

Gummesson closes his article with a warning, which is worth repeating verbatim:

> The 1970s was a breakthrough for Japanese products on the world market. The Japanese became market leaders in cars, motorcycles, cameras, stereo equipment, colour televisions, electron microscopes, and a long list of other products . . . They also developed totally new approaches to quality. We seem, however, to close our eyes to the fact that the same thing is now beginning to happen in services.

Of the ten largest commercial banks in the world, seven are Japanese.[33]

CEOs and their senior managers, faced with many complex factors, have little choice but to use strategic thinking. It is no longer sufficient to formulate a strategic plan once a year. Managers need to monitor the business environment continuously and must be willing to modify their strategic decisions whenever the need arises. Managers have a responsibility to understand the consequences of their actions when committing resources to a given strategic thrust. Given the complexity of coping with many strategic formulation problems, managers need to use tools (see Chapter 4) to aid decision making that will ensure that they have taken all the relevant facts into account and dealt with them appropriately.

Strategy formulation is concerned with long-term business plans for the effective management of environmental opportunities and threats, in light of a firm's strengths and weaknesses. Put another way, strategy formulation is concerned with deciding what the organisation should do. For many firms, the development of strategy formulation was motivated by several rationales:

- to develop organisational goals and objectives
- to help identify major strategic issues
- to assist in the allocation of strategic resources
- to co-ordinate and integrate complex business organisations
- to develop and train future general mangers
- to help forecast the future performance of the organisation
- to assist in the evaluation of senior and middle managers
- to help stretch the thinking of top management[34]

An organisation's strategy is a statement of the fundamental means it will use, subject to a set of environmental constraints to achieve its objectives. According to Hofer and Schendel, although this definition seems quite broad, it is circumscribed by two other observations. First, to take any action at all – and the accomplishment of objectives certainly requires action – an organisation must expend some of its resources. Thus one aspect of any strategy statement must be a description of the most important patterns of these resource deployments. Second, to accomplish any objectives, an organisation will also have to interact with an external environment. Thus, a second aspect of any strategy statement must be a description of the most critical of these environmental interactions.[35]

In essence strategy formulation differs from other types of organisational planning in the following respects:

- it involves critical decisions by senior management
- it involves ultimate allocation of large amounts of capital, labour and other types of physical resources
- it has long-term impact (and risk)
- it focuses on the organisations interaction with the external environment

In planning a firm's strategic formulation Andrews suggests ten key questions:[36]

1. Is the strategy identifiable, and has it been made clear either in words or in practice?

2. Is the strategy in some way unique?
3. Does the strategy fully exploit domestic and international environmental opportunity?
4. Is the strategy consistent with corporate competence and resources, both present and projected?
5. Are the major provisions of strategy and the programme of major policies of which it is comprised internally consistent?
6. Is the chosen level of risk feasible in economic and personal terms?
7. Is the strategy appropriate to the personal values and aspirations of key managers?
8. Is the strategy appropriate to the desired level of contribution to society?
9. Does the strategy constitute a clear stimulus to organisational effort and commitment?
1 0. Are there clear indications of the responsiveness of markets and market segments to the strategy?

Ansoff provides a strategic framework of strategic plans to aid in strategy formulation. The strategies contained in the strategic plan in Ansoff's book, *Corporate Strategy*,[37] are the basic guidelines for developing the firm's external posture and its internal capabilities. Before these guidelines becomes a bottom-line reality in terms of profits and growth, specific projects must be generated, planned, and executed. Furthermore, the strategic activity must be co-ordinated with the operating activities. Thus, the *strategic plan* is a starting point for three plans which translate strategic intent into specific plans for the strategic implementation:

1. **Capability and development plan**: contains project and supporting budgets which will change the internal configuration of the firm and its posture in the external environment. The bottom line of these projects is an enhanced potential for future profits.

2. **Operating plan**: is frequently comprised of both short- and long-term plans, and contains programmes and budgets through which the firm intends to continue making profits.

3. **Strategy development plan**: must be done through projects which have a limited time duration and which require participation of all functional competencies (discussed earlier).

The family of four plans is shown in Figure 5.4 below:

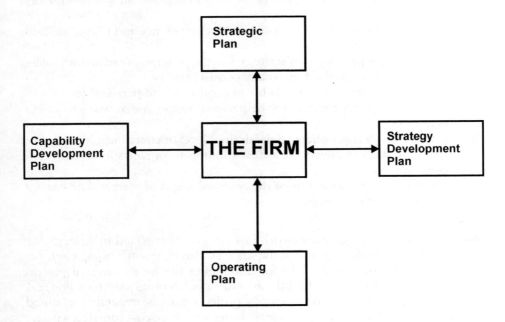

Figure 5.4   The Ansoff family of plans

Why programme strategy? According to Henry Mintzberg, the most obvious reason is for co-ordination, to ensure that everyone in the organisation pulls in the same direction, which may sometimes be facilitated by specifying that direction as precisely as possible. Plans, as they emerge from strategic programming as programmes, schedules, budgets, and so on, can be prime media to communicate not just strategic intentions, but also what each individual in the organisation must do to realise them (this point is also explored in the next section on strategy implementation). Quinn has referred to formal planning activities as 'fulfilling certain vital functions in co-ordination strategies',[38] including: awareness building, consensus generating, and commitment affirming. Planning thus forced managers to communicate systematically about strategic issues.

Other considerations in strategy formulation

These plans, of course, are not for all time: competitive strategies have to be formulated and reformulated; they are shaped and modified by circumstances, events, and opportunities as they unfold. However, by definition, they do not come about by themselves or without deliberation. Positions can unconsciously emerge, but competitive strategies, that is, plans about future positions cannot.[39]

While a rigorous, comprehensive strategy diagnosis, and analysis process does not wholly guarantee an effective strategy, there is, of course, a greater degree of probability of generating successful strategic options when the systems and methodologies that produce them are sound and complete. The first step in evaluating any strategy should be to assess the quality and totality of the processes by which it was developed. In this respect, it is possible to determine whether all the appropriate personnel within the firm were consulted and to evaluate the experiences of those who did participate, as well as the accuracy and reliability of the techniques and methods that were used to prepare the analyses and forecasts on which the proposed strategy is based.

The reader should remember from our earlier discussion that different organisations have different value systems. It is perhaps true to say that managers tend to adopt the values of the organisation that they are in or are attracted to. Attempting to implement a strategy which requires a shift from these values will meet with strong resistance. Individuals' value orientations can be mapped in the same way as that of organisations. Research by Johnson and Scholes points to a growing understanding that the strategy of a firm, its structure, the sorts of managers who hold power, its control systems, and the way it operates tend to reflect the culture of that organisation.[40] There are a number of firms in which the prevailing beliefs are essentially conservative, where low risk strategies, secure markets, and well-tried potential solutions are valued. Such organisations are referred to as defenders. In contrast, there are organisations in which the dominant beliefs are more to do with innovation and breaking new ground. Here management tends to go for higher risk strategies and new opportunities. Such organisations are referred to as prospector-type organisations. Prospectors and defenders do not behave in the same way even within similar environments. The strategies that such organisations follow are better accounted for by their prevailing beliefs than by the environmental stimuli.

According to Schwartz and Davis,[41] when considering strategic alternatives, senior management must assess the firm's compatibility with the corporate culture. If there is little fit, management must decide if it should take a chance on ignoring the culture or manage around the culture and change the plans or, alternatively, try to change the culture to fit the strategy or change the strategy to fit the culture. If the firm's culture strongly opposes a strategy, it would be foolhardy to ignore it. Further, a decision to proceed with a particular strategy without a commitment to change the culture or manage around it is dangerous. Restricting a firm, however, to only those strategies that are completely compatible with its culture may eliminate the most profitable alternatives from consideration.

Strategy implementation

Research undertaken by Bourgeois and Brodwin identified a variety of approaches to strategy implementation – from their research they categorised the various company approaches into one of five basic descriptions.[42] Namely:

1. The commander approach.
2. The organisational change approach.
3. The collaborative approach.
4. The cultural approach.
5. The crescive approach.

In each strategy, the CEO plays a different role and uses distinctive methods for developing strategies. The first two descriptions represent traditional approaches to implementation. The next two approaches, numbers 3 and 4, involve more recent attempts to enhance implementation by broadening the basis of participation in the planning process. The final approach takes advantage of managers' natural inclination to develop opportunities as they are encountered (see Table 5.2).

The commander approach

In this approach the CEO concentrates on formulating the strategy, giving little thought to how the plan will be carried out. He either develops the strategy himself or supervises a team of planners. Once he's satisfied that he has the best strategy, he passes it along to those who are instructed to 'make it happen'.

The organisational change approach

In this approach, once a plan has been developed the executive puts it into effect by taking such steps as reorganising the company structure, changing incentive compensation schemes, or hiring staff.

The collaborative approach

In this approach, rather than develop a strategy in a vacuum, the CEO enlists the help of his senior managers during the planning process in order to ensure that all the key players will back the final plan.

The cultural approach

This approach is an extension of the collaborative model to involve people in the middle and sometimes lower levels of the organisation. It seeks to implement strategy through the development of a corporate culture throughout the organisation.

The crescive approach

In this approach, the CEO addresses strategy planning and implementation simultaneously. He is not interested in planning alone, or even in leading others through a protracted planning process. Rather, he tries, through his statements and actions, to guide his managers into coming forward as champions of sound strategies. The crescive approach differs from others in several respects. Firstly, instead of strategy being delivered downward by senior management or a central planning department, it moves upward from the doers (the front-line staff) and lower and middle managers. Secondly, strategy becomes the sum of all the individual proposals that surface throughout the year. Thirdly, the top management team shapes the employees' premises, that is, their notions of what would constitute strategic projects. Fourthly, the chief executive functions more as a judge evaluating the proposals that reach his desk than as a master planner.

Trends

In studying the five approaches, Bourgeois and Brodwin noticed several significant trends. First, the two traditional methods are gradually being supplanted by the others. Second, companies are focusing increasingly on the organisational issues involved in getting a company to adapt to its environment, to pursue new opportunities, or respond to outside threats.

Additionally, at the time of writing Bourgeois and Brodwin saw a trend towards the CEO playing an increasingly indirect and more subtle role in strategy development. In the final analysis, the choice of method depends on the size of the company, the degree of diversification, the degree of geographical dispersion, the stability of the business environment, and the managerial style currently embodied in the company's culture.

Table 5.2   Summary of the five approaches to strategy implementation

Approach	The CEO's Strategic Question	CEO's Role
Commander Approach	How do I formulate the optimal strategy?	Master Planner
Change Approach	I have a strategy in mind– how do I implement?	Architect of implementation
Collaborative Approach	How do I involve top management in planning so they will be committed to strategies from the start?	Co-ordinator
Cultural Approach	How do I involve the whole organisation in implementation?	Coach
Crescive Approach	How do I encourage managers to come forward as champions of sound strategies	Premise setter and judge

Source: After L. J. Bourgeois and D. Brodwin, 'Putting your Strategy into Action', *Strategic Management Planning*, Mar.–May 1983.

The implementation process

The process of strategy implementation refers to the conversion of strategic plans into desired actions and results. In its broadest sense, strategy implementation is concerned with efforts to build an effective and profitable organisation. In essence, the two principal activities in implementing strategy are planning (programmes and budgets) and organisational design. Although each of these has implications for the other, they have often been discussed separately, as if successful strategy implementation could be accomplished through either. According to Hrebiniak and Joyce,[43] some researchers have productively focused on such issues as the implications of corporate level strategy for the development of business-level strategies specifying how the firm will compete in each of several, possibly related, businesses. Others have emphasised the implications of structural differences for achieving integration and the co-ordination of effort toward some desired organisational end. Planners and organisational designers, that is, have tended to confine their thinking about strategy implementation to their own separate fields. In contrast Hrebiniak and Joyce believe that both planning and organisational design are vital; both are interdependent and must be considered when implementing strategy.

It is one thing for CEOs and their managers to develop clear and meaningful strategies. It is, however, another matter – and one of great practical importance – to implement strategies effectively. Put another way, a strategy chosen and implemented badly is no strategy at all. According to Alexander the following ten problems were encountered by managers when attempting to implement strategic change.[44]

1. More time needed for implementation than originally planned.
2. Unanticipated major problems.
3. Ineffective co-ordination of activities.
4. Crises that distracted attention away from implementation.
5. Insufficient capabilities of the involved employees.
6. Inadequate training and instruction of lower-level employees.
7. Uncontrollable external environmental factors.
8. Inadequate leadership and direction by departmental managers.
9. Poor definition of key implementation tasks and activities.
10. Inadequate monitoring of activities by the information system.

Poor implementation of an appropriate strategy results in the failure of that strategy. A fine implementation plan, however, will not only cause the success of an appropriate strategy, it can also rescue an inappropriate strategy. One key reason why implementation fails is that CEOs and their managers have not always had (or taken into consideration) practical and sound models to guide their actions during implementation. Without adequate models, managers try to implement strategies without a thorough understanding of the multiple factors that must be addressed, often simultaneously, to make implementation work. Various researchers have noted that the problem is not that we know too little about strategy implementation, but that what we do know is fragmented among several disciplines of organisation and management study. This fragmentation may have hindered implementation-model development with such diverse components as organisation structure, control mechanisms, and reward systems included in various models (for example, see Quinn, and Hrebiniak and Joyce[45]).

Responsibility for strategy implementation

Depending on how the firm is organised, those who have responsibility for implementing strategy might be different from the people who formulate it – it is important to note that some people in the organisation who are critical to successful strategy implementation probably had little, or nothing to do with its formulation. The notion is to reach a state in which everyone in the firm understands what they are to do and why. This is the state of mutual understanding. There are four possible relationships that can exist between strategic managers and those they plan for. These relationships depend on how well the managers understand the needs, wants, and capabilities of the organisation's members, and how well the members understand the goals, objectives, tasks, and assumptions of the plan.

According to Rowe et al., managers can either make an effort to understand the members or not. Members can either be encouraged to understand the plan or not. This results in four possible outcomes. If the managers do not understand the members and the members do not understand the plan, then they are acting at cross purposes. Managers can attempt to implement the plan by decree, drawing on their authority, but this approach is unlikely to succeed. If, on the other hand, the managers understand the members, but the members do not understand the plan, the managers must sell the plan to the members and motivate them by means of rewards and incentives. Because the members do not understand the reasons for the plan, however, it is unlikely that the plan will be fully implemented or that the organisation will achieve its maximum potential. If the managers do not understand the members, but the members are educated to understand the plan and its underlying assumptions – a condition reached because of the participation and education activities that the organisation has engaged in – some of the plan will be implemented and some of the organisation's potential may be realised.[46]

Strategy implementation horizons

Strategies are usually subject to time constraints within which they must be implemented. The implementation horizon is determined by defining how long the firm will remain in business if it continues in its activities as it is today. If the answer to this question is several years, sequential strategy implementations may be appropriate. Managers in such circumstances can treat the strategy in segments, methodically moving on as each part is concluded. Alternatively, if the answer to the implementation horizon question is that time is crucial, then complex parallel interventions must be undertaken to implement strategy. The consequence of shorter implementation periods is to increase the number of elements that must be considered concurrently. Generally speaking, the shorter the implementation horizon, the more complex the change, and consequently, the more costly the adjustment in strategy. Under such circumstances, managers prefer to sequence implementation activities, starting with the smallest element that will produce a lasting solution to the strategic issue. The aggregation of these two attributes of strategy

– size of problem and implementation horizon – by and large determines the style chosen to implement strategy. Their combination indicates that even small problems can be difficult when joined with short implementation periods. The effect is a pace of change that produces costs approximating those of larger changes accomplished with longer implementation horizons.

	Members do not understand the plan	**Members do understand the plan**
Managers do not understand the members' needs, wants, and abilities	**Failed Implementation** Power and authority are the only available approaches	**Partial Implementation** Participation and education are possible approaches
Managers do understand the members' needs, wants, and abilities	**Partial Implementation** Motivation and selling are possible approaches	**Full Implementation** Requires full use of the social change process

Figure 5.5   Understanding strategic change

Source: After A. J. Rowe et al., *Strategic Management: A Methodological Approach*, 4th edn, Addison Wesley Publishing, Reading, Mass., 1994.

Measuring strategic success

Organisations need a balance between managing for short-term profits and for long-term strategic position (or future profits) From a belief that what is unmeasurable, you cannot measure – it is very difficult to manage for long-term position without some form of measurement for it. Firms need some specific measures of the progress of their long-term strategies to build into their control systems, for what a company chooses to control explicitly is what its people will focus their attention on.[47]

When Drucker published *The Practice of Management* in 1954,[48] measuring a firm's performance against its objectives was a new subject area. According to Drucker at that time: it was one of the most active frontiers of thought, research, and invention in American business. Company after company was working on the definition of the key areas (market standing, innovation, productivity, profitability, etc.), on thinking through what should be measured, and on fashioning the tools of measurement. Which measures will be used to assess performance depends on the organisation, as well as on the objectives to be achieved. Different measures are required for different objectives. In the last half century, financial ratio analysis has been widely used as a method of evaluating business performance and for comparing a firm with others in an industry. Such ratios (described in Table 5.3) have been used to determine:

1. The firm's position in its industry.
2. The degree to which strategic objectives are being accomplished.
3. The firm's vulnerability to decreases in revenue.
4. The growth potential of the firm.
5. The firm's ability to react to unforeseen changes in the environment.

Financial ratio analysis is also used in assessing a firm's internal strengths and weaknesses, and because considerable amounts of financial data are available about competitors, and for making comparisons within an industry. It is important to recognise, however, that these ratios reflect the past; therefore they are often more useful for evaluating past performance than for measuring ongoing strategic performance. This point is clearly undervalued, in *In Search for Excellence*, Peters and Waterman (the McKinsey consultants) turned their attention to excellent US companies, they selected six criteria over a 20-year period to measure long-term excellent performance. Their measures included: (1) growth and wealth creation; (2) compound asset-equity growth; and (3) the average ratio of market value to book value. The remaining three being measures of return on capital and sales: (4) return on total capital; (5) return on equity; and (6) return on sales. To qualify as a top performer, each company had to have been in the top half of its industry in at least four of the above six categories.

Table 5.3   Traditional performance measures

Performance Ratio	Performance Measure
Profitability	
Gross Profit Margin:	Measures coverage of operating costs.
Operating Profit Margin:	Measures operating performance excluding costs.
Return on Sales:	Measures overall cost-price structure.
Return on Total Assets:	Measures return on total investment excluding cost of capital.
Return on Net Worth:	Measures return on stockholder's cash investment.
Return on Equity:	Measures return on stockholder's cash investment.
Earnings Per Share:	Measures earnings available to common share owners.
Cash Liquidity	
Current Ratio:	Measures coverage of short-term creditor liabilities.
Quick Ratio:	Measures ability to pay off short-term creditor liabilities.
Inventory to Working Capital:	Up working capital.
Operating Effectiveness	
Inventory Turnover:	Provides measure of inventory adequacy when compared to industry.
Fixed Asset Turnover:	Provides measure of capital intensity and sales productivity when compared to industry.
Total Asset Turnover:	Provides measure of capital intensity and sales productivity when compared to industry.
Accounts Receivable Turnover:	Measures average length of time required to collect from credit sales.
Average Collection Period:	Measures average length of time (days) required to receive payment from sales.
Employee Productivity:	Measures labour productivity when compared to industry.
Capital Utilisation	
Debt to Assets:	Measures the use of borrowed funds to finance operations.
Debt to Equity:	Measures the use of borrowed funds versus owners' funds.
Long Term Debt to Equity:	Measures the balance between debt and equity in the long-term capital structure.
Interest Coverage:	Measures riskiness of firm in its ability to pay interest.
Fixed Charge Coverage:	Measures riskiness of firm in its ability to pay fixed charges.
Stockholder Returns	
Dividends Yield on Common Stock:	Measures annual return to shareholder.
Price Earnings:	Measures market perception of firm's riskiness and growth potential.
Dividends Payout:	Measures percentage of profits paid to shareholders.

Although Peters and Waterman's research led to a number of non-financial key performance criteria being identified, within 5 years over half of those excellent companies fell from stock-market favour. Why? Peters and Waterman's model was incomplete and therefore inadequate as a valid and reliable guide to excellence. Peters and Waterman used predominantly financial measurements as a preliminary judge of performance. The problem with analysis of this type is that samples are stratified on the dependent variable (a firm's success or performance), which may in turn bias estimates of the effects of factors expected to influence success of the firm. If business failure is commonplace, one can study it in order to shed light upon both the viability of various strategies and the factors leading to both good and poor company performance. Table 5.4 lists the most profitable of Britain's top 250 companies for each year from 1979–89. Of these 11 excellent companies, only five survived in their existing form to the end of the following year, 1990! Of these five survivors, only one could still be regarded as a strong performer. The majority had either collapsed or been acquired under depressed circumstances. According to Professor Peter Doyle, the explanation for this lack of robustness of these excellent companies is in the trade-offs made.[49] When management seeks extreme performance along one dimension, the trade-off against other goals becomes correspondingly extreme. Similarly, the conflict between stakeholders is amplified as one group expropriates the resources of others. The result is that excellent companies are prone to exceptional instability.

Table 5.4   Britain's top companies

Year	Company	Market Value (£m)	*ROI	Subsequent Performance
1979	MFI	57	50	Collapsed
1980	Lasmo	134	97	Still Profitable
1981	Bejam	79	34	Acquired
1982	Racal	940	36	Still Profitable
1983	Polly Peck	128	79	Collapsed
1984	Atlantic Computers	151	36	Collapsed
1985	BSR	197	32	Still Profitable
1986	Jaguar	819	60	Acquired
1987	Amstrad	987	89	Still Profitable
1988	Body Shop	225	89	Still Profitable
1989	Blue Arrow	653	135	Collapsed

* ROI: Pretax profit as a percentage of invested capital
Source: UK Management Today

Measuring strategic performance and growth

Writing in the Harvard Business Review, Professor Hamel refers to radically improving the value equation – in every industry, there is a ratio that relates price to performance where X units of cash buy Y units of value. The challenge is to improve that value ratio and to do so radically – 500 or 1000 per cent, not 10 or 20 per cent. Such a fundamental redefinition of the value equation forces a reconception of the product or service.[50]

Kim and Mauborgne, studied more than 30 companies around the world, in approximately 30 industries. They looked at companies with high growth in both revenues and profits, and companies with less successful performance records. In an effort to explain the difference in performance between the two groups of companies, they interviewed hundreds of managers, analysts, and researchers. They built strategic, organisational, and performance profiles. They looked for industry or organisational patterns, and compared the two groups of companies along dimensions that are often thought to be related to a company's potential for growth. Did private companies grow more quickly than public ones? What was the impact on companies of the overall growth of their industry? Did entrepreneurial start-ups have an edge over established incumbents? Were companies led by creative, young radicals likely to grow faster than those run by older managers?

Kim and Mauborgne found that none of those factors mattered in a systematic way. High growth was achieved by both small and large organisations, by companies in high technology and in low technology industries, by new entrants and incumbents, by private and public companies, and by companies from various countries. What did matter – consistently – was the way managers in the two groups of companies thought about strategy. In interviewing the managers, they asked them to describe their strategic moves and the thinking behind them. Thus they came to understand their views on each of the five textbook dimensions of strategy: industry assumptions, strategic focus, customers, assets, and capabilities, and product and service offerings. They were struck by what emerged from their content analysis of these interviews. The managers of the high-growth companies – irrespective of their industry – all described what they have come to call the logic of value innovation. The managers of the less successful companies all thought along conventional strategic lines. Intrigued by that finding, they went on to test whether the managers of the high-growth companies applied their strategic thinking to business initiatives in the marketplace. They found that they did. Furthermore, in studying the business launches of about 100 companies, they were able to quantify the impact of the value innovation on a company's growth in both revenues and profits. Although 86 per cent of the launches were line extensions – that is, incremental improvements – they accounted for 62 per cent of total revenues and only 39 per cent of total profits. The remaining 14 per cent of the launches – the true value innovations – generated 38 per cent of total revenues and a whopping 61 per cent of total profits.[51]

Alternative performance measures

In Chapter 1, it was suggested that organisations need to find alternative ways of measuring performance. Traditional methods, such as those specified in Table 5.3, are no longer adequate. This statement is backed-up by professor Robert Eccles, of Harvard Business School, who has questioned profit-based measurements on the grounds that they often distort the realities of a business and that they are necessary lagging indicators of success rather than leading ones. Eccles latter developed the theme in his book, *Beyond the Hype,* in which he and Nitin Nohria argue that there is no universal consensus on how best to measure financial performance – even on so basic a matter as how earnings should be calculated.[52] Citing the growing belief that sustainable long-term success is more likely to be attained when financial indicators are not the sole arbiter, Eccles quotes the example of Sealed Air Corporation, a speciality packaging company that changed its performance measurement criteria following leveraged recapitalisation. From using earnings per share as its primary performance measurement, the company developed a five-category ranking:

1. Customer satisfaction.
2. Cash flow.
3. World-class benchmarking.
4. Innovation.
5. Earnings per share.

The company came to believe so strongly in its new approach that its chief financial officer planned to introduce monthly statements of mainly non-financial measures, with financial statements relegated to quarterly publication. Such switches to non-financial indicators have the benefit, Eccles argues, of forcing managers to think freshly about 'the trade-offs between objectives and how to achieve appropriate balance among the different performance measures being employed'.

Increasingly stakeholders in the organisation's task environment are often concerned about performance. Each stakeholder has its own criteria to determine how well the organisation is performing. Such criteria characteristically deal with the direct and indirect impact of organisation activities on stakeholder interests. E. A. Freeman, a management theorist, proposes that senior management needs to *keep score* with these stakeholders:

it should establish one or more simple measures for each stakeholder category. For example:

1. Customers   Customer Satisfaction (retention policy)
2. Employees   Key Skills, Labour Turnover, etc.
3. Shareholders   Dividends
4. Suppliers   Payments, Discounts, etc.

In practice, reconciling the interests of stakeholders should not be difficult, as they are generally satisfiers rather than maximisers. Management's main concern should be watching for performance and environmental changes which can trigger active stakeholder disgruntlement. More positively, the firm can seek to broaden its tolerance zone by actively seeking to dampen excessive expectations. This requires developing a culture which respects and integrates the interests of the diverse stakeholders. Businesses that achieve consistent long-run performance build a sense of mission which reflects these mutual interests, and have a board of directors which oversees the conduct of its managers to achieve such consistency.[53]

Performance control

Lorange et al. propose that strategic management should contain a component dealing with the control of performance with respect to operating objectives.[54] Individual and group rewards play a vital role in strategic success because they control performance with respect to these ends. Performance measures, and the means of assessing such measures, can be established to focus either on actual performance results (outputs) or on the activities that generate the performance (behaviour). Behaviour controls specify *how* something is to be accomplished through a series of strategic objectives. This form of control appears more useful to the needs of CEOs in their attempts to control managers. Output controls specify *what* is to be accomplished by focusing on the end result of the behaviours through the use of objectives and performance targets. This form of control serves the needs of the organisation as a whole and is used largely because of the demand for quantifiable, measures of performance.

Behaviour and output controls are not considered interchangeable. Behaviour controls are most appropriate for those situations in which performance results are hard to measure and there is a clear cause-effect connection between activities and results. Output controls are most suitable for those situations in which there are specific agreed-upon output measures and there is no clear cause-effect connection between activities and results.[55]

A strategic control system ensures that the immense effort often put into preparing lengthy and detailed strategic plans is, in fact, translated into action and the learning process is consolidated. According to Bungay and Goold, there are a few important lessons about how to make strategic control work successfully.[56] It is necessary to:

- Invest in the training necessary and adopt an appropriate style in reviewing plans, especially in the early stages.
- Invest in careful preparation before review sessions, as good questions are vital.
- Set stretching targets, but only a limited number.
- Follow through, take it seriously, and make actions and words consistent.
- Create an explicit link with financial targets and budgets, integrating the two processes (or none of it will be taken seriously at all).
- Show that the operating company benefits from the process (e.g., through the business becoming easier to manage) and give strong support for success (so that another real benefit becomes the approval of senior management or a better relationship with the centre).

Although still rare, strategic control processes have started to make an impact in business operations. Without doubt, the use of alternative strategic measures (and the means of monitoring strategic performance) will increase as more and more organisations discover the true benefits of building long-term thinking into their business operations.

6 *Future Trends in Strategic Management*

INTRODUCTION

There can be no doubt that the world is entering a period of increasingly rapid change and that this is primarily due to technological drivers. Drucker has defined the development of the business world as passing through the stage of the Industrial Revolution, the Productivity Revolution, and the Management Revolution, until the situation we find ourselves in today, where the most important factor of production has become knowledge.[1] Shying away from describing our society as the 'knowledge society', he acknowledges that we have a knowledge economy. The increasing importance of knowledge has been brought about by a change in the way it is disseminated and used.

In the 1700s, knowledge of production processes was confined to members of Guilds, who fiercely protected their skills, and the English spoke not of crafts, but of 'mysteries'. The crafts or skills were taught, by example, through an apprenticeship scheme, with trainees indentured to a master. There was little understanding of the processes or science which underpinned the successful application of a particular craft or skill. However, between 1750 and 1800, the pattern changed and, rather than protecting the monopolistic profits of the Monarch's favourites, patents became a means of rewarding inventors for publishing knowledge and encouraging further development. This was the period during which the first Polytechnics were to start, not necessarily adding to the body of knowledge and skills, but adding to the body of people that could apply them. This heralded the Industrial Revolution, with the increase of large-scale private capitalist enterprise which came to dominate the West.

By the end of the nineteenth century, Taylor – using a technique that was to become known as work study – started to look at the processes by which work was actually done. This heralded the start of the Productivity Revolution, which was to become so important during World War II when the large-scale manufacture of weapons had to be increased so dramatically. The prospect of a five- or seven-year craft apprenticeship could not

be considered, and was successfully replaced by 60–90 day training programmes in the armaments factories of America. The approach had changed,
it was no longer enough to impart skill, it was now necessary to understand the best way to use those skills and impart best practice. However, it
can be argued that the Productivity Revolution was a victim of its own
success. With the changing patterns of employment that we referred to in
Chapter 1, less and less people were involved in manual work, skilled or
unskilled, and by the 1950s, the involvement and role of management had
changed. The role of management has become that of determining what
knowledge is needed and of applying knowledge and understanding to
knowledge itself.

The changes we are going through, and can expect to see, will impact
increasingly on organisations in a number of different ways. The first of
these will almost certainly be with information technology (IT) and its role.
With an increasingly computer literate population better able to communicate remotely and the dramatically increasing volumes of data available, IT
will at last realise its value as a component of the strategic-planning process.

With the ease of access to information on a worldwide scale driven by
the Internet, globalisation will increase and, with it, the nature of organisations will change. Some will seek to be larger, striving for increasingly
difficult to achieve cost efficiencies – others will seek to specialise, but
again seek the advantage of size. This may be achieved not by forming a
larger single entity, but by forming loose associations of enterprises that
will benefit from the skills of other members of the grouping. The increased knowledge that individuals will be able to access will bring about
changes not only in the nature of organisations and the way that people
choose to work, and are by definition managed, but also in the way they
view organisations. The public persona of enterprises will become increasingly important and reputations will need to be managed. Markets will
also change as cross-border alliances between organisations, and their sheer
size, have their impact on Governments and nation states. As knowledge
becomes the key resource, it will be increasingly difficult for nation states
to gain competitive advantage using the traditional resources of materials,
manpower, or money. It is likely that Governments will have to operate in
an increasingly co-operative manner with business, as technology increases
the mobility of the firm, and deregulation will become more and more
widespread.

The role of IT in business

The advancement of communications and computing technologies has increased the stature of information technologies from an operational resource,
unrelated to strategic goals, to a component in strategy formulation and

implementation leading to competitive advantage. The need to integrate technology into the strategic plans of a firm is widely recognised as vital to the health and longevity of the company.[2] If service organisations are to compete in a global arena, they must embrace the customer-driven concept and adopt those best practices that will satisfy customers and lead to market success. The information society implies the best use of technology as a strategic tool and its co-ordination with other factors, such as financial and human resources planning. For the UK and the European economies to grow, the same message and practice must be taken up widely throughout the business community, especially by the mass of service industries, in whom lies the greatest wealth-creating potential across the European Union.

The availability of global IT has altered the nature of business by increasing the speed at which things can be organised. A commitment can be made by telephone or electronic mail (e-mail) much quicker than by letter. Electronic means of ordering goods has made possible 'just-in-time' supply strategies. Product promotion can now reach a mass consumer market through the use of television advertising. Much information on your industry and competition is readily available on various databases from a variety of sources. All this has enabled business to be conducted at an increasing pace.

Consumers within the global community are demanding products and services irrespective of their national origin. Consumers with wider choice will develop more articulated demands and preferences. In response, businesses must provide best practice in meeting those demands, especially where the best practice has impact on customer relationships, for example, price, service, delivery. The need to provide greater customer satisfaction is more likely to be achieved by joint approaches between suppliers and *technology providers,* who can together take into account the wider global issues in order to find the most cost-effective solutions. Without doubt information technology is changing the way companies do business. It is affecting the entire process by which companies create their service offerings. Orlikowski and Gash define Information Technology as: 'any form of computer-based information system, including mainframe as well as microcomputer applications.'[3]

Table 6.1 shows the evolution of IT in the last 30 years. In business applications, the range and strategic impacts of such systems are vast; for example, in financial services the construction of customer-led information databases aims to improve levels of service quality by building long relationships with customers, thereby maintaining or increasing customer share.[4] In the financial-services sector, deregulation accompanied by increasing customer sophistication has led to mounting levels of competition. Building societies, in particular, have had to respond to encroachment from banks and other institutions into their core activities, such as mortgage provision and investment opportunities. As a means of combating competition from other players in the personal financial-service sector; building societies are adopting a more IT led approach. In 1997, the five major UK building societies spent close on £1 billion on new IT.[5] In a sector where excess capacity now exists, many building societies will be looking to the development of information systems which allow them to develop a competitive advantage as information providers.[6]

For IT, the 1990s have brought a turn toward flexibility as the dominant competitive thrust. Emerging IT strategies emphasis leveraging technology architectures to support the key success activities of the business. Organisation revolutions are under way at IBM and Digital Equipment Corporation (DEC), for instance. Both companies are forward integrating their businesses into software and support functions, to deliver application-based solutions rather than hardware boxes which have become a commodity product. On the information systems side, technology will focus more and more on the design of tailored workstations for service and knowledge workers within a highly networked information-based organisation. The environment for information processing is likely to be multimedia and to extensively use knowledge-based concepts and technology oriented to the individual cognitive needs and styles of knowledge workers.

In his book, *Intellectual Capital: The New Wealth of Organisations,* Thomas Stewart cites numerous statistics to show that the long-heralded new dawn has truly arrived. In the US, the proportion of knowledge workers – those working with information rather than things – will have risen from 17 to 59 per cent over the course of the century, while those handling material things will have halved to 41 per cent. Perhaps most revealing of all, in 1991 US business for the first time spent more money on IT – equipment to capture, process, analyse, and distribute information – than on production plant and equipment. The gap has steadily widened since. 'Call 1991', says Stewart, 'year *One* of the information age.'[7]

Table 6.1   The evolution of IT

Decade	Information Technology Strategy	Information Technology Systems
1960s	Maximise throughput Find economies of scale	High volume Mainframe Applications
1970s	Reduce overheads Support function Back office operation	Transaction processing Administration systems
1980s	Networking End-user computing Out of back office	Build technology architecture PC workstations
1990s	Leveraging technology Architecture IT supports Business thrust	Tailored workstations Knowledge-based technology Multimedia environment

Porter and Millar state that information technology offers organisations the opportunity either to lower costs or, perhaps more significantly within the financial services sector, to enhance differentiation.[8] In 1996, the Royal Bank of Scotland became the first bank in the UK to offer a full range of banking services on the Internet. The Royal Bank of Scotland offers Direct Banking by PC for its customers. According to Bill Bougourd, head of electronic services at the bank, some 50 000 of its 500 000 telephone banking customers have the technology to use the Internet. He said: 'We wanted to add a service as there is a growing expectation from customers for us to provide this channel, though we are not trying to pretend that everyone will be connected.' Strategic information systems and their capabilities play a significant role in the business domain and IT integration will equally be of vital importance. Both have significant customisation aspects and imply close links between customer and provider. For example, a Gallop survey conducted at the end of 1996 found more than 60 per cent of people in the UK would like to check their accounts and pay bills using a home computer. According to the survey, *Internet Banking in Europe*, by consultancy Booz Allen and Hamilton, 80 per cent of European banks will provide a full banking service over the Internet within three years. In the future of Internet banking there is scope for new services (see Table 6.2), new ways of doing things, and new ways for people to make money.[9]

A recent paper by Dutta and Doz discusses the case of Banco Comercial Portugues (BCP) which, in less than a decade since its inception in May 1986, has grown to become one of Portugal's largest and most profitable banks.[10] BCP's extraordinary growth has been marked by a series of innovations including extensive research of client needs in the target markets, careful segmentation of the bank groups, the appointment of a personal account manager for each customer, rigorously designed and efficient branches, and the introduction of new products. IT has played a crucial role in enabling such innovations as:

- strategic databases for prospecting and selling to clients,
- distributed processing with centralised data for the different bank groups,
- comprehensive information support systems for account managers,
- sophisticated automation in branches, and
- the flexible and rapid deployment of systems to support new banking products.

BCP is in many ways a leader in the strategic use of IT among European banks. However, its leadership position arises less from the use of cutting-edge technology as from a deliberate attempt to link IT to its business strategy and to build a competence in the business use of IT.

The initial decision by BCP to invest heavily in large-scale computer and software systems was painful, absorbing about a third of BCP's start-up capital. As one board member described it:

> We invest a lot in technology, but sometimes it is not easy to justify the investment for the future. It is a question of culture. If you spend a lot to buy a building the result is visible. But if you spend a lot to buy a computer then everyone complains - but the computer is more important for the company.

BCP's flexible technological infrastructure (Figure 6.1) gives it the unique ability to create and handle complex financial products that consistently appealed to the Portuguese market. For instance, BCP produced an account paying interest at different rates, depending on the average daily outstanding balance. Technology also helped to differentiate BCP in the eyes of its customers by enabling it to meet rapidly changing market conditions.

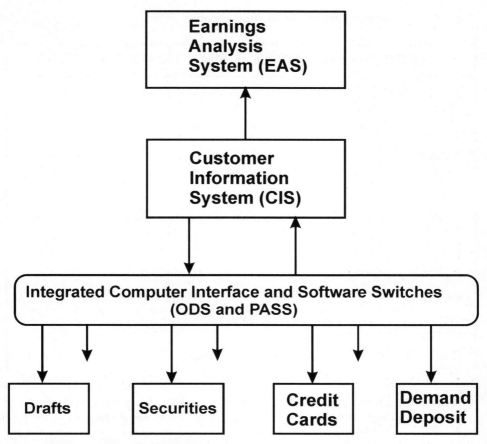

Figure 6.1   Software architecture at BCP

Source: S. Dutta and Y. Doz, 'Case Study: Linking information technology to business strategy at Banco Comercial Portugues, *Journal of Strategic Information Systems*, 1995, p. 102.

Table 6.2   Some predictions in banking services

SHAPE OF THINGS TO COME IN UK BANKING

Royal Bank of Scotland: The first UK banking service over the Internet. Customers will be able to print statements, pay bills to more than 750 companies, and transfer account data directly into home-banking software packages.

Lloyds TSB: Was the first bank to offer an on-line service in 1996, giving users full account services via on-line provider CompuServe. So far, 12 000 customers are using the service.

Halifax: The building society with more than eight million customers is looking closely at Internet, which it describes as inevitable. It recently began a £130 million five-year investment programme in new wide area-network technology so it can offer new services.

Barclays: Plans to launch a PC banking service to its customers this year. This will be a proprietary network, downloading account information into Microsoft's Money personal-finance package and then use the information off-line.

NatWest: Has an Internet-compatible trial running for a small number of customers. Participants use a browser but dial the bank direct.

Midland: Parent organisation HSBC is soon to test a home PC banking application in Hong Kong which could be trialled in the UK, potentially over the Internet in 1998.

Source: Taken from 'Top 100 Users,' *Computing*, 2 Oct. 1997, pp. 41–56.

Shifting IT investment boundaries

IT is not just affecting how individual organisational activities are performed, but through integrated networks, it is greatly enhancing a firm's ability to exploit linkages between internal and external value chains. For example, the UK state-owned postal service continues to exploit IT to increase its market share. Its four main businesses, Parcelforce Worldwide, Post Office Counters, Royal Mail, and Subscription Services, have recently been re-engineered to take advantage of technological economies of scale. The latest strategy identifies three areas of systems integration: the sales channel, which addresses the likes of call centres; the service channel, which looks at manufacturing-type systems; and business support. The group is looking to standardise its core processes, which will require a significant amount of investment over the next 2–3 years. In the sales channel, the Post Office – through its Pathway project – is installing 40 000 terminals in its 19 000 retail outlets in a bid to cut down fraud, boost efficiency, and open up opportunities for offering new services. In the service channel, it is focusing on mail automation, a new Integrated Mail Processing System is planned at a cost of £200 million. The group is also developing processes for getting computers to recognise addresses so that it can upgrade its mail-sorting lines without having to upgrade address-interpretation IT.

In 1986, Otis Elevator, a leader in the sale and service of elevators and related products in the French market, started reviewing the managerial and operational procedures surrounding the processing of customer orders. The resulting 'Master Plan' project aimed at simplifying the procedures, from the initial contact with the customer through to the installation of the elevator, with decentralisation of responsibility driving the design. Central to the master plan was the need to adjust the organisation structure to the decentralisation of responsibility, and to develop new IT applications to support business and management activities. These applications were developed between 1986 and 1993, and concerned negotiation, sales/contract management, invoicing/accounts receivable, purchasing management, and accounting. The five new IT applications include SALVE, a support system used by sales representatives in their negotiations with the customer from the initial contact to the booking stage. Once the order has been booked, it is forwarded to SAGA, a contract management system which creates and maintains the sales order. SAGA can be viewed as a special contract control system. Information gained from SALVE and SAGA serves as inputs to STAR, the purchasing and supplier management system. SAFRAN–N,S,K handles invoicing and other accounting functions related to the modernisation, as well as sales of new equipment. SAFRAN–O, handles the billing of maintenance services.[11]

From the above, it would appear that there is a wide range in the amounts invested in new technology, together with wide variation in the level of technical change taking place. Some organisations are producing in the same way as they have for many years, others are investing heavily in new technology. But technology is not an end in its own right and companies can invest for a variety of reasons. Butler et al. have classified the objectives of new technology investment according to whether companies are trying to achieve:

1. Efficiency objectives.
2. Development objectives in the sense of learning about new technology.
3. Market opportunity objectives.
4. Standardisation objectives, trying to standardise with customers and suppliers.
5. Regulatory objectives that have to be met, for example, health and safety.

6.   Grant and loan objectives from the EC or government.
7.   Image objectives, that is, the use of new technology to attract new customers.[12]

Technology and systems planning

Being a leader in IT innovation entails many risks such as: committing management to a new way of thinking; using new, and perhaps untried, technology; investing a large proportion of organisational resources; and ensuring co-operation from other parts of the firm's internal and external environment.[13] Experience with IT is one of the critical success factors in both establishing competitive systems and facilitating quick responses to competitive challenges (Figure 6.2). The major factor that prevents many firms from achieving their technical objectives, and therefore their strategic objectives, is lack of resources and a clear direction or vision.

A critical feature in the development of IT enabled competitive advantage is the integration of the firm's strategic and information system plans. In essence, a level of strategic validity is achieved when long-term corporate strategy is formulated, with both the existing and potential uses of IT considered. Without this integration, strategic options of the firm can be severely limited since IT architectures resemble the vision of technical rather than strategic planners. Conversely, a link between both corporate and information-system strategic plans facilitates competitive flexibility (the capability to respond to changing conditions, see Figure 6.2), as well as competitive innovation (the capability to change the rules of competition).[14] Thus the strategic use of IT can be conceptualised as technological architectures that are developed, deployed, and used as a result of, and in support of, the overall strategic objectives of the firm.

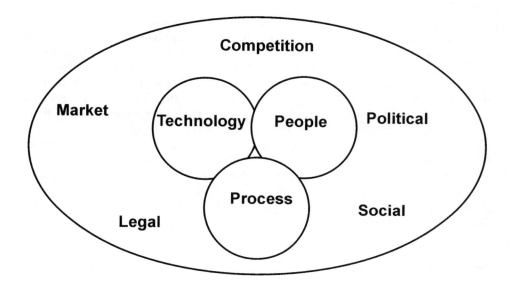

Figure 6.2   The main challenges of technology and systems planning

One school of thought is that Technology and Systems Planning (TSP) has gained steadily increasing organisational attention in the last decade. However, a recent survey among 245 of the 1000 largest manufacturing and service companies in the USA, showed that 54 per cent of those firms dedicated only 2 per cent of their staff resources to planning, while only 9 per cent dedicated 12 per cent or more.[15] Current research in this area suggests that the successful adoption of integrated business and TSP is still far from being common place. In fact, a study by Grover and Teng of large organisations indicates that the least effective data resource management function is the development of integrated, organisation-wide data models and data architecture.[16]

According to Hagmann and McCahon,[17] there is still some disagreement concerning what TSP accomplishes. Different planning methodologies, such as IBM's business systems planning (BSP) and information quality analysis (IQA), Andersen Consulting's strategic information planning, and Rockart's critical success factors (CSF), frequently lead to significantly different planning results and decisions because they use different techniques. BSP focuses on extensive analysis of business objectives and processes to create an 'information architecture' for information systems development, but CSF emphasises that priority should be given to TSP that supports the areas critical to organisational success.

According to Hagmann and McCahon, at present, a direct connection between strategic TSP planning and its implementation as a competitive tool is not clear, even among organisations which were the 'leaders' in establishing such systems. An exploratory study of successful implementations by Neo found that, for the firms classified as innovators and leaders in competitive systems, the most important factors leading to success were the perceived need to improve internal operations, the experience obtained from their existing TSP portfolio, and the stated objective of satisfying customer needs.[18] Experience with TSP applications allowed organisations to implement system improvements effectively and to modify and/or expand them when others sought to implement similar systems. The integration of TSP and business planning was found to be very important for start-up businesses, such as Federal Express and USA Today, which incorporated TSP into their strategy for success.

Information planning tools

By using a diversity of tools, ranging from assessing information flows and volumes, communication styles and patterns, to data entities and architectures, it is possible to build an 'information profile' of an organisation. This has several advantages:

1. Identification of what is corporate, divisional, and individual information.
2. Identification of what information must be shared and at what levels within the organisation.
3. Identification and qualification of the effort and cost of maintaining the various information bases.
4. Identification of the value information has or should bring to the organisation.
5. Identification of what decisions are required to invest in individual projects.

If we see IT as one of the building components of a firm's activities, information is the adhesive that comes in contact with all the other blocks that binds them together. The strength of the corporate structure will be determined by the quality of each of the blocks and of the adhesive which keeps them in place.

Technological alliances

Today's strategic planners must broaden their view of the global technology environment from the traditional perspective of individual firms competing against each other. The formation of strategic alliances means that strategic power often resides in sets of firms acting together. For example, Digital Equipment Corporation (DEC), like many of its competitors, crossed the ocean in an effort to increase its market share. DEC is buying 10 per cent of Italy's Ing. C. Olivetti and Company. The Olivetti purchase was DEC's third such arrangement to gain market position in Europe. DEC bought the computer division of Philips, the Dutch electronics firm, and also formed a computer company with Mannesmann AG, a German conglomerate.

Cross-border strategies are not the preserve of US companies. Stymied by small, insular markets and ever-escalating R&D costs, European computer manufacturers have been pursuing strategic alliances since the 1980s. The UK's ICL found a deep-pockets parent in Fujitsu of Japan. Finland's Nokia Data was later purchased by ICL, and Group Bull of France (already in partnership with Honeywell) accepted $100 million from IBM in exchange for a 'small' stake in the company. BCE, the Canadian telecommunications giant situated in a smallish home market, announced a major alliance with Cable and Wireless, a leading British telecommunications company. In one of 1993's biggest deals, British Telecommunications paid $4.3 billion for a 20 per cent stake in MCI Communications, the US long-distance carrier. The two companies also plan to pour $1 billion into the joint venture. Their objective is to make the new company one of the few global carriers in the fast-growing market of global corporate network services. They face some stiff competition. AT&T has already launched Worldsource in partnership with Kokusia Denshin Denwa of Japan and Singapore Telecom for the same purpose, and its purchase of McCaw Cellular puts it into wireless.

According to John Naisbitt, as computer, telephone, and cable TV companies come to realise that their markets will ultimately be one and the same, cross-border, cross-industry alliances will become the norm.[19] Joint ventures, mergers, and creative co-marketing arrangements of all kinds will quickly turn the three legs of the telecommunications industry into a single, global industrial sector, albeit made up of thousands of companies. Governments everywhere are liberalising, paving the way for the telecommunications revolution.

Because competitors are capitalising on the benefits of partnerships, they must be considered an option in the strategic array of alternatives. Hamel and Prahalad suggest some firms are unwilling to invest the enormous energy required to delve deeply into the emerging trends in technology and globalisation that point to new opportunities.[20] But unless the firm has built a sole and compelling view of the future, the firm will be caught within the orthodoxies of the past. If the goal is to shape the future rather than be its victims, the firm must live in the future. It must be as real and tangible as the present. The present and future do not adjoin each other. They are not neatly divided between the five-year plan and the great unknown beyond. The present and future are intertwined. Every company is in the process either of becoming something anachronistic and irrelevant to the future or of becoming the forerunner of the future. The long term is not something that happens someday, it is what every company is building, or forfeiting, by a myriad of day-to-day decisions.

Failure of technological alliances

The decision to form a technological alliance is visible under many circumstances. Much depends upon how the alliance is forged and managed. While the decision to enter into an alliance may be to gain access to capital or greater technology, there are still pitfalls for the unwary firm. Such risks include loss of: incompatible culture objectives, competitive knowledge, technical expertise, and competition instead of co-operation. As IT alliance decisions involve organisations on a more interdependent level, the issues of cultural fit and cultural conflict arise. In any type of inter-organisational alliance there can be a combination of the following factors:[21]

1. **Professional conflicts**: professional cultural conflicts arise when managers within the same company come from different educational or professional backgrounds. For example, the more scientific and engineering backgrounds of managers in the product development and R&D divisions can bring them into professional conflict with marketing managers, who may have more social backgrounds.

2. **Organisation conflict**: organisational cultural conflicts can often arise as corporations set up divisions in different parts of the country or abroad. For example, as many Japanese companies have shifted their R&D activities to Malaysia, there can be an 'organisational' cultural conflict. This is because the headquarters desire for control, as is usually the case with most Japanese corporations, can be in conflict with the Malaysian R&D division's desire to maintain its relative independence.

3. **Corporate conflicts**: corporate cultural conflicts can arise when two corporations from the same or different countries form a strategic partnership or any other type of co-operative agreement, including major IT outsourcing decisions. A strategic alliance based on differing cultures may become problematic, though there is evidence from the IT literature

that the differences can be worked through, for example, as in the alliance between major vendor EDS and the multinational glass manufacture, Pilkington.

4. **National conflicts**: national cultural conflicts can arise when companies begin to work in countries where they have had relatively little experience in the past. Differences ranging from languages to customs, traditions, business ethics – all can add up to substantial conflicts due to national factors.

Finally alliances that contain more competitiveness than co-operation are doomed to failure. Management should be wary of 'hidden agendas'. A partner may enter the alliance under the pretext of creating a commercial technology when, in reality, the alliance was formed to fund self-serving research interests. If the research is irrelevant to the strategic objectives of one of the partners, or there is feeling of uncertainty about the output value, the alliance will probably fail.[22]

Linking IT with the corporate strategy

A framework that describes linkages between corporate strategy and alternative IT strategies has been developed by Camillus and Lederer.[23] In this framework (Figure 6.3), three key dimensions are defined to describe alternative IT strategies. The first dimension is the type of system that is used, where transaction processing systems (TPS) is one extreme and decision support systems (DSS) is the other. The second dimension describes what type of computers are used and the extremes here are mainframes and single, independent personal computers (PCs). The third dimension concerns the procurement of hardware and software, where purchases can be either centralised with little regard to the needs of the single user, or they can be initiated by the individual user. These extremes are then linked with Porter's generic strategies cost efficiency and differentiation. The IT strategy that involves TPS mainframe-inflexible minimises the total cost of IT, and is therefore the appropriate alternative for a company that competes through cost leadership. For a company which competes through differentiation, the appropriate alternative is DSS-Micro-Flexible.

According to Bjornsson and Lundegard, it is debatable whether it is the corporate strategy that should be linked to strategic IT alternatives.[24] It may be more fruitful to describe the information structure in the company in terms of IT strategic alternatives. The needs of IT in two companies that compete through cost leadership (for example, Barclays and NatWest banks) in two different businesses can differ significantly because of variations in information intensity.

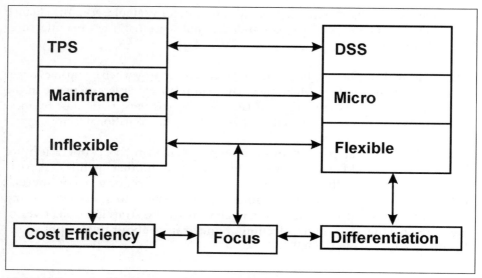

Figure 6.3   Camillus and Lederer's IT framework

A more comprehensive, procedural example of a business strategy framework is Wiseman's 'strategic options generator'. Wiseman believes that competitive edge results from strategic thrusts founded on the logic of both Chandler's growth strategies and Porter's competitive strategy frameworks. Figure 6.4 reproduces his strategic option generator. The strategic target equates to three of Porter's competitive forces. The strategic thrusts combine Porter's generic strategies with the mechanisms Chandler plotted in his theory of organisational growth. The mode indicates whether the thrust is being used to attack or to defend in the competitive arena. Direction describes whether the firm is using the strategic system option itself or providing it for the target's use. The potential value of the option generator is not only its conflation of a previous framework's analysis, but the logical list of analytical questions it provides. Like Porter's model, it therefore helps most in clarifying the firm's business strategy and suggesting the direction of IT strategy connection.

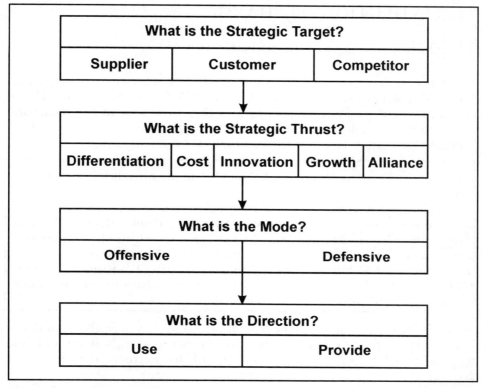

Figure 6.4   Wiseman's strategic options generator

Source: M. J. Earl, *Management Strategies for Information Technology*, Prentice Hall International
            1989, ch. 3.

In general corporate strategy, concerned with future directions and performance – and with identifying business types and organisation structure – is a
board responsibility and it suggests how IT should be positioned and managed. It is the main influence on the management information strategy.
Business strategies are the product-market analyses and the plans which each
strategic business unit formulates in pursuit of the mission it is given by the
corporate strategy. These are the main influences on information systems
strategy. Activity strategies are required to implement and support business
strategies, for example, finance or human resource strategies. The IT strategy is another, and is mainly determined by IT functional management, but
influenced and approved by business-unit top management.

THE EVOLUTION OF CHANGE

The changing shape of organisations

For many service organisations, which are dependent upon cost efficiencies for improved performance, increasing size will be a critical issue. This is evidenced by the takeovers and mergers that were seen in the banks and other parts of the financial services industries in the latter part of 1997. During that period, amongst the commercial banks:

> ING of the Netherlands bought Belgium's Banque Bruxelles Lambert (Europe's largest ever cross-border merger).
>
> The Finnish government announced the merger of Postipankki, the country's third-largest bank, with the state controlled Finnish Export Credit, a commercial lender. The new unit would be second only to Merita, until the latter announced a friendly merger with Sweden's Nordbanken.
>
> Banc One paid $3 billion for First Commerce Bank of Louisiana, the USA's sixth-largest bank was created when First Union of Charlotte acquired Core States of Philadelphia in a $16.6 billion deal.

Similarly, amongst the investment banking sector – where the boundaries between the different services of investment banking, stockbroking, and fund management has blurred – there was a rush for partners and targets for acquisition:

- Morgan Stanley merged with Dean Witter, Discover
- Merrill Lynch acquired Mercury Asset Management
- Travellers Group acquired Salomon Brothers
- Bankers Trust bought Alex Brown

Union Bank of Switzerland was effectively taken over by the smaller Swiss Banking Corporation to create the world's biggest asset manager. The new UBS will have close to $1 trillion under management, and will become Europe's leading competitor to Wall Street investment banks. It was estimated that approximately 13 000 jobs would be lost, half of them from investment banking operations.[25] The combined bank will stretch over more lines of business and more countries than most other competitors. Bearing in mind the previous conservatism and resistance to restructuring in Switzerland, Germany, and Austria, the last example is strong evidence of belief in the growing need for volume in this particular market.

Amongst the other examples of increasing globalisation, Zurich Group, a Swiss financial services company, raised its profile in the Far East with a $200 million investment in Peregrine Investments Holdings, a Hong Kong investment bank.

By contrast, a number of commercial banks have found it hard going trying to compete in the investment banking sector. Both Barclays and Nat West have withdrawn from most lines of investment business. Barclays by selling its European equity and investment banking operations to Credit Suisse First Boston for only $170 million, after attempting to auction its BZW investment bank as a complete unit, and NatWest by selling its NatWest Markets investment banking subsidiary's equity business for $301 million. America's Bankers Trust paid $217 million for the pan-European equities business, and Deutches Morgan Grenfell paid $84 million for the global equities derivatives and program-trading operations. Both Barclays and Nat West lost money on the respective deals.

The insurance market has also seen a similar volume of activity in the same short period. During October 1997, Zurich Insurance, Switzerland's largest insurer, merged with BAT in an agreed deal of $37 billion to create one of the world's largest firms, whilst Generali, Italy's largest insurer, made a hostile bid for AGF of France, but was beaten when Allianz, with an agreed bid of $10.3 billion, reinstated itself as Europe's largest insurance company.

The accountancy profession saw proposed mergers during the year with KPMG's proposed merger with Ernst and Young in a $16 billion deal, leap-frogging the $12 billion merger of Coopers and Lybrand with Price Waterhouse which would force Arthur Andersen Worldwide into third place. Aside from the cost efficiencies expected from these mergers, there would be the advantage of being able to offer a more complete service to clients as KPMG has the largest law practice associated with its French office.

Similar merger activity had been seen in telecommunications, television, advertising, parcel delivery services, shipping, and hotels. The majority of these businesses share the same characteristics: margins are relatively low, the service is difficult to differentiate, and competition is cut-throat. In the case of television and telecommunications, there are the added factors of spreading deregulation and convergence between the two industries.

Many of the mergers in the financial services sector have signalled an attempt by the players to offer a more complete service to their clients and to establish a presence in more stages of the industry value chain. Traditionally, investment bankers made their money by underwriting the sale, or by the floating of shares and debt, making markets in them for investors, and selling advice to investors, fund managers, and corporate clients. But the market has changed, with easier access to information and the rapid improvement in communications and technology referred to earlier, some of these roles have become less necessary. As clients have developed in size and sophistication, particularly the fund managers, they have found ways to bypass the investment banks' sole access to stockmarkets and have begun to deal themselves. The London Stock Exchange has now moved to electronic trading and now every major stockmarket in Europe uses computers where once it used traders. On most major stock exchanges, fund managers may not have direct access to the floor and must still deal through a member firm, an investment bank, or a broker, but now electronic traders match sales and purchases – automatically – off market, and the completed transactions are reported to an exchange once completed. This has brought increased downward pressure on the commission rates charged. The size of fund managers, and their power, has increased dramatically and they now routinely employ their own analysts and traders, again eroding a source of income for the investment banks. A number of investment banks have moved to protect this source of income by acquiring their own fund mangers, and the merger of UBS and SBC referred to earlier is an example. However, the clients that the fund managers are dealing with are also getting larger and exerting downward pressure on margins as they expect an improved service, and more of it, for lower commissions.

Within the investment banking industry, a large proportion of the cost structure is devoted to staff, as the new entrants to the market force up the costs of hiring and retaining talented staff to trade and to advise. Typically, half the operating costs of a bank are made up of salaries and bonuses. Even with the layoffs that accompany the mergers, these spiralling costs – together with the squeezed margins – will make it harder for the banks to enjoy the profits that they have in the past. It is possible that with less competitors and higher barriers to entry through increased capital, the banks may be able to pay their staff less, charge clients more, and return to a more profitable future.

However, this may not be the case, as evidence has shown from other industries with similar operating characteristics. As can be seen with the global airlines, oligopolies can be fiercely competitive and usually operate on very thin margins. The effect on staff may be another problem for the financial services industry, particularly in the case of the more talented individuals who have received high salaries and bonuses. After enjoying the experience of business process engineering and 'downsizing' as their organisation concentrated on short-term results and extracting as much value as possible from all assets, including the staff, how will they react to further attempts to reduce salaries and bonuses? With the improvements in telecommunications, the more talented individuals may leave to start their own small, but profitable firms.

Evidence, gathered and described by Ghosal and Bartlett in *The Individualised Corporation*,[26] suggests that the time has come for a new style of management which will build on the learning organisation proposed earlier by other authors. Based on interviews in a number of organisations including, amongst many others, McKinseys and International Service Systems (a Copenhagen-based cleaning-service company), they suggest that to be successful a company will need to:

- create a sense of ownership amongst the staff to encourage entrepreneurial effort
- foster self-discipline amongst staff to prevent chaos
- build a supportive culture that tolerates, but learns from failure

This will become increasingly important for those industries where the only way of differentiating the service offered is by the quality and performance of the staff. As services become more like commodities, it will be harder to maintain margins and to build in switching costs, even emotional ones like branding.

To create a sense of ownership there will need to be a dramatic reduction of the power held in the centre of the organisation. The authors describe dramatic levels of delegation, both of power and assets, with significant reduction in head-office staff levels and a change in the way that management information systems work. Front-line functions, such as operations, development, marketing, and sales, should be controlled in the units. Although there will always be a need for central policy on support functions like logistics and personnel, their implementation will also be local – unless there is a significant loss of synergy by doing so. In general, the greater the degree of external dynamism compared to functional dynamism, and the greater the synergy between the functions rather than within the functions, the more attractive the unit structure becomes. This kind of arrangement will require strong managers at the centre, confident in their ability and well respected by those that report to them. Relationships between central managers and unit managers should revolve around strategic issues, not operational ones. With operating companies controlling the majority of the budget in the organisation, and the relative freedom to retain earnings and to borrow, decisions can be made closer to the customer by front-line managers. By definition, operating units would need to be smaller and based around technologies or markets. Fostering the degree of trust implied in this kind of organisational environment will not be easy, releasing control will be a difficult step for many established senior managers.

Traditionally, the processes and procedures of capital budgeting, and other methods of project appraisal in organisations, are heavily standardised and exclude the soft data which is often essential for an effective decision. This lack of essential detail, which we have referred to earlier (Chapter 3), has been heavily criticised by Hayes, Wheelwright and Clark for its destructive effect on American industry.[27] There is also the problem that by the time a proposal has gone through the layers of management hierarchy to reach a level senior enough to commit the funds, it is likely to be quite distant from the 'champion' who has gathered the data, completed the analysis, produced the report, and believes in the project. However, as organisations become larger, it must be recognised that senior managers cannot hold all of the rich detail and tacit knowledge necessary to make the decisions in the various markets in which the organisation chooses to operate. The changing role of IT, that we have referred to earlier, will be necessary to collate and disseminate knowledge and information as widely as possible, and inform the decision-making process at all levels of the organisation.

Traditionally, the budgetary process defines the power base, the relationships, and the behaviour within the firm, and only now are managers beginning to realise the damaging effect that managing within the annual budget can have on their responsiveness to competitive threats. It is difficult to focus on technological breakthroughs and new market entrants if the task is defined as meeting the monthly or annual budget, as defined by a complex computer model derived on a sophisticated spreadsheet, produced by head office on a high powered PC. In a recent survey of American companies quoted by Hope and Hope, fully 97 per cent used budgets to control performance and 67 per cent required written explanations of the causes of deviations.[28] The implication is that the process is too rigid, too internally focused, adds little value to the firm, encourages the wrong management behaviour, and uses too much of the respondent's time.

There is also much evidence to suggest that true control, even if worthwhile, is relatively impossible with accounting systems anyway. It is too easy to shift expenditure from one budget to another, to use contract labour to avoid over-runs on headcount, and defer needed expenditure to stay in target for a particular time period, all of which are potentially damaging to the effectiveness of the organisation. Whereas a traditional budget and control system will place the emphasis on control of costs, the need is for a system that will encourage cost reduction by focusing on delivering customer value, whilst removing waste and educating staff to identify and understand what work adds value. The need therefore is not for the diagnostic controls offered by budgeting, but for interactive control systems. Whilst a diagnostic system supports single-loop learning and encourages people to keep within boundaries, interactive control systems are designed to promote double-loop learning, whereby the learning process will facilitate further questions about the validity of the strategy followed and how it can be improved upon.

There will similarly be a need for different forms of appraisal and reward systems within this type of company, as the emphasis will change to one where the size of budget and the headcount managed can no longer be the criteria for reward. Similarly, if the company is to reward entrepreneurial spirit, the reward for success must be tempered with a tolerance for failure. Kanter describes the traditional paycheque, based on status and not on contribution, where any merit element was a small percentage, as bankrupt.[29] With the growing emphasis on teamwork, co-operation, entrepreneurship, and synergy across operating units, the size of a paycheque cannot be based on an individual's length of service or position in the hierarchy. The change to paying the person rather than the position will be driven not only by entrepreneurial pressures, but by cost, equity, and concerns about productivity. The present system is too expensive to maintain, perceived as unfair; and unlikely to motivate high performance. There are, of course, problems with designing a suitable scheme of reward since, it has been suggested by Grint,[30] whatever criteria are used for determining performance may lead to a Pavlovian response, with detrimental effects on other factors important to the firm. If, for instance, employee morale is considered important and rewarded, managers may treat staff well to the detriment of productivity. The need for subjective measures, as opposed to the 'hard' measures associated with profit and product numbers, may well be resisted by some managers, but measures unrelated to profit have been used in voluntary and non-commercial organisations with success for a number of years.

With a performance measure of share of market capitalisation rather than ROCE or profitability, the effects of creative accounting are avoided. Thus the company can measure what contribution it has made to the new wealth created by the whole industry in the market over the last year. At Svenska Handelsbanken, for instance, where traditional budgeting processes were dispensed with in 1970, staff bonuses relate to team working and mutual support, and are related to the whole organisation's performance, benchmarked against the industry average. However, instead of being paid periodically, bonuses are paid into a retirement fund. The final payment received depends not on final salary, but on length of service – any employee leaving after 25 years may expect to receive approximately £200 000. Arne Martesson, the chief executive, says the company has beaten this average every year since 1972, and puts the success down to the dismantling of the budget and control system, and replacing it with an encouraged atmosphere of thrift and improvement, together with the open-management information system which allows one branch to compare its results with another. With a cost/income ratio of 45 per cent, it compares well with the 70 per cent achieved by most industry competitors, such as Nat West, ABN-Amro, and Deutschebank.

Although each branch sets its own targets and effectively runs its own business, the federated approach creates a pressure to perform because the branches are part of a league table. However, as the rewards relate to the organisation as a whole, there is a similar pressure to share knowledge and resources as underperforming units affect the rewards of all others. This aspect of Bartlett and Ghosal's new management style can be found in other Scandinavian companies, such as Ikea, Volvo, ISS, Electrolux, and Asea Brown Boveri, all of whom are abandoning traditional budgetary control methods. ABB started to implement the new organisation model when Percy Barnevik took over as chief executive in 1988, and the emphasis is on a federation of small businesses that share knowledge and resources. There are at present 1300 small businesses in ABB, each with approximately 200 staff and an annual turnover of $25 million.

The concept of the balanced scorecard with a large selection of variables may well be the answer, as long as the measures used are regularly reviewed to ensure that they assess and encourage behaviour appropriate to the corporate aims. Introduced in 1992 by Robert Kaplan and David Norton,[31] the technique views performance from the perception of four different user groups, shareholders, customers, internal operations, and innovation. The measures chosen are designed to relate performance to an organisation's strategic direction. Since introducing the concept, they have conducted research with more than 100 companies and have found that although the companies did not set out to develop a strategic management system, this has effectively happened. The scorecard has supplied a focused framework for many of the critical management processes necessary for success. Goal setting for departments and individuals, feedback and learning, business planning, and capital allocations are amongst the processes expected to gain from its implementation. Typical connected and interrelated measures that might be included in a balanced scorecard designed for an insurance company are:

Financial	increase shareholder value reduce loss ratio reduce expense ratio
Customer	improve policyholder satisfaction reduce policyholder loss improve producer satisfaction
Operations and process	reduce claims handling cycle time reduce loss frequency reduce loss severity improve quote-to-sell ratio
Learning and innovation	increase % new segment business

Very few of the measures relate to only one of the stakeholder groups, but have an impact on the satisfaction and performance of more than one of the categories of financial, customer, operations and process, and learning and innovation. The attempt to move to what is often described as a 'third wave' company by this approach is not always successful.[32] Companies that have tried, and failed, include Digital, Wang, Olivetti, Bull, and Air France. In every case, they have been pulled back to their original form by the strength of the traditional budgeting system, which has reinforced old patterns of behaviour and power systems.

Similarly 360 degree feedback schemes are likely to gain acceptance and importance in the new organisations. Traditional appraisal schemes operate on, at most, two dimensions, self-appraisal and appraisal by ones boss. However, if a manager has one boss, leads a team of five, and deals regularly with four peers of similar grade, who is best placed to comment upon their effectiveness in the areas of people management skills and interpersonal relations? Clearly, the people who work for and with that manager could make a very useful contribution to their training and development. The circumstances of the assessment are not based on exercises or simulations away from the workplace, but relate directly to what the manager concerned does in their working cycle. This means that the results of the process are more likely to be realistic, credible, perceived to be fair – and are thus easier to accept. Usually collected confidentially by questionnaires on paper or directly onto disc, the system may be multipurpose or specific to one aspect of managerial development or behaviour, although generally, they are used for a group of competencies. Where the comments chosen for the questionnaire are descriptive rather than judgmental, the feedback becomes more balanced and that – together with the nature and variety of the assessors, and the face validity of the activities measured – make it easier for the participants to accept the outcomes. With each questionnaire comprising a number of comments followed by a rating scale, they will often consist of as many as 150 such comments and can be used at all levels of the organisation from chief executive through to the whole of the organisation. The technique was successfully introduced as long ago as 1987 at Tesco (the UK supermarket chain) by the director of training, Peter Ward,[33] who has gone on to use the technique with other retail clients who are grooming middle managers recognised as having the potential for board-level appointments. The technique has also been used successfully in other companies such as Rhone Poulenc Agricultural.[34] Ward feels that the technique will gain increasing acceptance since many of the UK's leading management colleges are now using 360 degree feedback as a component of their training and development programmes, and organisations such as the National Health Service already use peer review in the assessments of professional staff.

Although the idea will be to genuinely empower staff to make entrepreneurial decisions about new products and services, the wishes of the corporate centre and the general direction that company wishes to follow cannot be ignored. General standards of behaviour and an atmosphere of mutual respect will need to be second nature to all members of staff. There will be strong similarities to the relationships formed in the partnerships that Cannon enters into to promulgate its laser-engine technology, or Microsoft enters into to spread acceptance of its software. Whereas departments and divisions in an organisation have traditionally competed with each other for limited resources controlled, and apportioned, by the corporate centre, there will be a need for a more co-operative and complementary approach to the relationships between the operating units. Nalebuff and Brandenburger have coined the word 'co-opetition' to describe the relationship that we outline here, and use the term 'complementors' to describe the players.[35] They contrast the view of Gore Vidal:

> It is not enough to succeed. Others must fail.

with that of Bernard Baruch, a leading American financier:

> You don't have to blow out the other fellow's light to let your own shine.

and point to relationships which lead to mutual success rather than mutual destruction. Although the emphasis of their work and the examples they quote describe relationships between unrelated companies, the situation is often the same between the operating units of a large company.

In addition to the increased versatility and market awareness in the operating units, there will need to be a raised awareness of both profitability and the financial impact of the decisions made. This will mean that the management information system will need to provide appropriate information at lower levels in the organisation, rather than just function as a command and control mechanism for senior management. The staff of the operating units will need training to be able to understand the reports that they will be able to call up, to review their performance, and to compare it to other parts of the organisation. With the reporting system designed to produce information aggregated at only the unit level and freely available to all units, cross-unit benchmarking becomes possible. By comparing to other similar, but more successful operations, they will be able to learn from those other units and transfer successful ideas into their own operations. The information systems we have referred to earlier in this chapter will help to facilitate this air of co-operation. The improved business literacy will not only develop the competitive spirit, but, through a desire for mutual success, will increase the sense of membership of the whole organisation.

There will need to be a clear sense of purpose, possibly spelt out in a mission statement, and its development and communication will be part of the role of senior management. Rather than a cliché about 'higher quality' or 'commitment to customers', there will need to be clear and, if possible, measurable statements of direction and intent. To be effective, mission statements need to be brief, clear enough to be understood by everyone involved, and set a communal sense of direction. Memorable examples of statements of 'strategic intent' include the Japanese corporation Komatsu's aim to 'encircle

Caterpillar', Cannon's intention to 'beat Xerox', and President Kennedy's famous wish to 'put a man on the moon'. Possibly one of the most effective was that formulated and used during the 1980s by SAS, the Scandinavian airline, which was simply to be 'one of five in 95'. With no explicit statement of what was being measured, it gave a sense of direction, of survival, and of success. Such mission statements, coupled with clear corporate objectives based on overall financial performance such as a target return on capital employed, will allow freedom to act, but within guideline responsibilities.

Although the changes outlined above will go some way to bringing about an entrepreneurial spirit within an organisation, the hardest step will be to build a supportive culture in the firm. It is a slow and difficult process to develop a truly learning organisation, where managers have the self-confidence to question assumptions and to act independently. The role of the senior management must change from one of controller to coach, from allocator to facilitator, and from deciders to mentors. Goran Lindahl, chief executive of Asea Brown Boveri, the Swedish power generation company with over 1200 operating units, is quoted as saying that, when he perceives an unexpected problem in one of their businesses, he asks the mangers responsible three questions:

- What is the cause of the problem?
- What are you doing to fix it?
- How can I help?

When a company tries to introduce this approach into established businesses with established reporting arrangements, it is going to require a significant change in the mindsets of the managers concerned. The role of the senior manager has become to 'develop the mangers to develop the businesses'.

We have said earlier (in Chapter 3) that one of the principal causes of failure is complacency due to success, but this is more poignant when those in the operating units can see the problem coming and even have ideas as to how it could be avoided. With the development of a supportive culture, this is less likely to happen as managers of small decentralised units have the self-confidence to question policy decisions, and senior mangers have the self-confidence to let them. Similarly, there is a need to build a tolerance to well-intentioned failure into the culture of the company. The statement that 'the only way not to make mistakes is not to make decisions' should be replaced by the words on the plaque in Ed Land's (the founder of Polaroid) office: 'A mistake is an event, the full benefit of which has not yet been turned to your advantage.'[36] However, the implication is not that individuals should learn from their mistakes, but that the organisation as a whole should learn from the mistakes made by individuals. This will require a particularly strong and supportive culture to overcome an individual's fear of failure, and subsequent embarrassment, as their mistakes are not just known to their boss, but are widely disseminated around the organisation. Kanter produced a set of 'rules for stifling initiative' which detail the steps necessary to ensure that this culture does not exist:[37]

1. Regard any new idea from below with suspicion – because it's new and because it is from below.

2. Insist that people who need your approval to act first go through several other layers of management to get their signatures.

3. Ask departments or individuals to challenge or criticise each others proposals. (That saves you deciding – you only need to pick the survivor.)

4. Express your criticisms freely, and withhold your praise. (That keeps people on their toes.) Let them know they can be fired at any time.

5. Treat the identification of problems as a sign of failure to discourage people from letting you know when something in their area isn't working.

6. Control everything carefully. Make sure people count anything that can be counted, frequently.

7. Make decisions to reorganise or change policies in secret, and spring them on people unexpectedly. (That also keeps people on their toes.)

8. Make sure that requests for information are fully justified and make sure that it is not given out to managers freely. (You don't want data to fall into the wrong hands.)

9. Assign to lower level managers – in the name of delegation and participation – responsibility for figuring out how to cut back, lay off, move people around, or otherwise implement threatening decisions you have made. Get them to do it quickly.

10. And above all, never forget that you, the higher ups, already know everything important about this business.

Spelt out like this it is unlikely that any manager recognising these traits in themselves would continue to follow these 'rules', or that any organisation would tolerate this kind of behaviour by its management.

There will need to be a change of emphasis on the investment in the human assets of the organisation. In many companies, when managers wish to invest in tangible assets, there is a need for senior management approval, but not so when the investment is made in recruiting a new employee. The very terminology used when we describe the tangible asset as a 'fixed' or 'capital' asset implies the importance and permanence of the decision. But in terms of the effect on the organisation, a successful recruitment can have just as much effect on the future of the organisation as the piece of equipment purchased, particularly in the knowledge-based industries where there is rapid change. Having bought the fixed asset, the company will take care of its maintenance to ensure it continues to contribute to the profits and prolong its useful life. Eventually, however, because of the inflexibility of the machinery, it will need to be replaced by the next technology and new equipment will be bought. However, the situation can be different when we hire new staff. Even if significant emphasis and expenditure is placed on the recruitment of the best possible people from those available in the market place, without 'maintenance' they will, like the plant and equipment, have a finite shelf life. Yet unlike the machinery with investment in maintenance, they will actual grow and adapt to the changing requirements placed upon them by the company and the environment. As well as developing the environment, where there is co-operation and mutual development across unit boundaries, both Arthur Andersen and McKinsey encourage the development of individual expertise within their staff. The slogan in the recruitment brochure for Arthur Andersen, 'after training with Andersen, you could work for anyone, anywhere – or you could work for yourself', gives an indication of the firm's investment in self-development.

For these companies who have invested larger amounts of money in finding the best recruits, it makes sense to maintain them at the forefront of their specialisms. Many companies have effectively formed universities for their staff, and they encourage them to elect to take courses which will develop their skills or they have supported them in taking courses externally. This is particularly important for industries where there is rapid change in the environment, such as software, media, communications, and management consultancy. McKinsey recently advertised in the UK for recruits who had been accepted on selected MBA programmes to come for interview, happy to cover their fees for the programme they were about to start. However, the development of staff is not just about education and training – be it internally or externally delivered. There is much value in a formal mentoring and coaching system whereby, in addition to a line manager, staff will be assigned another senior manager who will have responsibility for fostering that individual's career and self-development.

Barley and Kunda have suggested that organisations do not evolve into an optimum operating structure and pattern, but that progress is best described by a pendulum motion whereby the nature of management oscillates between a normative approach and a rational approach.[38] Considering the past century in the US, they identify the following periods:

1870–1900	industrial betterment	—	normative
1900–1923	scientific management	—	rational
1923–1955	human relations	—	normative
1955–1980	systems approaches	—	rational
1980–1992	organised culture	—	normative

To this we can add that 1992 to the present has continued in a normative approach very much focused on the development of staff as the most important asset of the organisation, particularly with the work of Ghosal and Bartlett.[39] Whereas the rational approach can be said to involve securing control over employees, the normative approach involves securing their commitment to the organisation and its values. The fact that these two extremes cannot be reconciled means that organisations will oscillate between variants of the two polarised positions. In discussing this work, Grint comments that the increasing use of psychometric testing and balanced scorecards may signal a return to rational methods.[40] However, it can be argued that this will surely depend on what measures are included in the balanced scorecard. He further notes that although rational approaches have been dominant over the time considered, the normative influences are more visible and have attracted more attention. Barley and Kunda go on to correlate the application of rational and normative approaches to management, with the position in the long-run economic and technological cycles described by Kondratieff and Schumpeter. They suggest that the rational approach occurs at the growth phase, when capital investment is increasing and particular technological development spurs economic expansion. When expansion starts to slow and there are declining returns for investment, then the period of consolidation that results is managed in a normative fashion. If we are to see a return to the rational approach, it would imply that we will see significant capital investment and the development of significant, and novel, technologies.

Our discussion has so far concerned large organisations and their characteristics. They have been described elsewhere as a fishing net,[41] the boundaries of which contain groups of staff in small federal organisations – which change direction collectively within those boundaries when the whole organisation is subject to environmental change. In the transitional phase, as these companies transform to a genuine third-wave firm, this description may be true. However, once the transformation is complete, the net may no longer be necessary – if all the characteristics described by Bartlett and Ghoshal are in place, perhaps a shoal is a better description. As the belief systems, boundary systems, and interactive control systems become second nature to the firm and the information flows become rapid and accurate, the need for the net will disappear because all employees are aware of the strategic direction to be followed by the firm. To carry on the metaphor, not all fish will stay in the shoal forever. Handy describes the shape of the organisation of the future as that of a shamrock – a trefoil plant with each leaf divided into three leaflets or lobes. There will be three distinct groups of people in this structure, who will be managed and organised differently.[42] The core staff will be professional, highly paid, working long hours, and essential to the organisation. These are the people who are left after any downsizing that has occurred – who are still in the shoal.

The second group of staff are the flexible workforce, those whose competencies are so specialised as not to be in constant demand by the firm. They will swim away from the shoal of permanent employment by the organisation, selling their time on a contractual basis to the organisation, only as and when required. If the flexible workforce tire of casual work, they may set up loose organisations of their own and, with a number of associates who have the same or complementary skills, they will effectively be small consultancy firms or providers of interim management, a separate shoal in fact. The practice of interim management is well established in Scandinavia and the Netherlands. The client base for these embryonic consultancies will broaden as the associates sell their time to more than one organisation, as befits their skills. However, their skill base will not be the only criterion for additional business. They will take extra work to suit their needs, and personal objectives, for both financial and interest reasons.

The third group of people will also be outside the organisation, but will be working for specialist contractors who provide services such as cleaning, catering, and maintenance. These will be the tasks that cannot be performed easily or successfully by the previous group, where economies of scale are still important. These companies may be quite large (such as ISS, to whom we have referred earlier) or relatively small. The small firms will arise where a company decides to outsource the work of a service department, and the staff of that department leave, bid for the work and get it. With local authorities in Britain, this has already happened to a great extent and not all contracts have been won by large companies. Similarly, where a company decides that a business is no longer core to its activities, management buyouts will create a new small- to medium-sized enterprise (SME).

There will therefore be an increase in the number of small companies operating for the main organisation, but outside it. These firms will be characterised by the work they do. The work that is boring and repetitive and relatively low-skilled will fall to the part-time labour and to the large companies, but knowledge work that is outsourced will increasingly fall to SMEs. This will be driven by the digital age and, with this change, there will come a change of boundaries. Rather than markets defined by geography and proximity, the market will now be defined by communication – the Internet and the quality of telecommunications links will have a significant impact on this form of work. There are already examples of companies using better or cheaper sources of labour, and expertise, on the other side of the world in the bulk-increasing industries of manufacturing. Where the nature of the work is bulk reducing, this will become more and more prevalent. The local tax forms for Westminster Council in London were processed on the Indian subcontinent – it being cheaper to fly the forms out to India and to send the processed data back by wire. The New Jersey claims' office of the New York Insurance Company is based in Castleisland in County Kerry, Eire, not only because the staff are cheaper and just as skilled as those in New York, but because the Irish telephone system is one of the best in the world.

Kinsman has described the company F International,[43] which was started by Steve Shirley in 1962 to capitalise on the expertise of women who left work to start families, or others who could not fit their life into a 'conventional' working day and environment. Increasingly there will be doubt over what constitutes a conventional working day or environment in these small service companies. When Steve Shirley started the company as Freelance Programmers, it was small and run from her own home. Two years later, there were four full-time staff and the name had changed to F International. By 1988, it had become FI Group plc, had a turnover of approximately £20 million, and 1100 employees. However, less than 200 were salaried, the large majority were self-employed and working from home. The company believes that those people are fully 30 per cent more effective, since many of the distractions of the office – lunch, coffee breaks, personal phone calls, and people dropping by the office for a gossip – are removed. The self-employed workers are networked into the organisation with e-mail, and they work in flexible and shifting teams built around specific projects. The published charter of the company is:

> . . . to develop, through modern telecommunications, the unutilised intellectual energy of individuals and groups unable to work in a conventional environment.

Support from the organisation is strong, with training investment and regular contact through a number of small branch offices and 'free speaks', where senior members of the small head-office core management team will tour the country to attend question and answer sessions with the staff. There are regional work centres where, when necessary, the self-employed staff can go to meet with their colleagues on a face-to-face basis.

The changing shape of external relations

The increasing globalisation of companies, together with the increase in world communications and a more aware and vociferous population, will increasingly expose those organisations to criticism when they are perceived to have abused their size and power. Although world politics have changed since the days of the 1960s and 1970s, when many Governments were Socialist in ideology, and the concept of multinationals ran counter to the ethos of central planning. The governments may have accepted that co-operation with multinationals may lead to joint prosperity, but they have been replaced in opposition by the increasingly aware and powerful pressure groups within those countries. For companies, it is not only important to maintain the value of their brands, it is also important that they manage their reputational capital. With the transparency of global communications, it is quite easy for the increasingly sophisticated and professional pressure groups to get the information that they feel will support the case they wish to make against the target company. It can be an expensive process to have to go to law to defeat the claims of those who are intent on damaging the name of the firm. In many cases, although judgement is made in favour of the company, the damage limitation is ineffective and the company still suffers.

McDonald's, the burger chain – which, together with its competitors, is regularly criticised for only providing low-grade work – had to defend an action in England against activists who had mounted a campaign against them. In a high-profile protest, the activists claimed that McDonald's was responsible for the destruction of rain forests in its production processes. Although the company was able to satisfy the court that this was a libel, the result was inconclusive and there was far more press coverage for the action – and the evidence – than there was for the end result.

Similarly, Shell was criticised for its suggested lack of action in Nigeria in the case of the hanging of Ken Saro-Wiwa, a playwright and political activist. Although he had been a critic of the large oil companies that operate in Nigeria, nobody suggested that Shell had played any part in his death. The criticism was that they did not use their economic muscle to persuade the Nigerian Government to reverse its decision and commute the death sentence. Whereas in previous times multinationals had been criticised for using their economic power in bringing pressure to bear on Governments, in this case they were being criticised for not doing so. This is likely to be a tactic that will be used increasingly in the future, as the company concerned pays a heavy price if it chooses to ignore the threat. During 1995, when the Saro-Wiwa affair occurred, Shell's position in various surveys of the most respected companies slipped and there can be no doubt that this, together with the protests by Greenpeace about the sinking of Brent Spar, had been a contributory cause. Shell has recently acknowledged that it had not been as clear on human rights as it should.[44] Mark Moody-Stuart was quoted as saying that

> We have always been strong about not bribing people and not interfering in party politics. But when we get into human rights, it's been a much more hidden thing. We need to get those values out in the open.
>
> Shell's statement of business values has been amended and for the first time includes the statement: 'it supports fundamental human rights in line with the legitimate role of business.' Although there are distinct advantages to being a global company – increasingly, there will be different challenges as sectors of the population that cannot get satisfaction directly from their government will use the power of the organisation to do so.
>
> The management of reputational capital can have far-reaching consequences for a company, whether it is a global player or not. Relationships with all of a company's stakeholders are likely to be soured if the company develops an adverse reputation in any area, be it as a bad employer, bad supplier, or bad member of the community.

This becomes particularly important in times of crisis.

> During 1982 and 1986, the pharmaceutical company Johnson and Johnson (J&J) was the victim of a poisoner who injected cyanide into packs of Tylenol, the company's best-selling pain relief drug. As soon as it was recognised that the poisoning was due to taking Tylenol, the company immediately withdrew all stock from the market, launched an expensive advertising campaign, set up free telephone hot-lines, and offered a reward for information leading to the arrest of the murderer. The quick and decisive action, the assumption of responsibility (although it was the act of a third party), the concern for the victims and their dependants, together with the open relations with the media, worked well for the company. Although many commentators had condemned the brand and suggested it would not recover from the disaster, the opposite was true, J&J received enormous public sympathy and consumer trust, and subsequently recaptured 90 per cent of its previous sales volume. When interviewed subsequently, the company said that their actions had been driven by 'The Credo',[45] a set of principals specifying the company's obligations to consumers, employees, local communities, and stockholders, which are widely circulated and form the core of the company's identity. It was thus the everyday practices at J&J that helped them to turn a potential disaster into a relative success.

Research by the French Dragon group is quoted as providing the following findings about consumer motivation:[46]

- Consumers are increasingly interested in corporate reputation and are able to evaluate corporate behaviour – but so far have little information to do so.

- They are willing to be favourably influenced by good corporate behaviour, but they do not expect companies just to be altruistic, they understand that they are driven by commercial motives.
- They value environmental performance, employment record, and community involvement, and are particularly influenced by their perception of what it would be like to work in the organisation.

It is not only at times of crisis that managers need to be aware of the effects that decisions have on the firm's reputation. There is an increasing need to build procedures and practices into the company processes that will protect and enhance the good name and standing of the firm in the various communities within which it operates. With the advent of increasingly influential pressure groups, as described above, it will be necessary for organisations to proactively take steps that will build respect for themselves amongst those who have influence. Many organisations have now started to play a more active and philanthropic role in the communities around them. Whilst those communities may not represent their customer base, they will almost certainly consist of employees and potential employees. Recruitment is much easier if you are well respected in the community in which you work and – since more are likely to apply for positions – you are likely to not only attract better applicants, but also to have more to chose from.

The idea of corporate citizenship is not lost on companies like J. P. Morgan, the New York bank, Ben and Jerry's ice-cream parlours, and the Virgin Group.

Amongst other ventures of a similar nature J. P. Morgan has, since 1988, funded and run a professional development office for teachers at two New York schools. The facility was set up to improve public provision of education by giving teachers growth opportunities, peer feedback on teaching methods, and the possibility to work with volunteers from the bank's staff in skill-building workshops. In 1992, the independent programme, designed by J. P. Morgan, was adopted by the city's Central Board of Education for implementation in all of the schools under its control.

Ben Cohen and Jerry Greenfield formed an alliance with Harlem entrepreneur Joe Holland and HARKhomes, a homeless shelter founded by Holland, to start Partnershop. This was designed as a neighbourhood business, in a distressed part of town, to provide some of the disadvantaged local population with job training and employment opportunities. J. P. Morgan was also involved in the project and had helped arrange financial support for the venture.

> In the UK, Virgin Group has set up and supports the work of HELP, a counselling organisation which every week helps hundreds of young people with a variety of problems related to drugs and sex. The company is also part of a consortium of entertainment companies which fund and support a school for the performing arts and technology in Croydon, on the outskirts of London.

Although it could be expected that an ice-cream vendor and an entertainment company would need to keep a high profile in the local community, since this could impact directly upon their sales, this is not so true of an investment bank like J. P. Morgan. The bank operates mainly as a wholesale bank, providing banking services and loan facilities to blue-chip companies and governments throughout the world, but only to individuals with a high net worth. However, this 'enlightened self-interest', or philanthropy, goes back to Pierpoint Morgan, the founder of The House of Morgan – from which the current J. P. Morgan and Morgan Stanley were formed and have continued ever since. The company now 'does well by doing good' in two main ways: not only does it donate considerable sums of money to nonprofit groups, it also involves itself in community projects.

Increasingly, it will be necessary for companies to manage their reputation with their various stakeholders in a more effective way, and this has been recognised by the founders of some of the more successful companies. Anita Roddick, Body Shop founder, says in her book *Body and Soul*: 'All I want is a high profile in the community, I'm not interested in seducing the consumer with expensive images. We've got better things to do with the money.' We have already discussed the changing nature of the relationship between the company and its staff, there will also be changes in the way that companies interact with their community, both local and international. The management of reputational capital is possibly best summed up by the statement made by Arthur Ashe, the late tennis champion:

No matter what I do, or where or when I do it, I feel the eyes of others on me.[47]

For organisations this will become increasingly true.

The changing shape of the market

As we have shown earlier, there has been a high degree of consolidation in a number of the service industries over the last few years and this has, in part, been driven by the need for critical mass as the players have sought to drive down transaction costs. There are, however, other factors which have driven the increasing globalisation of businesses. Increasing deregulation in a number of industries and countries has meant that global markets have opened to foreign organisations that were formerly unwelcome. Agreements reached within the General Agreement on Tariffs and Trade (GATT) have meant that nation states must open their borders to fair competition from abroad, and may no longer protect their 'own' companies. The freedom of communication now enjoyed by potential customers has meant that they are more aware of what is on offer from an international variety of sources, and will seek the product or service that will suit them best – regardless of source. The changing life styles of consumers have also led to increased requirements for different forms of service, delivered in different ways.

In 1978, the Airline Deregulation Act radically altered the rules of the market for the industry in the US. This has been followed some 20 years later by similar legislation within the EU, which has now been followed by the 'Open Skies' discussions between the two trading blocks. These talks have raised some vital issues for national flag carriers and the already privatised companies, such as British Airways. These issues are covered, together with the strategies that the players may adopt, in Case Study 1, (Chapter 7). The forces that have impacted upon that industry, and brought about such major change, can also be seen in the other industries which are being forced in the direction of free markets.

We have referred elsewhere to the impact of technology on the business to business market, but it is also argued that there will be a significant impact on the services provided for the consumer market. This is noticeable in the sphere of personal banking, where recent developments in computing technology and the increasing commercialisation of computer networks, such as the Internet, have allowed the development of on-line services. It has been claimed that there are potential advantages for both the customers – a convenient 24-hour service – and for the banks which offer the service – a reduction in the need for an extensive bricks and mortar network, and reduced overheads.

The UK retail banking industry has undergone considerable change over the past 20 years, with the deregulation of financial markets, the liberalisation of building societies, and the wholesale restructuring that has occurred, due to mergers and acquisitions, between not only the banks, but also between the banks and the building societies as the services they offered have converged. In 1995, the retail banks Lloyds and TSB merged, after Lloyds had previously merged with the Cheltenham and Gloucester Building Society. The total number of banks operating in the UK fell from 244 in 1988 to 124 in 1994,[48] although this number is forecast to increase as more and more building societies take advantage of the changed legislation and convert to bank status. During 1997, four building societies, Halifax, Alliance and Leicester, Woolwich, and Northern Rock followed the Abbey National, which had converted some years before, and became banks. On a total assets basis, Halifax and Abbey National now rank amongst the top ten UK banks.

In other parts of Europe, a similar effect can be seen. In Germany for instance the major banks had concentrated during the 1980s on becoming *allfinanz* [capable of offering all kinds of financial services], such as personal banking and insurance services from each branch. In the public savings banks and credit co-operative banking sectors, which are both typified by having a large number of small local, branch networks there had been considerable consolidation through mergers and closures. The total number of banks in Germany fell from 13 300 in West Germany in 1960 to 3800 in unified Germany by the end of 1996,[49] but it is claimed that Germany is still over provided with banking services,[50] with on average one branch per 1500 customers, compared with the UK where each branch serves 2900 customers. However, the banking system in Germany is somewhat different to that in Britain since not all banks are driven by the profit motive. Whilst the private commercial banks do seek to maximise profits, the savings banks and credit co-operatives seek a reasonable surplus, but aim to support their customers and members at the same time.

For the banks and remaining building societies in the UK, there is pressure to find new customers and to retain or even build their market share, and to add value to those customers by offering additional services to provide one-stop shopping. A critical volume of current accounts is important for the clearing banks because the funds gathered from commercial and retail customers form the basis of the funds that are lent out as loans. They are a cheap and important source of borrowing for the banks, which is underlined by the fact that banks do not normally charge for retail current accounts that are kept in credit. The mobilisation of cheap funds through the network of branches is an important business metric for clearing banks. A further feature of current accounts is that they represent a database of potential customers which can be used for the cross-selling of a variety of services, such as investment and insurance products. Whilst corporate banking aims to find individual solutions for business customers, retail banking is mass marketing – still offering tailored products, but now standardised to suit large market segments easily educated both in their concept and in their use. The substitution of ATMs for bank tellers is a point in case, as is the use of debit cards instead of cheque books, heralding the cashless society and increased convenience. The latest development in ATMs involves combined retinal identification and the use of a card, with trials in Reading, England, by the Nationwide Building Society and NCR.

The potential of technological change for the retail banking sector in Europe has, to date, mainly been realised within the banks, which have seen the rationalisation of work processes and speeding up of payment clearances. National Westminster Bank, for instance, has cut its branches from 3100 to 1900 in the ten years to 1996, with a reduction of staff from 75 100 to 47 600 over the same period. For the customers, progress has been largely limited to credit cards, debit cards, and the availability of cash points or ATMs. Whilst the number of retail branches has fallen to around 10 000 in 1996, the number of ATMs has increased sixfold between 1980 and 1996 to some 16 000.[51] However, the high market penetration of the home market by PCs, due to the declining cost of computer hardware and software coupled with an increasingly computer-literate society, has been forecast to bring significant change to this sector. Retail bank customers have the potential to make use of electronic banking via telephones and on-line computers, rather than visiting their branch and using paperwork methods of conducting transactions.

Although the German banking industry is considered to be one of the most conservative in Europe, on-line banking has had a more pronounced impact over the last three years than in the rest of Europe. The German on-line provider T-On-Line is now the market leader of banking services with some 1.4 million registered users.[52] In fact, Germany is a larger user of on-line services generally (including e-mail and home banking), with 6.2 million users in mid 1997, compared to 5.8 million in France and 4.9 million in the UK.[53] The German banks have attempted to satisfy this demand for direct services by a twofold approach – as well as offering on-line services themselves, they have established stand-alone direct banks offering telephone banking and on-line banking via PCs. Since the stand-alone banks have been remotely located, it has been possible to take advantage of the tax incentives and grants available for companies setting up in areas of high unemployment. Commerzbank set up their Comdirect subsidiary under such a scheme in Quickboen, outside Hamburg. German current account customers typically have to pay £4 a month in bank charges and, increasingly, they are becoming more cost conscious and critical of the service offered – particularly its speed. Current account management can typically include 24-hour banking, with the ability to check and print copies of previous transactions, and a brokerage service allowing share trading and the downloading of chart analysis and reports.

There are presently 16 direct banks in operation, four of which were set up by the major commercial banks in an attempt to take control of the retail market away from the competing private savings (*Sparkassen*) and credit co-operative banks (*Volksbanken* and *Raiffeisenbanken*), which between them account for 50 per cent of the total assets of German banks. Charges for the use of on-line services are typically one third cheaper for the customer, but the German consumer organisation, *Stifung Waretest*, reported that the cost advantages were not so significant for the customers as had been claimed.[54] With additional costs amounting to as much as £100 per annum for the on-line providers' charges and the increase in the telephone bill, together with the prospect of taking up to 30 minutes to make a successful connection with the bank, the service was considered to be not so attractive. At present, all the on-line banking in Europe is being conducted through closed, private service providers, such as CompuServe, rather than with open access on the Internet since there are customer concerns about security. As yet the customers using direct banks do not have access to the full range of services that would be offered by the traditional bricks and mortar branch network.

Although on-line banking has become established in Germany, the 1.4 million registered customers holding 2.5 million accounts do not represent a significant penetration of the market at only 3.5 per cent of all accounts,[55] and any impact so far is limited. Relatively few German banks have opted to enter the Internet with their own web site, partly as a reflection of the limited interest shown by customers. At the end of 1996, only 35 banks of a possible 3800 were represented on the Internet, with the majority of those limiting its use to that of a marketing tool with information only.

Recent research has shown that the reasons for the limited success of direct banks in Germany are as follows:[56]

- Only a limited number of customers have converted to on-line banking and the expensive advertising campaigns to convince them to do so has meant that direct banking has not, as yet, made a profit.

- The limited number of customers has not allowed the banks to reach a critical mass of funds for lending on.

- Not all of those who opt for on-line banking close their in-branch facility, thus keeping open the facility of face-to-face advice. The need for advice becomes stronger in the customer's mind when the financial markets enter a period of instability, as they did during 1998 with the events in the Far East.

- The cost savings for the customer are not as high as initially believed, and the argument is not particularly strong or effective in promoting this service to the target segment.

- The security concerns about the Internet are still strong in people's minds. The problems of encryption are preventing a number of banks offering their services worldwide and denying them the opportunity of globalisation.

- The services offered are considered to be limited by the majority of potential customers. Whilst the direct banks offer current, deposit, and share-trading accounts, they do not offer mortgages or personal loans thus limiting the opportunities for cross-selling.

The situation is broadly similar in the UK, where the British Bankers Association state that there are currently only 3 million telephone banking accounts, and analysts believe that First Direct, which was launched by Midland Bank (part of the HKSB Group) in 1989, only became profitable after five years of operation.

As retailers attempt to maintain their growth by broadening their appeal to a diverse and relatively fragmented customer base, they have entered the area of financial services in an attempt to capitalise on their strong brand names. Although a number of large retailers in Britain have operated credit cards for many years, it is only recently that the supermarkets have started to become involved. Tesco has a loyalty-card scheme, Club Card Plus, which was developed from the original reward card, on which points were earned for purchases. The new card now draws regular amounts from the customer's ordinary bank account and pays interest at 5.5 per cent on credit balances, significantly higher than that available from the clearing banks. The card can be used to draw cash at stores or NatWest Bank ATMs up to an agreed credit limit. The scheme is a joint venture between Tesco and the Royal Bank of Scotland. Safeway's ABC bonus card operates in a similar fashion.

The cost of setting up these operations has not, however, been cheap. Sainsbury spent an estimated £30 million in a joint venture with the Bank of Scotland to set up a bank and offer an instant-access savings account, a Christmas savings account, and personal loans up to £15 000. Card holders receive reward points on the card – even when they use them to make purchases at rival retail outlets. The new bank had attracted 350 000 customers with a total of £600 million by the end of August 1997, apparently attracted by the high interest rates of 6.15 per cent. Tesco have recently announced that they will soon follow suit and open full telephone-banking facilities with a new telephone call-centre employing 300 people, in an extension of their joint venture with the Royal Bank of Scotland. Other organisations with strong brand names are also entering the banking arena. The Virgin Group, in partnership with AMP, recently announced that it would invest a further £290 million in Virgin Direct to set up full banking facilities.

The potential is there for market-driven technological change in the personal banking sector, but unlike the advent of ATMs, it will need to be customer driven. The skills base and facilities that the customer has to have available to use on-line banking represent a larger jump than did those required for the introduction of cash and debit cards. Similarly, it will also be necessary for the telecommunications system to make rapid and efficient connections between the banks and their customers. As yet, these conditions have not been sufficiently met to threaten the in-branch banking system, but retail banks cannot afford to ignore direct banking – to do so would erode their market share albeit, at the moment, slowly. Stand-alone telephone financial services and banking will continue to increase, although it is likely to be limited to a small, but lucrative customer segment. It is most likely to exist as a part of a multi-channel method of access for the customer. At present the most significant change for the sector is likely to be the emergence of powerful new players in the industry as retailers seek to capitalise on their strong brands, large established distribution networks, large customer bases – and to some extent captive audiences. This will pose a threat to the existing traditional banks, for whom growth by acquisition and merger must be reaching its limits. Lloyds TSB is already close to its regulatory limit of 25 per cent on current accounts and business accounts,[57] and domestic growth opportunities are limited.

Overseas growth may not be the answer, and the attempts during the 1980s to move into Continental Europe foundered as the regional and cultural differences were too strong to overcome. Local regulations are significantly different, as are customer expectations and product preferences. Peter Birch of Abbey National, which has expanded its financial services business into several other European countries, has said that the home-loan market has local features which cannot be ignored: 'For a mortgage in the UK, you go through a solicitor and that's it. If one has a mortgage in Italy or Spain, one has to have a notary present on completion.' This means that not only is the process slower, but even the design of waiting areas is different in those countries, where whole families are likely to be present for the mortgage process. The differences between the German banks and the UK banks that we have described above also means that although the margins enjoyed by the UK retail banking system may appear attractive, the prospect of a German bank moving into the sector successfully are remote – unless they adopted local custom and practice. This may slowly change with increased deregulation and the common market, but progress is likely to be slow. Where banks have been successful in developing an internationally recognised brand, such as Citibank, they have tended to concentrate on a particular market niche. Citibank has concentrated on a more sophisticated clientele, often expatriate, who themselves have an international perspective. In other cases, local branding has been essential for success.

The UK retail sector itself has seen considerable change over the last decade with the relaxing of regulation on trading hours and, more recently, Government attempts at curtailing the development of hypermarkets and out-of-town shopping. Pressure to prevent the development of further retail parks increased as the environmental impact of additional car use, and the use of land, became more important in the public's perception. Further improvements in profits for the players in the sector are not likely to be available by increasing the distribution network other than by acquisition, by the development of specialist stores in urban areas, or by overseas expansion. It is more likely that the existing supermarkets will need to concentrate on:

Diversification:	The major supermarkets are moving into financial services, and Tesco are opening new formats of stores, such as Metro and Express stores in urban/ commercial areas.
Capitalising on their brand name:	Own brands have changed over the last decade from a cheap and cheerful product offering a product of acceptable quality at a competitive price. The strong brands have helped the companies diversify into other areas.
Overseas development:	Both Sainsbury and Tesco have acquired retailers abroad, Sainsbury in America and Ireland, and Tesco in Continental Europe and Ireland.
Building customer loyalty:	Most major supermarkets now have loyalty or reward cards, and staff are trained to be increasingly customer focused, with the recognition that many consumers are not driven by price alone. There is an increase of in-store facilities for customers such as product panels.
Increasing like for like growth:	Store refurbishment with the intention of making the space work harder has been a priority, as has the use of the database from loyalty schemes to target offers to consumers. The use of improved scanning technology to process customers more quickly through the tills has improved the shopping experience.
Price competitiveness:	The major supermarkets maintain price bases of their competitors, and promotions which refund differences over competing retailer's prices are not uncommon.
Improving margins:	The impact of technology in this sector has been pronounced on the management of the supply chain.

Just as with the financial services sector, advances in communications technology are having a noticeable, but limited effect on the consumers. Telephone and Internet shopping have started in the UK, as has the availability of QVC, the shopping channel on cable television, but as with financial services, these developments will need to be driven by consumers' changing life styles. One area where Internet shopping has had a more noticeable impact has been that of book purchasing. With the demise of the Net Book Agreement within the UK, and the resulting freedom for bookshops to discount publishers prices, many smaller bookshops have failed and the industry has seen significant consolidation. As with personal banking, the Internet has had a relatively small, but increasingly important impact on the book trade. The virtual bookshop, Amazon, has built a network of 15 000 associate sites which are connected to its own web site. With an electronic sales force to whom it pays commission, it has very low administrative costs and sources books from all over the world. Such a global service is possible because the product offered by the service is completely standardised, there is no need for 'localisation', a book title by a particular author in a particular language cannot be diversified in any way.

Whilst it has been affecting other industries, communications infrastructure and telecommunications is, itself, another industry which is undergoing dramatic regulatory change. It is only recently that telephone companies around the world have started to move from the state-owned bureaucratic organisations to fully commercialised operations. Most regulation has been to control who entered the market, but with the privatisation of the services, the intent of the regulators has shifted to ensuring that a monopoly position is not abused, that there is relatively free entry to the market, that customers do not suffer predatory pricing, and that an agreed level of service is provided. The situation in America was slightly different in that AT&T, the main trunk provider, was never under state control, but started out as a private monopoly, and the local services were supplied by Bell Telephone, a similar private monopoly.

Within America over the past 50 years, regulations have changed from cost of service regulation of the private monopoly of AT&T to reliance on competitive forces supplied by new players, augmented by limited controls on AT&T's prices. Whereas entry to the market for long distance transmission was regulated, together with the price that could be charged, technological change after the war led to greatly reduced costs and the possibility of others entering the market. Traditionally, the local calls, which were primarily serving a domestic market, were cross-subsidised at the expense of the business and long-distance calls. This attempt to satisfy a public policy objective of universal service continued by virtue of pressure from politicians representing consumer interests. As technology made possible microwave and satellite transmissions, together with electronic switching, various large organisations were able to build their own systems, and had the potential to set up their own private telecommunications networks and bypass the Bell network. This alternative was sufficiently economically attractive to put the cross-subsidy at risk.

At the same time, new players were allowed to enter the market in America and companies, such as Sprint and MCI, started to take a share of the inter-state telecommunications market. The break up of the Bell system further complicated the issue and made for an increasingly competitive market. For the regulator, the problem was to reduce the value of the cross-subsidy, but for the players it was to raise their market share, since the industry is characterised by cost efficiency. Within Europe, most telecommunications companies were not only monopolies but were also state owned, often as part of the postal company. Amongst the first to be privatised was British Telecom (BT) when it was separated from the postal company, which remained in state control, and the Dutch PTT, where the telecommunications and the postal-delivery company were privatised together. BT was one of the first of the state companies to be privatised by the conservative government led by Margaret Thatcher.

With the stated intention of reducing bureaucracy and increasing cost efficiency by ensuring that such companies were run in a businesslike fashion, the government recognised that there would still be a need to regulate both the service provided and the prices charged by the newly commercialised company. There would also be a need to ensure that free market forces would prevail by making it possible for there to be new entrants to the market. The regulatory system for pricing decided on by the UK government was one based on a price cap, such that BT would be free to price in any way that it chose, but the annual increase for the price of a basket of its services could only rise by the rate of inflation less an agreed figure for improved productivity, set at 3 per cent per annum for five years. This, it was felt, would encourage efficiency, and a similar system proved popular with the US regulator, the Federal Communications Commission, who applied it to AT&T – who were more enthusiastic for this than for the old system. Wendell Lind, AT&T's administrator of rates and tariffs, was quoted as saying:

> . . . with price-cap regulation instead of rate of return, prices will go down more because we will have the incentive to really try to be more efficient. We would pass some of the saving on to the customers.[58]

There was therefore little argument from the telephone companies with the concept of price restraint, since productivity increases could and were achieved. However, many of those gains were dependent on large volumes, and so fierce competition to gain market share was encouraged by the legislation. It was not so easy for the UK regulator to encourage new entrants to the market and ensure that BT did not abuse its monopoly position. In areas with a low population density, any new telecommunications would depend on mobile technology, but where population density is high, fixed installations are the most cost effective. Any potential entrant to the market would need either access to the existing carrier's system or a system of their own. There are few cases where a new player can afford the high capital cost of installing the infrastructure necessary, and these have been limited in Britain to: the cable companies, who are offering television as well as telephony; the railways, who have a private-use telephone infrastructure already; and the electricity transmission companies, whose pylons could be used for the wiring. Other entrants have had to use BT's trunk network and the regulator has had to ensure not only their access, but also that prices are charged which allow them to make a reasonable profit. Cable and Wireless attempted to enter the market to by capturing sufficient market share through public telephones on high-volume sites, and by supplying telephone systems to high-volume clients at the end of a BT trunk line. They withdrew from the public telephones market when they were unable to capture sufficient market share.

The market for international calls is becoming increasingly competitive and is an area where regulation plays a large part. A strong presence in the international market, estimated at $400 billion per annum, is essential to satisfy the increasingly demanding corporate clients which the telephone companies need to satisfy. The pricing for international calls includes 'accounting rule charges', whereby the telephone company in the originating country makes a payment to the telephone company in the receiving country. These charges are currently artificially high and do not reflect the true cost of the call. The charges are agreed by international negotiations between the regulatory bodies of the participating countries. Since many of the countries involved still have nationalised telecommunications companies and the charges are based on the typical cost of an operator-assisted call, there is often a 'trade balance deficit' between those companies in countries with fully liberated markets and those that are not. This is particularly true of AT&T in America who, on some calls, were losing $0.16 a minute on calls made to Germany, this being the difference between the charge they made to their customer and the payment they were required to remit to Deutsche Bundespost.

In general, calls made from America to most other countries are cheaper than the equivalent call made in the opposite direction. This has encouraged the recent attempts at globalisation through partnership, as the larger telecommunications companies around the world attempt to expand the reach of their infrastructure by acquisition, merger, or alliance. AT&T, already partnered with the Swiss national phone company, is currently rumoured to be looking for acquisitions such as Cable and Wireless rather than alliances,[59] as Spain's Telephonica having abandoned them and joined BT.

There is a need for any truly global telephone company to be present in three key markets – Europe, America, and Asia – and it has been said that if a telephone company does not belong to a global alliance, it will not exist in the next decade. The importance of globalism and consolidation was underlined when WorldCom beat BT with its successful bid for MCI at £37 billion. The position has been worsened by new technology,[60] which allows cheap call-back services to be provided by companies such as International Telecom (ITL) in America. Offering a service called Kallback, overseas callers telephone a number in America and hang up after one ring. A computer receives the call and, from data encoded in the signal, dials the number back – allowing the caller access to the cheap rates currently charged in America. Whilst overseas regulators keep the 'accounting rule charges' above those charged by the FCC and markets are not fully deregulated, this service will be a major thorn in the side of the larger global players.

The media industry is also enjoying the same double impact of deregulation and rapid technological change as that experienced in telecommunications. One of the principal effects of the technological change that both of those industries are experiencing is that of convergence. Increasingly, the networks that are used to transmit voice and data via telephony is also capable of transmitting the higher volumes necessary for picture transmission. This has given consumers the opportunity to switch away from the traditional telecommunications providers, now buying their telephone service from cable companies along with their subscription to a multitude of television channels. This, together with the rapid increase in the number of channels offered by digital broadcasting, will increase competition for viewer figures and ratings amongst the broadcasting companies. In the UK, competition was restricted to four terrestrial channels, two of which were public-service television broadcast by the BBC. That was the situation until the launch of Channel 5 in 1997 – satellite reception compliments of BSkyB and a cable company per geographical area. With the advent of digital broadcasting, the number of channels available to those prepared to pay a subscription will increase by a factor of approximately fivefold.

Changes to the media ownership rules (which were based on the number of broadcasting licenses held, but are now based on size of audience) reached across all media, bringing consolidation to the industry and the emergence of increasingly larger and larger players. All of the cable broadcasters operating within the UK are owned by American, or Canadian, parent companies, who saw the opportunity to capitalise on their extensive back catalogues of programmes and use them again on British audiences. No cable company operates across all of the UK, but each have regional franchises, and it is for this reason that BT has been prohibited from offering video on demand and other 'media-type' services down its telephone network. Although BT campaigned vigorously against this prior to the 1997 elections, the ruling is not expected to be overturned until the year 2000 thus giving the cable companies a chance to establish themselves.

Digital technology will also give the first opportunity for truly interactive television and, at that time, convergence of broadcast technology and computing technology is likely to occur in a meaningful way. There were rumours that Microsoft was considering the acquisition of BT,[61] whose attempts to grow had been frustrated by its failure to acquire Cable and Wireless while its search for global status had been frustrated by its failed attempt to buy the US group, MCI. Bill Gates has said:

> The fact that Microsoft has been a leader in the PC era should mean that we won't be a leader in the communications era. I'd like to defy that tradition.[62]

Microsoft has succeeded in making Windows the *de facto* software standard for personal computing by making the product readily available to all who would use it in the development of their own products and working with them. A merger or, more likely, an alliance of Microsoft, possibly through the new development they have opened in Cambridge with the BT laboratories at Martlesham, would allow both companies to leapfrog the first stage of convergence between television and telecommunications which is currently under way. Microsoft has already made strategic investments in the US in telephone companies and cable TV, and has bought a specialist producer of set-top boxes, WebTV.

There are also examples of cross-media ownership, for example; the Murdoch empire of newspapers and satellite television; EMAP, a large publisher of magazines, as well as being one of the largest radio-licence owners within the UK and Europe; and Pearson with its involvement in newspapers, publishing, and television production. The consolidation of interests will help create economies of scale and increased negotiating power with those wishing to buy advertising time or space in the programmes or the publications. However, the proliferation of channels may mitigate this since, as the broadcasters claim, the increase of channels allows better and tighter targeting of audiences and thus more effective advertising, those audiences will, by definition, become smaller and advertising is usually paid for by the size of audience reached. The impact of digital technology is not only going to be felt at the broadcast end by the large firms, it will also present an opportunity at the production end for small companies. Digital technology will allow dramatic improvements in the way that tape is edited and will facilitate small companies producing programmes edited on PCs. There has always been a history in the film and television industry of small companies being successful on low budgets, this can only be improved by digital technology.

As we have described earlier, driven by the deregulation of domestic financial markets and the improvement in communications, there has been a rapid internationalisation of the financial services industry. Banks that less than 20 years ago confined themselves primarily to their domestic markets now have offices in all of the world's important financial centres. The following statistics underline this dramatic growth:[63]

1. In 1980, the stock of international bank lending (cross-border lending plus domestic lending in foreign currencies) was $324 million – by 1991, it was $7.5 billion.

   In 1982, the total of international bonds outstanding was $259 million – by 1991, it was $1.65 trillion.

2. Between 1980 and 1990, the volume of worldwide cross-border transactions in equities grew, at a compound rate of 29 per cent per annum, from $120 billion to $1.4 trillion per year.

   In 1989, cross-border equity investment amounted to approximately 14.5 per cent of world stock turnover.

It is no longer unusual for investors to diversify their portfolio by investing overseas in foreign equities or bond markets, nor for companies to attempt to reduce their cost of capital by borrowing from foreign banks or raising their funding on foreign stock markets. As a consequence of the use of international sources of finance, many companies are becoming less recognisable as national corporations. By obtaining listings on more than one stock market, many companies are losing their national identity and the prospect of the 'stateless corporation' proposed by Reich is becoming a reality.[64] For companies like Hanson, traditionally labelled as a large British conglomerate, its dual listing on the London and the New York Stock Exchanges has allowed it to raise funds in both countries, to buy companies using shares in both countries, and to reward staff with stock options in both countries. It also helps to satisfy any regulatory or emotional considerations of local ownership. As more stock markets have reached international status and their opening hours have overlapped, the possibility of financial trading as an integrated continuous operation has opened up. The last gap of just one hour, between San Francisco closing and Tokyo opening, disappeared when New Zealand started to trade.

This continuous trading has its problematic side as events in the Far East have shown where, at the end of 1997, the economic growth slowed and the currencies of Malaysia, Thailand, and Indonesia came under pressure. The Japanese financial sector came under pressure and there were reports that the government would step in, using public funds to support both the banks and the stockmarket.[65] South Korea was granted a rescue package of $55 billion by the IMF, the World Bank, and others, and suspended operations at nine of the country's 30 merchant banks, whose lax short-term outlook was blamed for the country's economic crisis. Samsung, a Korean multinational conglomerate, cancelled an investment project in the UK worth £450 million because of the instability of their home market. The effect of the problems in the Far Eastern markets had their effect on international markets, depressing stock markets around the world, and it was only the robustness of the Hong Kong market which calmed the situation. The potential for bad news to travel fast from market to market is high, and the potential for crashes is higher with the size of the fall being higher also. With this in mind, it has even been suggested that there is a need for the regulation of foreign exchange markets – Dr Mahathir, Malaysia's prime minister, blamed currency traders and, in particular, hedge funds for all of the problems. However, it is unlikely that this will be possible as the wealth of increasingly large financial institutions continues to get larger than the economies of the countries in which they trade. The only country probably large enough to do it, the USA, is unlikely to do so for ideological reasons.

From what we have seen from the companies described above, for the service industries, the changes to the market over the next decade are likely to be brought about by increasing deregulation, the impact of various technologies and their convergence, and the changes in consumers' life styles.

The changing shape of Europe

The prospect of a single European currency and the combined countries of Europe acting in agreement may bring about a large enough trading block to wield similar economic influence to that of the US. There have been a number of arguments put forward for the gains that would be made by firms if this were to occur. Certainly, the removal of the exchange rate differences from transactions made by the members of the common currency would bring more stability to the companies in the countries involved, and significantly reduced exchange transaction and hedging costs. However, the reduced cost of currency conversion has been estimated at only 0.4 per cent of the GDP of the EU as whole.[66] Moreover, the single currency will create a larger market, particularly if a common economic policy can be adopted. In addition, according to an Andersen Consulting survey, two thirds of senior executives believe that competition will increase in their home market because of the transparency of prices.[67] This will further permit a pan-European price list, with the possibility of rationalisation to single-site production for companies. According to Johnson, the discipline of the European Central Bank should keep down the rate of price inflation, allow the economy to grow, and be strong enough to rival the dollar and the yen.[68]

There are, however, counter arguments and risks associated with the introduction of the single currency. By far the largest of these is the risk associated with the failure of the venture, the effects of which have been described as 'chaotic' and leading to the collapse not just of the currency, but of the whole EU.[69] Certainly, there will be disadvantages compared to those countries which do not immediately join, but retain their own currency since, by devaluing their currency against the Euro, those countries will gain competitive advantage. Similarly, if, through lack of political will, there is fudging of entry criteria, some countries who join will gain competitive advantage by virtue of the achieved exchange rate on entry. The political considerations will continue to be important as the member states decide a common policy on taxation, employment conditions, and state intervention in business.

> The fundamental question becomes: 'On a worldwide basis, there are now more countries in the world than there have ever been.'[70] So, is it better nowadays to be a small nation rather than a big one?

In summary, we can say that the issues facing those who plan for the future in organisations and have the responsibilities for ensuring success are as follows:

- Technological change will continue to be rapid and will involve the convergence of telecommunications, broadcasting, and computing.
- Harnessing the use of this converged technology will be essential for survival in companies which will need to have an increasingly global reach.
- The nature of employment and the relationship with staff will change, with management and leadership becoming more of a facilitating role in loosely organised 'shoal' firms.
- Firms will need to become more aware of knowledge building as a core competence.
- Alliances will become even more important, particularly for those firms where a global reach is not feasible or effective by wholly owned subsidiaries.
- Just as the relationship with employees will be more co-operative, so too will the relationship with communities and a broader church of stakeholders.
- Financial markets may continue to be volatile, but will become independent of nation states, as will the larger global companies.
- The feasibility of full political and economic integration within Europe – and how large 'Europe' actually turns out to be – is, as yet, unknown.

7 *The Case Material*

Our first study, 'Competitive Strategies in the World Airline Industry', was originally published in 1993 and, although still relevant today in 1998, it is interesting to consider how the airlines have applied the strategies described therein as the themes described in earlier chapters have evolved. The strategies adopted by Air France, British Airways, Delta, and Singapore Airlines in reaction to the trends described in Chapter 6 are described. The airlines have 'suffered', particularly from increasing globalisation, deregulation, and cut-throat competition, leading to reduced margins. Increasingly, privatisation has also had an impact on the players in the industry, although Air France, one of the companies described, is still receiving state support despite the protestations of British Airways to the European Court. In most cases, where it has not been possible to develop market share and the resultant cost efficiencies by merger or acquisition, the airlines have developed strategic alliances of varying degrees of formality. The strategies, described in Chapter 5, of competing globally and differentiating with a cost focus have allowed the airlines to offer passengers a seamless transfer between hub and feeder airports as they swap from one airline to the other, partnered, carrier.

The control of slots at hub airports is of vital importance to the principal carriers, hence the pressure referred to in the case for British Airways to release its stranglehold on the access to Heathrow and Gatwick, and the EU insistence on the release of more than 250 transatlantic slots before the alliance with Atlantic Airlines goes ahead. The development of loyalty schemes with ever-increasing benefits has also reflected their attempt to differentiate and thus build repeat business. This has depended upon the increased integration of IT systems (which we refer to in Chapter 6) into the operations of the carriers, and easier check-in, earlier in the journey, is a major point of differentiation. This presents one of a number of common points with the second case, where BAA, having recently launched the Heathrow Express, allows passengers to check in and secure their luggage in Central London, before travelling out to the airport at Heathrow in enhanced comfort. Both the airlines and BAA gain a significant advantage from the detailed marketing database of customers (BAA also has a loyalty scheme) to better assist them in servicing customer needs.

Our second case, BAA, reflects the importance we have placed on quality and continuous improvement in Chapter 6. BAA continuously monitor and measure customer satisfaction and their own performance, looking for ways that improvements can be made that benefit travellers and those concessionaires that serve them. Their partnership approach with suppliers and contractors shows many of the hallmarks of relationship marketing, and the recent launch of the Heathrow Express after a tunnelling setback could only be achieved by what is best described as a short-run strategic alliance with the contractor concerned. By empowering employees in a prizewinning performance, referred to in the case, they demonstrate the need for the new ways of working described for ABB and ISS in Chapter 6. This is further demonstrated by their approach to the staff in Indianapolis, for whom they assumed responsibility. To quote from their latest report:

> Our mission is to make BAA the most successful airport company in the world.
> This means:
> - Always focusing on our customers' needs and safety.
> - Achieving continuous improvements in the costs and quality of all our processes and services.
> - Enabling our employees to give of their best.

To achieve this they describe their strategy as being to:

> Concentrate on the core airport business, be prudently financed, continuously improve quality and cost effectiveness, become excellent in information technology, fully develop our property and retail potential, achieve world class standards in capital investment and develop an international business which enhances the quality and growth prospects of the Group.

This reflects the approaches that world-class companies are having to take, described in Chapter 5, to capitalise upon many of the trends we have referred to in Chapter 6. For example, the proposed advantages of a single currency and closer integration with mainland Europe are, for BAA, muted by the proposed abolition of duty- and tax-free (DTF) sales. By acquiring an American competitor, BAA have taken steps to reduce the impact of this by extending their global reach. The company has leveraged its core competencies of the management of airport operations and the management of retail operations by successfully bidding to operate overseas airports, capitalising on the deregulation trends referred to earlier as countries follow the UK example of privatising their airport utilities. The emphasis on cost efficiency is also an important one for the company in their property arm, Lynton, as they attempt to achieve world-best performance on price and deadlines in their construction projects.

1: COMPETITIVE STRATEGIES IN THE WORLD AIRLINE INDUSTRY*

The case study

This case examines the strategic response of leading international carriers to the competitive challenges currently facing the world airline industry. Three main strategies are being followed including: the expansion of global rout networks; customer/marketing-oriented strategies aimed at improving service quality and securing brand loyalty; and cost strategies. Maintaining a distinctive competitive advantage in any of these areas is becoming more difficult because similar strategies are being followed by all leading airlines. A major consolidation of the airline industry, both globally and in Europe, is already under way – a trend that will continue for the remainder of this decade. As a consequence, the sector will become increasingly dominated by a handful of global mega-carriers. In Europe, airline deregulation is unlikely to lead to more open competition or reduced airfares.

Introduction

The early years of this decade had been a watershed period for the world airline industry. For the first time in half a century of continuous growth, passenger volumes fell significantly in 1990 and over half of the 50 largest international airlines recorded losses. The immediate cause of such difficulties was the rapid decline in passenger volume as a consequence of the Gulf War. While the worst effects of this have now passed, the industry is currently facing a number of longer-term challenges which will have a more profound effect than anything since the 1960s, when jet power transformed the sector into a mass-transport industry. By the end of this decade, a major restructuring of the world airline industry will have occurred. In response, the major carriers are introducing a range of strategies in an attempt to ensure their long-term competitiveness.

The European airline industry is in the forefront of these developments. The establishment of an 'open skies', Common Air Transport Policy is a step in the process of European integration and the 'free movement of goods, persons, services, and capital'. This will create major opportunities for EC carriers to expand services into other member states. Attractive opportunities exist, too, in the newly opened markets of Eastern Europe and through

* This case study by Jim Hamill is reproduced by kind permission of the Editor, from *European Management Journal*, Vol. 11:3, pp. 332–41. Copyright EMJ 1993.

expanding transatlantic and Asia-Pacific routes. These opportunities need to be balanced against the competitive threats currently facing European airlines arising from market liberalisation; the entry into Europe of US and Asia-Pacific mega-carriers; rapid technology change; and industry restructuring through mergers, acquisitions, and strategic alliances. Scope for expansion is further limited by the highly congested air-traffic control system in Europe and the lack of availability of takeoff and landing slots at major airports.

This paper examines the main competitive challenges currently facing the world airline industry, taking into consideration both the global and European dimensions, and the strategic response of leading carriers to these challenges. Brief case studies of the competitive strategies of two leading European carriers (Air France and British Airways) are presented and compared with two of their global rivals, namely Delta of the US and Singapore Airlines. The issues examined in the paper are summarised in Figure 7.1A, which establishes a clear link between competitive challenges (industry trends) and strategic response. Table 7.1A, shows the ten largest international airlines by passenger revenue in 1991.

Industry trends and competitive challenges

The major competitive challenges currently facing the international airline industry include:

● **Gulf War** – this had a 'scissors' effect on the airline operations by increasing fuel prices and reducing passenger volumes. In the year to January 1991, passenger traffic worldwide fell by 12 per cent (compared to a forecasted increase of 7%); 15 400 flights were cancelled; and the industry reported total losses of $2.7 billion. Although essentially a short-term crisis, the effects of the war had longer-term implications for industry structure. Several carriers, already suffering from severe financial difficulties, were eventually forced into bankruptcy, including Continental, PAN AM, and TWA. As a consequence, the industry became even more highly concentrated, especially in the US where American, United, and Delta have become the undisputed 'Big Three'.

● **Recession** – the worst effects of the Gulf War have now passed and passenger volumes have increased. Mainly as a consequence of the current worldwide recession, however, passenger volumes are considerably lower than previous forecasts – especially in the high price business travel segment. A number of the leading international carriers remain in severe financial difficulties.

● **Long-term growth** – despite the current difficulties, long-term growth prospects for passenger travel remain good. The increasing globalisation of business; closer economic integration between countries; and the opening of new market opportunities (e.g., in Eastern Europe and China) will ensure a steady increase in passenger volumes through-out the 1990s. A doubling of air traffic is forecasted by the year 2000, although the actual increase may be constrained by air-traffic control problems and airport congestion.

● **Deregulation** – the gradual trend towards more 'open skies' is one of the most important developments currently affecting the competitive structure of the world airline industry, especially in Europe. The industry has long been highly regulated by national authorities, in bilateral and multilateral agreements which have controlled market access, limited competition, and fixed prices. Beginning in the US in the late 1970s, however, a gradual liberalisation of airline competition has taken place, which is now being extended to Europe. While actual progress has been slow, the EC is gradually moving towards a more liberal air transport system, a process that will continue during the remainder of the decade. Three 'packages' of air traffic deregulation in Europe have been introduced – in 1987, 1990, and 1992. The most radical is the 'Third Package' which is currently the subject of detailed negotiation and bargaining. When fully implemented, this will allow European airlines to set their own prices; the freedom to fly between EC countries; and to establish cabotage rights, i.e., the right of European airlines to operate domestic flights within any EC member state.

The liberalisation process will have a major impact on the competitive struc-ture of the European airline industry. The Third Package is designed to stimulate more open competition and reduce European airfares, which, on average, are still one third higher than in the US. Much detailed negotiation remains to be done, however, and the extent to which fares will be reduced and compensation increased will be constrained by several factors including mergers, acquisitions, and alliances; air traffic congestion; and the limited scope for a price war given the financial problems of many carriers. In the US, deregulation encouraged the entry of many new carriers into the indus-try. The resulting price war left many airlines in a financially weak position leading to a wave of mergers and acquisitions. As a consequence, the US airline industry is more concentrated now than before deregulation.

● **Global competition** – the last few years have witnessed the globalisation of airline competition, partly as a consequence of deregulation. The leading international carriers are engaged in a competitive battle covering the main global routes linking Asia, Europe, and North America. Established European carriers, such as British Airways, Air France, and Lufthansa, have expanded their transatlantic and Asia-Pacific services. US mega-car-riers (American, Delta, and United) have followed by aggressively expanding into Europe and the Far East. Smaller- and medium-sized airlines have responded to globalisation pressures by entering into strategic alliances, for example, the European Quality Alliance linking Austrian Airlines, Finnair, SAS, and Swissair designed to achieve scale efficiencies and joint marketing of services in an attempt to compete with the mega-carriers.

● **Privatisation** – several of the entrenched market leaders in the international airline industry achieved that position as a legacy of being state-owned 'flag carriers' granted a virtual monopoly of international routes. Over the last decade, however, carriers such as British Airways, Air France, Lufthansa, and Japan Airlines (JLA) have been privatised. The removal of state support has forced these companies to become much more customer/service orientated and to introduce cost control measures to improve efficiency. It has also provided them with greater flexibility to expand international routes, further globalising industry competition. Privatisation is also becoming an important issue in Eastern Europe, with Western carriers expressing interest in equity participation in airlines such as CSA of Czechoslovakia, Malev of Hungary, LOT of Poland, and Aeroflot of Russia. The emergence of more efficient and customer-orientated carriers from these countries will add to the competitive pressures currently being faced by the industry.

● **Congestion** – the extent to which the process of air deregulation will stimulate more open competition is severely constrained by congestion, especially in Europe. The European air-traffic control system is already overstretched and many of the major hub airports are operating at full capacity. This has the effect of squeezing out potential new entrants due to the lack of available takeoff and landing space. Slot access therefore is a crucial aspect of competitive strategy in the industry as is evident in the recent friction between British Airways and Virgin Atlantic concerning takeoff and landing rights at London Heathrow.

● **Overcapacity** – as a consequence of the above trends, there is significant overcapacity in the world airline industry, resulting in a large reduction in passenger load factors. A major consolidation and rationalisation of the industry is expected over the next few years through mergers, acquisitions, and strategic alliances. Forecasts predict that by the end of the decade, global routes will be dominated by a small number of carriers.

● **Technology** – the rapid pace of technology change is having a major impact on the competitive structure of the industry in at least two main ways. First, through improvements in computer reservation system (CRS) which have become crucial to achieving high load factors and the most efficient balance between price-sensitive economy passengers and the highly profitable business-class sector. Second, improvements in aerospace technology leading to the development of larger, more fuel efficient aircraft.

● **Safety/security** – overriding all of these trends is the continued threat of international terrorism, creating the need for large investments in airport safety and security.

Competitive strategies

In response to the competitive challenges arising from the broad trends summarised in the previous section, the leading international carriers have adopted a range of strategies to maintain and create competitive advantage. This section provides a broad overview of the main strategies being followed; the next section examines strategy in the four case companies. Figure 7.1A lists 11 main strategies currently being followed by the leading international carriers. These can be divided into three main categories covering: competitive positioning strategies; marketing and customer orientated strategies; and cost control.

Competitive positioning strategies

As in many other industries exhibiting globalisation trends, competitiveness in world airlines is increasingly dependent on size, market share, and geographical coverage. Carriers who stand to gain most from globalisation are those with high market shares and extended geographical route coverage. As a consequence, the leading international airlines have adopted a series of measures to consolidate and strengthen their competitive market positions. These include the expansion of global route networks, which is being greatly assisted by the progressive deregulation of the industry. As stated in the previous section, the leading international airlines from the US, Europe, and the Far East have been aggressively expanding their route networks into each other's markets. Closely related to the above, new market opportunities are being exploited, especially in Eastern Europe where political reforms have opened up previously restricted markets with major growth potential long term. The last few years have witnessed a wave of cross-border (and domestic) mergers, acquisitions, and strategic alliances (MAAs) in the industry. While cost control and rationalisation have been prime motivating factors, the boom in MAAs has also been brought about by attempts to consolidate and strengthen global route coverage, as shown clearly in the case examples to follow.

Two strategies crucial to achieving a strong competitive position on global routes are the establishment of a co-ordinated hub and spoke system and slot access. In a hub and spoke system, services from smaller airports (spokes) are fed into a much larger central hub. The hubs are then linked by direct flights. Especially on international routes, hub and spoke systems have a number of important advantages over point-to-point direct linkages.[1] These include the enormous potential for gaining multiplier effects on the number of city-pairs served (market coverage); high load factors through interconnecting flights; more effective carrier control of traffic; reduced dependency on the other carriers for connecting traffic; greater efficiencies in operations through increased aircraft utilisation and lower unit costs per passenger. Hub and spoke systems also provide the opportunity for establishing significant market power through controlling feeder flights and departures. As a consequence of these advantages, all of the case study companies examined later have aggressively tried to expand their hub and spoke networks in recent years. The main disadvantages of hub and spoke is airport congestion, especially during peak periods, arising from waves of almost simultaneous arrivals and departures.

The second factor crucial to achieving a strong competitive position through expanding global route coverage is slot access. Most of the major international hub airports are dominated by one (at most two) large carriers. Given the already high level of congestion at most hubs, extension of route coverage can often be achieved only at the expense of other carriers. Slot access is controlled by the air transport regulatory authorities. As a consequence, the leading international carriers have devoted considerable resources to bargaining for additional landing and takeoff rights at leading airports. This can be seen clearly at London Heathrow, where British Airways is coming under intense pressure from both US mega-carriers and from smaller UK competitors, such as British Midland and Virgin Atlantic, to relax its dominant control over landing and takeoff slots.

Marketing/customer-orientated strategies

The more competitive environment facing airline companies, deregulation, and privatisation of previously state-owned companies, have made it imperative that the leading international carriers adopt more marketing-orientated strategies aimed at securing customer satisfaction and loyalty. A range of strategies is being followed to achieve this objective. The development of efficient CRSs has become a key marketing weapon in the industry. They are a source of invaluable marketing information, as well as of profit through subscriptions. Their vast databases allow passengers to obtain a complete travel package including flight, hotel and car reservations, theatre bookings, etc. Probably their main advantage is the opportunities created for efficient market segmentation and positioning strategies to achieve the most profitable balance between first, business, and economy fare passengers. As a consequence, participation in a global CRS is now essential to provide a complete service to customers. The huge capital costs of setting up and operating these systems, however, has focused major airlines to pool resources and recent years have witnessed a consolidation of reservation networks through mergers and alliances. TWA and Delta, for example, merged their system with the largest Asian system (Abacus) to form Worldspan. In February, 1993, two of the worlds largest CRS (the European Galileo system and the US Cavin-Apollo) merged to form Galileo International. Ownership of the new group, which claims to be the first truly global CRS, is shared equally between major European and US carriers. Participating airlines include British

Airways, United Airlines, US Air, KLM, Swissair, Alitalia, Aerlingus, Air Canada, Olympic Airways, TAP, Air Portugal, and Austrian Airlines.

To support the above, the leading carriers have invested substantially in improving customer ground and in-flight services, while employing competent, trained, and highly motivated staff to implement this policy and deliver increased customer satisfaction. Global branding has become an important marketing tool for competitor differentiation involving large advertising expenditure.

Cost control

Given the more competitive environment and the weak financial position of many leading carriers, cost control strategies have been introduced aimed at achieving efficient, profitable operations. These have included mergers, acquisitions, and strategic alliances to share the costs of developing global routes; the purchase of larger, more fuel-efficient aircraft; and, in some cases, large-scale redundancies and radically changed working practices to control labour costs.

Some cases

Following the review of broad industry trends and strategic responses, this section examines the competitive strategies of four of the world's leading international airlines. Each case comprises three main sections covering competitive positioning strategies, marketing/customer orientated strategies, and cost control/efficiency measures. Figure 7.2A provides a summary of the main strategies being followed by each of the four carriers in each area.

Case 1: Air France

Air France is Europe's largest airline and the third largest in the world. Despite its size and extensive international route network, Air France has not been immune to the wider problems of the industry. The world recession and Gulf War led to heavy losses in 1990, and full recovery is not expected for some time. The company is facing much stronger competition in two of its major areas of operation, namely North American routes and Europe. The former is a consequence of the aggressive transatlantic expansion of US mega-carriers; the latter, a consequence of deregulation. Air France's major strategic response to these challenges include:

Competitive positioning strategies

Air France has made considerable efforts to strengthen and consolidate its already extensive international route network. This has included the opening of new routes and increasing the frequency of certain flights, but has been achieved mainly through acquisitions and strategic alliances. On transatlantic routes, new services have been started from French regional airports (Muhouse, Lille, Lyon, and Strasbourg) to New York; and several co-operative agreements have been established with US carriers (United, US Air, and American Airlines) to improve connecting flights within the US, joint promotional activities, and co-operation in information technology. In Europe, 39 new services from Paris and 45 from French regional cities were launched following the first deregulation package. Strategically important partnerships have been negotiated with Sabena of Belgium (involving a 37.5% equity stake) and Lufthansa, involving widespread co-operation of both flights and ground services. The agreements were aimed at achieving operating synergies, improved competitiveness, improved customer service, and economies of scale and scope. Air France has also entered the newly opened Eastern European market through its purchase of a 40 per cent stake in the Czechoslovak airline CSA and the creation of EuroBerlin – a joint venture between Air France (51%) and Lufthansa (49%).

The most important acquisition was the purchase of a 70 per cent stake in the large French carrier UTA in 1989, through which Air France also gained control of the domestic airline Air Inter. It was this agreement that established Air France as the largest carrier in Europe and the third largest in the world, giving the company a 95 per cent domestic market share. Prior to the acquisition, Air France lacked a strong domestic market base, being restricted to flights to Nice and Corsica. The link with UTA and Air Inter to form the Air France Group was aimed at creating an airline large enough to compete globally with the other mega-carriers from the US, Europe, and Asia. In addition to size, the three main strategic motivations underlying the merger were that it filled the major gap which existed in Air France's domestic route portfolio, allowing the group to develop a hub and spoke system similar to its major international competitors, a major strengthening of international route coverage, and operating synergies through streamlining and integration of the three companies. An important feature of this agreement was that it was approved (with conditions) by the European Commission. This was seen as a precedent encouraging other amalgamations in the European airline industry, supporting the view that the sector will become increasingly concentrated.

Marketing/customer-oriented strategies

Although few criticisms can be made against the quality of Air France's pre- and in-flight services, there is little in the group's customer orientation that distinguishes it from competitors. Carriers such as Delta and Singapore Airlines put much greater emphasis on service quality. The company has recently announced that its future strategy is to invest heavily in enhancing customer service, but little detailed information is yet available. Neither is there a distinctive competence or advantage in the area of personnel relations. Being a state-owned carrier, Air France is highly unionised and operated on the basis of rigid collective working agreements which have resulted in numerous industrial disputes.

Air France's major strengths in the marketing area lie in its CRS and market segmentation policies. Regarding the former, the group is one of the main participants in the European Amadeus system which is linked globally to Worldspan. The recent formation of Galileo International has created a major global competitor to Worldspan. Regarding the latter, Air France's extensive international route network allows considerable flexibility in pricing strategy, and segmentation. Several discount and promotional fares have been introduced including: 'Jeunes' aimed at young people travelling in Europe; 'Vacances' aimed at leisure travellers; and 'Temps Libre' for the over-65-year-old giving a price discount of 65 per cent. Market segmentation and positioning strategies were significantly improved following a merger with UTA and Air Inter. The combination of the three carriers allowed the Air France Group to provide different services depending on market requirements, for example, three-class Air France services to the US, UTA services to Africa and the South Pacific, and one-class Air Inter flights to Mediterranean leisure destinations.

Cost control strategies

As a consequence of the competitive challenges facing the airline industry, as summarised earlier in this paper, and problems with the postmerger integration of UTA and Air Inter, Air France has been experiencing financial difficulties and declining market share. This has encouraged the group to examine the efficiency of its operations. In the autumn of 1991, a major cost-cutting and restructuring programme was introduced including a freeze on recruitment, capital expenditure controls, a 6 per cent reduction in staffing level, reduced headquarters overheads, a major revision of salary scales, and so on. To support these measures, the group received a financial injection of FFR 2 billion from the French government and a further FFR 1.2 billion from Banque Nationale de Paris, who acquired an 8.8 per cent stake.

This led to claims of unfair competition from Air France's main competitors.

Case 2: British Airways (BA)

More than any other leading international carrier, British Airway's strategy has emphasised the importance of globalisation. The stated strategic objective of the company is to become the global industry leader. To achieve this, BA has been rapidly expanding its global route network, mainly through an aggressive acquisition and alliance policy; considerable emphasis has been put on developing a strong global brand image, quality and customer service, with cost control measures being introduced to improve efficiency. In achieving its global objectives, BA is facing a major competitive challenge from US mega-carriers who have considerably expanded their transatlantic routes (which account for over two thirds of BA's operating profit) and from smaller independent airlines such as Virgin Atlantic and its main domestic UK rival, British Midland.

Competitive positioning strategies

Even before privatisation in 1987, BA operated a global route network based on its hub at Heathrow airport. Subsequent acquisitions and strategic alliances have consolidated and strengthened this network. The process, however, has not been without problems and BA has on several occasions been frustrated in its attempts to find suitable global partners.

The first major acquisition following privatisation was the 1987 takeover of British Caledonian at a total cost to BA of £353 million. This considerably strengthened the company's domestic market position. Attention is now focused on finding suitable foreign partners to expand BA's network both in the US and Europe.

Due to the importance of transatlantic routes and the attractiveness of the large domestic market, BA established a link with United Airlines (ULA) in 1987. The alliance established one of the most comprehensive 'one-stop' services covering 305 destinations worldwide. In 1989, BA attempted to reinforce this relationship by taking a 15 per cent stake in UAL, but this did not take place due to the US partner's inability to raise its share of the $750 million investment. The marketing alliance with UAL was to prove to be one of several frustrated attempts by BA to expand globally through acquisitions and collaborations, and was terminated in 1990 when United bought Pan Am's London routes for $200 million. This gives it a major base at London Heathrow, in direct competition with BA on transatlantic routes.

United has since established a strategic partnership with BA's main UK competitor, British Midland, to provide feeder flights for its transatlantic Heathrow service.

Other frustrated attempts to expand global routes through MAAs include aborted merger negotiations between BA, KLM, and Sabena; the later unsuccessful attempt to acquire KLM; and the aborted alliance with Delta in the US, under which BA flights from Gatwick to Dallas-Fort Worth would have provided daily connecting services with 23 Delta destinations. This alliance broke down when Delta formed its 'Global Excellence Partnership' with Singapore Airlines and Swissair.

BA's most recent attempt to expand its transatlantic network has also run into serious difficulties. In July, 1992, the company announced it was spending $750 million to acquire a 44 per cent stake in US Air, the sixth largest domestic carrier. This would provide BA with feeder flights to 204 US cities compared to the 91 it already operated. The proposed deal was bitterly opposed by other US carriers during the presidential election campaign. As a consequence, BA had to settle for a more limited partnership with US Air. Even this deal may be blocked by the new Clinton administration, which is under intense pressure from UAL, Delta, and American Airlines to veto the deal with the US carriers, demanding greater slot access to Heathrow in return. Finally, BA has recently acquired Dan Air of the UK and a small equity stake in Quantas of Australia.

In addition to the MAAs discussed above, BA has attempted to expand its route network in other ways including expansion into Eastern Europe. In the short term, BA's main concern is to retain its dominant control over slot access at London Heathrow. In 1991, the British government partially opened up Heathrow to new competition, which encouraged 17 new carriers to move into the airport. A further relaxation of BA's dominant position, especially allowing greater access to the US mega-carriers, may be necessary to ensure the US Air deal is not blocked by the US authorities. At the time of writing, Richard Branson's Virgin Atlantic is threatening legal action against BA in both US and European courts concerning allegations of anti-competitive practices and a 'dirty tricks' campaign. Given the uncertainty regarding the US Air deal, BA could well do without a lengthy US court case.

Marketing/customer-orientated strategies

Even before privatisation, BA's most important marketing challenge was to change a corporate image in which the initials BA were widely seen as standing for 'Bloody Awful'. In the early 1980s, a major staff training programme entitled 'Putting People First' was introduced to gain a quality advantage over competitors. This was latter supported by a major promotional campaign under the theme of 'The World's Favourite Airline'.

In more recent years, a series of marketing initiatives and product enhancements have been aimed at improving market share in response to the recession and stronger competition being experienced, especially on transatlantic routes. These included a radically changed branding policy covering different market segments. Following extensive passenger research, the standard terminology of first, business and economy-class passenger segments was replaced with a sevenfold classification which was more customer oriented, including Concorde, First Class, Club World, Club Europe, World Traveller, Euro Traveller, and Super Shuttle. In 1991, the 'Winning for Customers' campaign was launched modelled on the earlier 'Putting People First'. All employees in the group were involved in the scheme which was aimed at improving customer service, thereby differentiating BA from its competitors. Providing a superior service and good value for money in each of its market segments is a prime goal of BA as stated in its mission statement. The effects on the group's image of the current dispute with Virgin remains to be seen.

Finally BA's ability to provide an efficient, global service to customers has been enhanced by the fact that it is one of the major participants in the newly formed Galileo international computer reservation system.

Cost control

BA, like most other leading international carriers, has introduced a range of measures to control costs and improve efficiency. These have included a substantial reduction in employment levels, new working practices, and wage and salary controls. As a consequence, there has been a substantial improvement in productivity levels. The changes, however, have not been without cost. In late 1992, cabin crews threatened industrial action over plans to reduce minimum rest breaks on short-haul flights and increase maximum flight times on long-hauls. A recent survey of all employees highlighted major problems in staff morale and motivation. For the future, BA's ability to achieve further cost savings depends on how successfully it integrates its various mergers and alliances.

Case 3: Delta

Until 1978, Delta was a purely domestic US airline. In the ten years following deregulation, the company's strategy was focused primarily on strengthening its domestic market position in response to the more severe competitive environment and ensuing price war. The company is now one of the largest US mega-carriers. Since the late 1980s, Delta's strategy has focused on further consolidating its market position in the US, combined with a major attempt to internationalise its operations. Although significant internationalisation has taken place, the bulk of the company's operations is still concentrated in the US.

As with the other airlines examined in this paper, Delta has adopted a range of strategies in response to the major competitive challenges facing the industry. Particular emphasis has been placed, however, on the quality of the company's personnel and on customer service. The main strategies pursued under the three headings identified earlier include:

Competitive positioning strategies

Delta's initial attempts at strengthening its route network were concentrated in the US. By the mid 1980s, the company had already established a strong presence in the Eastern Seaboard, with Atlanta being its largest hub. The acquisition of Western Airlines in 1987 extended this market coverage to the western half of the US, and the company now operates a highly integrated national hub and spoke network based around Atlanta, Salt Lake City, Los Angeles, Dallas-Fort Worth, and Cincinnati. The company's competitive position in the US was further threatened in 1987 with the signing of a ten-year agreement whereby Delta became the 'Official Airline' of Disney World. This provided Delta with major marketing opportunities, including the development of on-site ticketing and packaged vacations.

In more recent years, Delta's route network strategy has focused on internationalisation, which has been achieved through both internal expansion, but primarily through acquisitions and alliances. These have included expansion into Canada and Mexico, following its acquisition of Western Airlines and the establishment of connecting flights to the Caribbean jointly with JAL.

The two most important deals, however, were the acquisition of major transatlantic routes following the liquidation of Pan Am and the 'Global Excellence' alliance with Singapore Airlines (SIA) and Swissair. New routes added as a consequence of the former include: New York to various European destinations; Miami to London; Detroit to London; and Pan Am's Frankfurt hub. The latter is particularly important as it will allow Delta to develop Frankfurt not only as a transatlantic hub, but also as a base for intra-European services in a deregulated market. The alliance with SIA and Swissair was aimed at achieving cost savings and strengthening Delta's market position in Europe and the Asia-Pacific region through co-ordination of flight schedules, improved connecting services, joint marketing, sharing ground-handling facilities, cabin crew exchanges, and joint fuel purchases. In the longer term, there is scope for Delta to develop a Pacific hub based in Taipei (Taiwan) to provide connecting services between its US gateway cities and points in Asia. Finally, Delta is one of the three large US mega-carriers currently in dispute with BA over slot access at Heathrow which is crucial to the further expansion of the group's transatlantic routes.

Marketing/customer-orientated strategies

Delta was an industry leader in establishing a revenue control system to manage the allocation of seats among different fare categories – a system of extreme importance in the postregulated market characterised by frequent competitive price changes. Other major marketing initiatives include a Frequent Flyer Programme to gain customer loyalty and market segmentation strategy aimed at broadening its customer base by focusing on special passenger markets, such as Walt Disney, family and senior citizen travellers, groups and conventions (Democratic and Republican Parties), and so on. In the area of CRS, Delta is a leading participant in Worldspan.

The most important customer-orientated strategy, however, and the way in which Delta attempts to differentiate itself from its competitors is the quality of its personnel. The company's philosophy is that effective management of human resources will promote productivity and greatly benefit the quality of customer satisfaction and loyalty. The main elements of its human resource management approach include a no-redundancy policy promising job security and creating staff loyalty to the company, non-unionisation, flexible working practices, extensive staff training, and Customer Service Awards to exceptional staff which include share of stock. Delta believes that it is the quality of its relationship with employees which distinguishes it from competitors and this is reflected in the groups promotional campaign which emphasises employee commitment. The major challenge facing Delta in this area is the integration of 7000 ex-Pan Am employees into the corporate culture.

Cost control strategies

Delta operates one of the most modern, fuel efficient, and technologically advanced fleets giving it a major operating advantage over US competitors. The company, however, recorded significant operating losses in the financial years 1991 and 1992. This has led to a major cost-cutting programme including a reduction of more than $5 billion from its capital expenditure programme, and including the purchase of 100 fewer aircraft; cutting personnel through attrition; consolidation of facilities; a streamlining of flights; and more use of part-time and contract staff – aimed at a fundamental change in its cost structure.

Case 4: Singapore Airlines (SIA)

SLA first flew under its own colours in October 1972 following the break-up of Malaysia-Singapore Airlines. The new carrier has had an outstanding record of growth and profitability since the de-merger. In terms of passenger revenue, SIA ranks as only the twentieth largest airline in the world. It is the tenth largest, however, in terms of international passenger volume – an impressive performance given the extremely small domestic market (a population of less than three million). More significantly, SIA is one of the world's most profitable airlines.

The success of SIA has been due, more than for any other airline, to the importance it attaches to a customer-oriented philosophy and service culture. However, the continued ability to differentiate its services is being threatened by stronger competition and the adoption of more customer-focused strategies by other leading carriers. Especially in the growing Asia-Pacific routes, SIA is facing more severe competition from Western airlines and from other Asian carriers, including Cathay Pacific, JAL, Thai International, Malaysia Airlines, and a new Taiwanese start-up called Eva Air. As a consequence, SLA has formed several strategic alliances to strengthen its global route coverage; has introduced cost control measures, while attempting to retain the quality of service on which its reputation has been built.

Competitive positioning strategies

SIA's emergence as a leading international carrier was greatly assisted by the long-term economic boom in the Far East and its strategically well-located home base, which is a natural hub for East–West and North–South traffic. Despite its locational advantage, the company has avoided the strategy of developing as a major global mega-carrier, characteristic of the other airlines examined in this paper. The company's mission statement emphasises the importance of customer service and cost efficiency rather than the development of global route networks. In the last few years, however, greater attention has been paid to strengthening route coverage given the growing intensity of competition being faced from the other mega-carriers, especially on the highly lucrative Asian routes. This has been achieved mainly through strategic alliances with other leading airlines including KLM, Air

Canada, and Lufthansa. By far the most important co-operative agreement, however, is the 'Global Excellence' alliance formed between SIA, Delta, and Swissair. The trilateral alliance established a co-ordinated global route network covering 288 cities in 82 countries. Partners were chosen because they exhibited the same commitment to service excellence as SIA.

Customer-orientated strategies

SIA's commitment to service excellence and customer care is now world famous. The company's philosophy has been to differentiate itself from competition by offering the best quality service available. Until recently, this has been built around a soft service image based on the natural warmth and hospitality of Singaporeans, supported by a large advertising budget (e.g., Singapore Girl). Global competitive pressures have led SIA to complement this soft image with the application of advanced technology to provide service excellence. The group's use of technology to improve customer care has been examined in detail in a case by Vandermerwe and Lovelock,[2] with major improvements being introduced in the quality of both on-the-ground and in-flight services including:

- The Abacus computer reservation system now merged into Worldspan.

- An innovative Priority Passenger Service (PPS) whereby the recorded preferences of such passengers (seats, meals, etc.) are automatically retrieved from the computer.

- Major improvements in Departure Control Systems through simplified check-in procedures, machine readable boarding passes and baggage tags, etc.

- Analysis of survey data for input to the Quality/Productivity Index.

- Other innovations including video screens on each seat, satellite linked air-to-ground telecommunications systems (e.g., video games), on-board business facilities (e.g., faxes, computers, etc).

Cost control strategies

The application of technology as described above has allowed SIA both to differentiate itself from competitors and, at the same time, follow a cost-leadership strategy. As stated previously, SIA is one of the most profitable airlines in the world. This is mainly due to rigid attention to cost control and the fact that it operates one of the most modern and cost efficient fleets of aircraft in the world rather than to market power.

Conclusion

The industry trends and competitive strategies examined in this case have major implications for the future of the airline industry in Europe. The three requirements for airline competitiveness in a turbulent global environment are:

1. The establishment (either internally or through MAAs) of an extensive global route network supported by a strong hub and spoke system.
2. Continual improvements in service quality and customer satisfaction.
3. Rigid attention to cost control to achieve efficient, profitable operations.

Maintaining a distinctive competitive advantage in these areas is becoming much more difficult as similar strategies are being followed by all leading airlines. The most likely 'winners' are the already well-established global mega-carriers. The most likely 'losers' are smaller- and medium-sized airlines, who will be confined to exploiting niche markets or will be acquired by larger carriers. A major consolidation of the European (and global) airline industry through MAAs is already under way – a trend which will continue for the rest of the 1990s. As a consequence, it is unlikely that European deregulation will result in a more openly competitive airline industry or reduced fares. Rather, the sector will become dominated by a handful of global mega-carriers.

Table 7.1A   The ten largest international airlines by revenue in 1991

Carrier	Country	Revenue ($m)	Profits ($m)	Passenger Miles in Billions	Rank by Revenue	Rank by Passenger Miles
America (AMR)	US	12 993	(240)	82.3	1	1
Air France Group	France	11 823	(122)	33.3	2	8
United Airlines	US	11 784	(332)	82.3	3	1
Japan Airlines	Japan	10 627	(100)	32.6	4	9
Lufthansa	Germany	9 713	(251)	32.6	5	10
Delta	US	9 170	(324)	62.1	6	3
British Airways	UK	9 064	685	40.9	7	6
Northwest	US	7 534	(3)	53.2	8	4
All Nippon Airways	Japan	6 634	55	23.0	9	12
US Air Group	US	6 533	(305)	34.1	10	7
Singapore	Singapore	3 044	521	21.7	20	13

Source: IATA

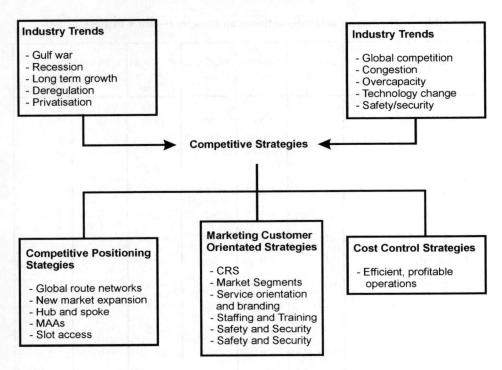

Figure 7.1A Competitive challenges and strategies in the world airline industry

Competitive Positioning Strategies	Air France	British Airways	Delta	Singapore Airlines
	Expansion of Transatlantic and European routes; to establish domestic/ international hub and spoke system; alliances with Sabena and Lufthansa	Rapid expansion of international route network aimed at becoming global industry leader; aggressive MAA strategy, but not always successful; protection of slot access at Heathrow is vital	Strengthening of domestic route network followed by internationalisation; acquisition of Western Airlines and Pan Am's transatlantic routes; Global Excellence alliances with Swissair and SIA; competitive battle with BA for slot access at Heathrow; development of Euro-hub at Frankfurt	Emphasis on customer satisfaction rather than development of global routes; competitive pressures on most profitable routes encourage the formation of Global Excellence alliances with Delta and Swissair; strategic location as major hub for North/South, East/West traffic
Marketing/ Customer Orientated Strategies	Major investment to take place in improving quality and customer service; particularly in Amadeus and Worldspan CRS	Major promotional campaign to change corporate image; strong emphasis on branding; participant in Galileo international CRS	Strong emphasis on quality of its personnel, customer service and satisfaction; efficient global CRS	Strong emphasis on service excellence and customer care; recent use of advanced technology to improve customer satisfaction
Cost Control Strategies	Major cost cutting and restructuring programme; financial investment from French government and Banque National de Paris	Major cost cutting and rationalisation measures introduced following privatisation; further cost savings dependent on successful MAA integration	Modern, fuel efficient and technologically advanced fleet; major cost cutting programme introduced following losses in early 1990s	Highly profitable airline due to application of technology, newness of its fleet and rigid control of costs

Figure 7.2A   Competitive strategies of four leading international carriers: summary

CASE STUDY 2: BAA PLC*

Introduction

In 1987 the British Airport Authority changed its name to BAA plc and was floated on the UK stock exchange, as one of the first of a number of privatisations made by the Conservative government. Immediately after World War II, the Labour government had nationalised all commercial airfields and airlines, and brought them under the control of the new Ministry of Civil Aviation. At that time three airlines were created: BEA serving UK domestic and short-haul European destinations; BOAC serving the Commonwealth, North America, and the Far East; and BSAA flying to South America. BOAC subsequently absorbed BSAA and was later merged with BEA to form British Airways. During the mid 1960s, the bureaucracy of government-centred management was considered inappropriate to run airports, particularly one the size of Heathrow, and the British Airport Authority was created. The 1965 legislation, The Airports Authority Bill, brought together Heathrow, Stanstead, and Gatwick airports in England and Prestwick in Scotland under one management structure. BAA acquired Edinburgh airport from the Government in 1971, and subsequently bought Glasgow and Aberdeen airports from the Corporation of Glasgow and the Civil Aviation Authority respectively. Prestwick Airport was subsequently sold and Southampton Airport acquired to give the present portfolio of UK facilities.

In preprivatisation days, the organisation was run with a fairly high degree of autonomy from central government, which made the transition to the commercial world somewhat easier. In addition to these UK facilities, BAA is in the third year of a contract to manage the Indianapolis airport system, manages the shops and catering facilities at Pittsburgh airport, is the controlling partner in the management of Naples airport, and in 1997, won the contract to manage Melbourne airport for 99 years.

The company is now the world's largest commercial operator of airports. Heathrow and Gatwick are truly international airports, whilst the other five service mainly the UK and European market.

---

*   Research for this case study was funded by a grant from the Company of Firefighters

Table 7.1B   Passenger destinations 1995/96

Passenger destinations (%)	Heathrow	Gatwick	Aberdeen	Edinburgh	Glasgow	Stanstead	Southampton
UK/Channel Isles	18.0	8.0	85.3	86.2	53.9	50.0	82.0
Rest of EU	32.0	49.6	9.0	13.0	33.3	44.0	18.0
Rest of Europe	12.8	12.0	5.7	7.0	5.5	6.5	
North America	17.4	9.4		0.1	7.2		
Middle East & Far East	13.0	3.1				0.1	
North Africa	3.4	3.6			0.1		
Rest of World	3.4	4.3				0.1	

Source: Retail report, 1996

Since privatisation BAA has shown steady year-on-year growth both in traffic statistics and financial results, as is shown in Table 7.2A.

Table 7.2B   BAA performance statistics

Traffic statistics	1987	1988	1989	1990	1991	1992	1993	1994	1995	1996
Passengers (millions)										
Terminal	55.3	63.7	68	71.3	72	72	77.7	82	87.7	93.6
International	44.2	51	54.4	56.6	56.9	57.4	62.9	66.4	71.2	75.7
Movements 000s,	626	680	715	766	791	815	847	871	895	931
Cargo (000s tonnes)	864	951	1 021	1 090	1 082	1 079	1 156	1 305	1 480	1 552
Profit and Loss	£M	£M	£M	£M	£M	£M	£M	£M	£M	£M
Revenue	439	523	630	746	834	903	952	1098	1159	1253
Profit for the year	78	105	137	185	189	153	211	240	279	315
Balance Sheet										
Fixed assets	956	1 212	1 987	2 605	2 916	2 952	3 039	3 604	4 099	4 545
Net current liabilities	(88)	(129)	(109)	(206)	(246)	(247)	(133)	(238)	(491)	(237)
	868	1 083	1 878	2 399	2 670	2 705	2 906	3 366	3 608	4 308
Creditors due after 1 year	(174)	(185)	(472)	(515)	(794)	(825)	(859)	(823)	(763)	(1 141)
Shareholders' funds	694	898	1 406	1 884	1 876	1 880	2 047	2 543	2 845	3 167
Earnings per share (p)	7.8	10.5	13.7	18.5	18.9	15.2	20.9	23.5	27.2	30.5
Dividend per share (p)	-	3.6	4.5	5.8	6.5	7.3	8	9	10.1	11.3
Net asset value per share (£)	0.7	0.9	1.4	1.9	1.9	1.9	2	2.5	2.8	3.1

Source: BAA annual reports.

Heathrow is by far the most important contributor to both the company's revenue and profit.

Table 7.3B   Revenue, profit, and net assets, 1996

£ million Airports	Revenue	Operating profit	Net assets
Heathrow	760	323	2 174
Gatwick	268	80	827
Stanstead	54	(11)	589
Glasgow	65	19	200
Edinburgh	33	11	54
Aberdeen	25	8	59
Southampton	9		51
Total Airports	1 214	430	3 954
Non-airport property	23	14	273
Other	5		(23)
Total UK	1 242	444	4 204
US	11	(1)	8

Source: BAA annual report, 1996.

As Table 7.4B indicates, the majority of the revenue for BAA comes from airport and traffic charges and retail operations, and the retail operations play a larger part in the income generation of the group.

Table 7.4B   Revenue by source

£ million *Airports*	Airport/traffic charges	Retail	Property	Other	Total
Heathrow	258	347	133	22	760
Gatwick	84	138	36	10	268
Stanstead	14	27	10	3	54
Glasgow	35	23	5	2	65
Edinburgh	22	8	2	1	33
Aberdeen	16	5	4		25
Southampton	5	2		2	9
Total Airports	434	550	190	40	1 214
Non-airport property			23		23
Other				5	5
Total UK	434	550	213	45	1 242
US		6		5	11

Source: BAA annual report, 1996.

Consequently:

- BAA now makes more money from its retail, car parking, and other concessions than it does from landing fees for aircraft. In general, the retailing operations in recent times have shown better performance than their traditional High Street counterparts.

- The company can be described as currently established in four main spheres of activity: running major airports; offering high-quality retail and catering outlets; the management of a substantial property portfolio; and maintaining a continuous programme of capital development projects – the latter three revolving around the core function of airport operation.

- The company handles more than 100 million people annually and the figure is expanding every year. Public demand for air travel from its three southeast airports alone – Heathrow, Gatwick, and Stanstead – is expected to double by 2013.

- Sir John Egan, the chief executive, has made it clear that to meet the rapid growth in air traffic, BAA needs to build the equivalent capacity of a new passenger terminal every two or three years.

- In the run up to privatisation, BAA was investing a little over £150 million per annum in new facilities and equipment, such as Terminal 4 and the massive expansion of Stanstead in the 1980s. Capital expenditure has mushroomed since then, rising to almost £1 million per day in the early 1990s.

- The company is currently engaged in a three-year programme to invest £1.4 billion, with the outlay expected to be maintained if formal approval is received for Terminal 5 at Heathrow. Terminal 5 would be BAA's largest single capital project, accommodating nearly 30 million additional passengers a year and costing around £1.5 billion. Because of the heavy capital commitments, there is a continual effort to secure better value for money from the large projects with which it is involved.

Table 7.5B   World rankings

Position	Total international passengers	Total terminal passengers	Airport charges
1	London (Heathrow)	Chicago	Tokyo
2	Frankfurt	Atlanta	Frankfurt
3	Paris (CdeG)	Dallas	Vienna
4	Hong Kong	London (Heathrow)	Chicago
5	Amsterdam	Los Angeles	New Jersey
6	Tokyo (Naria)	Tokyo (Haneda)	Berlin
7	Singapore	Frankfurt	Munich
8	London (Gatwick)	San Francisco	New York
9	New York	Miami	Amsterdam
10	Bangkok	Denver	Brussels
11		Seoul	Paris (CdeG)
12		New York	Athens
13		Paris (CdeG)	Oslo
14		Detroit	Helsinki
15		Hong Kong	Moscow
16		Las Vegas	Copenhagen
17		Phoenix	Stockholm
18		Minneapolis	Lisbon
19		Paris (Orly)	Dublin
20		Newark	Johannesburg
21		St. Louis	Orlando
22		Amsterdam	Miami
23		Houston	Singapore
24		Boston	Washington
25		Tokyo (Narita)	Madrid
26		Honolulu	London (Heathrow)
27		Singapore	Milan
28		Bangkok	Los Angeles
29		Seattle	Budapest
30		London (Gatwick)	Vancouver

The core business is driven by passenger volume and air traffic volume, both of which have been rising continuously over the years since privatisation. Passenger volume itself is driven by both domestic and international demand for travel either for business or pleasure. The strength of demand for these travel reasons can be directly related to economic activity and personal incomes. The growth in demand is primarily due to substitution, where travellers will compare the respective prices, and convenience, of all available modes of transport. At present, the falling real price of air transport relative to other forms of transport means that the substitution threshold is approximately 450 kilometres and falling.[1] Whilst domestic demand at BAA is driven by the economic well-being of the UK, international demand is driven by world GDP. This offers an advantage to BAA at Heathrow and Gatwick, where a large proportion of its passengers are travelling from outside the UK and transferring between flights. This puts these two airports in competition with the other European hub airports of Charles de Gaulle (Paris), Schipol (Amsterdam), and Frankfurt – all of which are competitors for international transfers. A comparison of financial performances across these five airports is difficult since BAA is the only operator not in public ownership. However, it can be seen from Table 7.5B that Heathrow simultaneously has both the highest number of international passengers in the world and airport charges amongst the lowest.

Regulation

As a regulated quasi-monopoly, BAA is subject to price control on its airport charges. This economic regulation is the responsibility of the CAA, under advice from the Monopolies and Mergers Commission. Price controls apply to airport charges which include takeoff, landing, and parking fees which are calculated by reference to the weight of the aircraft, plus a per capita fee for every departing passenger carried. The fees for cargo are based on weight.

The regulation of airports is governed by International Treaty and, under these agreements, airport charges must be calculated at cost. An additional condition of the treaties, known as Bermuda 2, dictates that airport charges should be arrived at by a 'single till' approach and calculated as follows:

> Asset value x reasonable rate of return = current cost operating profit
>
> Current cost operating profit + operating costs = revenue required
>
> Revenue required – commercial revenue = airport charges

Commercial revenue includes earnings by incidental operations, such as duty-free sales and the sale of services to the airlines. The principal points of negotiation at the five-yearly review relate to the capital base in terms of its value and the fair rate of return that should be expected. There are other formulae by which regulation could be imposed and the government has suggested that the price-cap method may not continue after the present five-year period. However, other methods such as direct-tariff regulation and dividend regulation are respectively applied to complex pricing of utilities or they are not suitable to companies with large capital investment programmes.

The price-cap regulation as described has the characteristic that the firm regulated cannot have weighted-average price increases which are greater than the retail price index less x per cent (RPI minus x). The RPI is used rather than the specific industry cost index because the latter could be manipulated by a monopolistic player that the regulator was trying to control and because it gives customers' a clear prediction of prices. The main advantage to both firm and customers is that they know the inflation-adjusted average prices for the coming five years and that during that period, any savings will flow directly through to profits. This incentive to cost efficiency for the firm will last until the end of the five-year period, during which time the operator can retain the benefits, but after which the regulator can pass on savings to customers by setting a higher value to x. Paradoxically, because of the 'single till' approach, the more profitable BAA becomes at airport retailing (and they are already the best in Europe), the further down their permitted airport charges will be driven at the next review. There would seem to be little long-run incentive for the company to put too much emphasis into retailing. However, in discussions between the UK and US Governments in 1994, it was suggested that the single till might not apply indefinitely.

Quality of service is not formally regulated and it is argued that costs could be reduced by lowering the quality of service. Not all services provided by BAA are subject to price-cap regulation, and check-in-desk rental falls into this category. For the first five years after privatisation, the maximum charge was set at RPI minus 1 per cent. For the second quinquennium, the CAA originally proposed a tariff of RPI minus 8 per cent for each of the five years, but after representation from BAA and a number of user airlines which felt that such a regime would deter investment, this was reduced to RPI minus 8 per cent for two years, RPI minus 4 per cent for one year, and RPI minus 1 per cent for the last two. The MMC had originally proposed a price cap of RPI minus 4 per cent for Heathrow and Gatwick, with the caveat that charges could be increased at Heathrow if work commenced on Terminal 5, but that overall, the southeastern airports would be capped at RPI plus1 per cent. There is a similar ruling to allow for the cancellation of duty-free allowances which has been proposed by the EU. Thus Heathrow and Gatwick can have separate pricing policies, and Stanstead is only subject to the overall formula applied to the three airports.

Since security standards are imposed by the Department of Transport, any required increases that relate to security issues are exempt from the price cap and can be passed on.

Some airlines have argued that passenger volumes are not the only variables involved and IATA (International Air Travel Association) have suggested that the RPI minus x per cent price cap should be supplemented by adjustments for the value of mail and cargo.

Although the UK Government no longer has an equity stake in BAA, it does hold a 'golden share'. This share ownership prevents any party from holding more than 15 per cent of the voting rights, and prevents BAA itself from disposing of Heathrow, Gatwick, or Stanstead without the consent of parliament. Similarly, BAA can only be forced to dispose of an airport by an act of parliament.

As a result of the expansion of Manchester airport, BAA's market share for air passenger volume and cargo tonnage have declined from 73 per cent and 85 per cent to 71 per cent and 81 per cent respectively since privatisation in 1987. Because of BAA's dominant position, virtually any significant expansion of its activities in the UK or EU would require approval by the competition authorities. However, even though RPI minus x per cent is a maximum permitted price, predatory pricing is not allowed and Stanstead, which charges marginal cost, has given an undertaking not to target airlines which operate from Luton, with which it competes.

Airport management

Airport management can be divided into terminal management and airfield management. Terminal staff have responsibility for security, engineering, and customer services, whilst airport operations range from snow clearing to firefighting. Approximately one third of BAA employees work in security, mainly in the screening of passengers and hand luggage prior to going airside. At a cost of £175 million, a system to screen hold baggage for international passengers departing UK airports is substantially complete, making the company a clear leader in airport security. The system, the world's most advanced and effective, was developed by a team comprising the Departments of the Environment and Transport, the regions, and BAA, with the development led by BAA. Capitalising on this expertise, the company have developed consultancy and training services to guide other organisations who wish to enhance their security.

More than 90 airlines have established a base at Heathrow, enabling the airport to offer an unrivalled choice of destinations and services. Each year 390 000 flights bring more than 58 million passengers to and from the airport – and around 30 per cent of these are transferring to other flights. At peak times, there is a takeoff or landing every 90 seconds to meet the continuous demands from airlines and passengers for Heathrow's services.

Each airport is licensed by the CAA under the Air Navigation Act 1985, and this legislation ensures that, in addition to being competent, the operator provides takeoff and landing facilities to all aircraft on equal terms. Under the license, BAA has the responsibility for monitoring noise and air pollution on behalf of the CAA.

Additionally the CAA will, on behalf of the Department of Transport, exercise limits on aircraft movements, for example on night flights, and has the power to redistribute air traffic between airports to minimise congestion.

Airport capacity is determined by several factors, the principal of which are: runway layout, number of runways, gates at the terminal, and number of positions on the apron. Within each terminal, the check-in capacity depends on access to the airport, the number of check-in counters, and the capacity and sophistication of the baggage-handling system.

British Airways estimate that the European single market has helped increase the volume of transfer passengers by approximately 20 per cent,[2] and this has had the effect of increasing the pressure on the baggage-handling systems at its main hub, Heathrow – sometimes, passengers will only have 30 minutes between connecting flights and their luggage has to keep up with them. BAA are solving this problem with the completion of a £60 million investment in developing an existing tunnel between Terminals 1 and 4 as a high-speed luggage link. Baggage will be transported on automated carts in an estimated 11 minutes. The system is being built by the same company, BAE Automated Systems of Dallas, that designed and built the system for Denver, one of the largest hubs in America. Most airports use bar-code tags now for luggage, where the reader will automatically direct luggage. However, these tags will often suffer mechanical damage on conveyor belts and Heathrow is already investigating the possibility of using tags which contain memory chips, in anticipation of the opening of Terminal 5.

Within Europe, one of the most significant current limitations on capacity, both for airlines and airports, is the present state of the air-traffic control systems. In 1993, the 23 member countries of the European Civil Aviation Conference had 31 different air-traffic control systems, relying on 18 different types of computer and 30 incompatible programming languages. It will be some time before a harmonised system exists which will be comparable to the one currently operating in the US. This will, however, be speeded up if the 33 members of the International Civil Aviation Organisation approve the development of a satellite navigation system as a replacement for the current terrestrial ones. In addition, such a system is forecast to save the airlines as much as ECU 7.8 billion in improved routings and reduced delays.

Additionally, there is a need for improvements in infrastructure, since ground congestion resulting from slow road and rail access is a problem at a number of airports. Airports try, in co-operation with regional authorities, to attract economic activity to develop into significant business centres. Amsterdam Schipol has, together with regional and local bodies, drafted a strategic plan for the development of both the airport and the region into a main complimentary port, similar in concept to the port of Rotterdam. Similarly, the Airport Authority of Copenhagen has a master plan for a second terminal and improved rail links. Paris Orly and Frankfurt have each opened new terminals in 1993 and 1994 respectively, raising capacity by approximately 10–12 million passengers in each case. Schipol is in the middle of modifications which will raise capacity to 40 million passengers by 2015.

Within the EU, the major airports compete with each other for passenger and freight traffic that is not destined for the countries in which those airports are based. The airports are acting as hubs and the traffic is often passing through. Estimates for Heathrow suggest that at least 30 per cent of arrivals on extra EU flights are transferring to other flights, whether for intra-EU connections or even extra-EU connections. Hence airports such as Charles de Gaulle or Schipol could easily supply the same service. The major airports, and the airlines that operate from them, compete aggressively for this transfer market. Although competition between major hubs is largely international (for instance between Heathrow and Schipol), there are a number of examples of competition between hubs in the same country (Gatwick and Heathrow) and, increasingly, regional airports are not restricting themselves to the role of feeders of major hubs, but are starting to offer direct routes. Currently, Manchester airport is building a second runway to expand capacity and capture traffic generated from the North of England which had previously been fed into Heathrow, either by local flight or other means of transport. Manchester will build market share at the expense of other northern airports and London Heathrow, but will also attract new induced traffic. Between 1984 and 1993, Manchester saw an increase in passengers from 6 million to 13.5 million, and in freight from 29 000 tonnes to 89 000 tonnes. Similarly, there has been an increase to 7 per cent – from 2 per cent – of hubbing passengers over the last 6 years.

Across Europe, there are increased efforts to link airports to rail networks, During 1996, BAA launched a £500 000 feasibility study into ways of linking Heathrow into the national rail network to avoid passengers from the provinces having to travel through central London. A survey of 45 leading airports by IATA during 1996 rated Dulles airport amongst the worst with high taxi fares from Washington to the airport, Schipol scored highest with its fast train link to Amsterdam, with Gatwick coming fifth, Heathrow eleventh, and Manchester scoring higher with trains running every ten minutes from the city centre. The problem of transport, together with the forecast passenger increase of Terminal 5, was behind BAA's £450 million venture, the Heathrow Express, linking Paddington in Central London with the airport in a journey time of 15 minutes. Originally, this had been a joint venture with the British Railways Board, but their partner withdrew before completion. BAA own the infrastructure and rolling stock and are operating four trains an hour. Customers will be able to check in at Paddington and travel in air conditioned carriages, via a five mile tunnel, to one of two stations serving the terminals at Heathrow. Expected to attract six million passengers in its first year of operation, the service will reduced the airport-related traffic around Heathrow by 3000 vehicles per day. Previously, passengers would use the Underground system, mingling with commuters and stopping at all stations, and be faced with delays when few ticket windows were open and ticket machines had insufficient change.

One of the UK's largest private sector construction projects suffered a severe setback in October 1994 with the partial collapse of three tunnels being built under the central terminal area. Through the highly successful partnership approach (described later) and by working as a single team, BAA, Balfour Beatty, the tunnel contractor, and the suppliers agreed a common goal of opening on time in mid 1998 without further incident. This approach won them the Institute of Personnel and Development's people management award, recognising that the Heathrow Express project has concentrated strongly on processes and people.

Similarly, National Express, having won the franchise to run the Gatwick Express in the recent privatisation of the railways, are running services every 15 minutes until midnight and hourly services thereafter. Before the privatisation, there were infrequent trains after 9.30 p.m. and no trains at all at night.

Generally, airports which are too far out of town have proved to be failures. The 1970s proposal to build the third London airport at Maplin Sands, on the Essex coast, was shelved by the disruption and cost of a high-speed rail link to the centre of London. Similarly, Mirabel was built too far from Montreal and has never taken the position of premier airport for the city as had been intended. However, despite the fact that Schipol airport has approval for a fifth runway and sufficient land for extra terminals, the Dutch Government has opened a debate on the construction of a new airport to be constructed either in the North Sea, the port of Rotterdam, or on the Zuider See. Having been forced to restrict passenger volumes to 44 million by a powerful environmental lobby, the Government now needs to decide whether it wishes to continue to compete for transfer passengers, who constitute approximately 40 per cent of Schipol's business. The amount of revenue that such passengers bring into the national exchequer is a point which is being debated both by the Dutch and those involved in the long running enquiry into the construction of Terminal 5 at Heathrow. Heathrow are convinced of their importance and recently constructed, at a cost of £100 million, a new centre for work and relaxation between flights.

In 1996, just over 34 per cent of all passengers to Heathrow travelled by public transport, while the stated target is that this should rise to 50 per cent. If Terminal 5 goes ahead, it will be served by an extension to the Piccadilly Line, part of the London Underground. Additionally, there are plans to link the airport more closely to the existing rail network, over and above the construction of the Heathrow Express, by building two stations at a cost of £5 million each and providing dedicated bus services.

Those opposing the construction of Terminal 5 argue that Heathrow is a monster whose development has got out of hand. However, this is certainly not true of its size, at only 3000 acres it is only about a tenth of the size of the recently opened Denver International in Colorado. Handling 420 000 takeoffs and landings a year, it employs some 55 000 people on the airport, approximately another 25 000 in related businesses just beyond the perimeter, and supports another estimated 191 000 jobs elsewhere.[3] It is proposed that the terminal be built between the two runways on land which is currently occupied by a sludge works. Arguing that its construction will lead to more efficient use of existing runways so that, with its capacity to handle larger aircraft, there will only be an 8 per cent increase in flights with no additional night flights. BAA believe that the need for an additional runway in the southeast of England could be delayed by up to five years. BAA have said that if Terminal 5 does not go ahead, £600 million annually in export earnings will be lost to Paris, Frankfurt, or Amsterdam . The completion of Terminal 5 would allow Heathrow to handle approximately 80 million passengers a year.

BAA has adopted the approach of being an environmentally responsible neighbour and of achieving a balance between the interests of the growing number of those who wish to fly and those who live near airports. There is strong commitment to minimise the impact of the airport operations on the environment and on local residents. The company has formed and registered its own charity '21st Century Community Fund', committed £10 million to a voluntary noise-insulation scheme for more than 7000 homes, and donates approximately £100 000 per annum to local environmental projects and charities. By a constant review and monitoring process, the noise contours have been reduced such that the number of people living within them has shrunk over the last 20 years. Environmental responsibility rests at Managing Director level, the company developing the Environmental Management System in-house and producing a separate environmental performance report for public distribution. There are established community-relations programmes focused on promoting education, environmental issues, and economic regeneration. The importance of public opinion, the high level of regulation, and transparency of accounting and reporting procedures have been recognised by the company, which has chosen to take the stance of being a progressive organisation aware of stakeholders' interests and expectations towards whom they act responsibly.

Retail management

The BAA chief executive, Sir John Egan, is clear about the primary objective, having declared:

> It is our intention to be the most successful airport company in the world, by focusing on our customers' needs and safety, and by seeking continuous improvements in the costs and quality of our services.

Each year the company goes through a massive public consultation exercise by asking more than 500 000 passengers their views about service at the airports. In addition, there have been two major achievements during the tenure of Sir John Egan – the creation of a powerful group presence in the retail sector and the ability to cut the cost of the group's massive capital expenditure bill.

Expansion of retail has been prompted partly by the Government imposed regulation of landing charges and partly by the resulting slower growth of revenue from the traditional airport activities in recent years. Despite the huge increase in passenger traffic, the level of retail revenue had risen relatively slowly from £212 million at the time of privatisation to £550 million by 1996. This has, however, reduced the dependence on airport activities as a source of income, and, by 1998, for the first time more than 50 per cent of total revenue came from retail activities.

Having seen the enormous potential of providing high-quality services to the 100 million people landing at and taking off from BAA's airports annually, the company has set about becoming the most effective airport retailer in Europe. By recruiting high-quality managers with retail experience, they have been able to attract the retailers that their research had shown them would maximise passenger spend at the airport concessions. Potential retailers are invited to take up concessions after extensive market research to determine their attractiveness to the travelling public. The company has placed great emphasis on developing its retail interests by investing heavily in new facilities and by attracting the best-known High Street businesses to open up shops and catering outlets at the airports. Today, many familiar High Street names can be found alongside each other at BAA airports. To underline the company's commitment, BAA's aim is to almost treble retail space by the end of the century to around 100 000 square metres. Recently, some 7500 square metres of new shop-floor space was added in a single year to the portfolio, which then boasted some 60 000 square metres of retailing space in nearly 300 shops and 100 restaurants. The company uses quality service monitoring and continuous improvement groups to ensure the highest standards of service to the concession holders.

The range of specialist shops is broad, ranging from Austin Reed and

Aquascutum through Churches Shoes and the Disney Store to Thomas Pink, the shirt makers. For all specialities, the best end of range is represented and the British Museum also has a concession at Heathrow Terminal 4. Added to this, after a successful experience with the management of Indianapolis, BAA invited the Sunglass Hut to take up concessions at its UK based airports, which has also been done successfully. The bureaux de change are managed by, amongst others, Thomas Cook – possibly one of the most famous names in the industry.

BAA's shops sell 20 per cent of all perfume sold in the UK, sell 800 000 ties a year, and a pair of socks every two minutes.[4] During the summer months, the McDonald's outlet at Gatwick sells more food than any other outlet in the UK. Mappin and Webb sell more Rolex watches at Terminal 4, Heathrow, than any other branch. The TGI Friday outlet at Pittsburgh Airport has the highest revenue of any in the US. In 1996, Heathrow was voted 'Retail location of the year' by *Retail Week,* a leading industry journal, in 1997, attention to customer service was commended in the *Daily Telegraph*/BT Customer Service Awards, whilst for the second year running, *Business Traveller* magazine voted Heathrow the best duty-free shopping centre in the world.

Both the retailers and BAA can gather extensive market research from the relatively affluent, captive passengers in the terminals. Of the passengers passing through Heathrow over 53 per cent are in the AB socioeconomic bracket with a further 36 per cent in the C1 category. In their research, BAA asked women passengers what additional products or services they would like to see provided whilst they waited for flights. The fact that 60 per cent would be prepared to pay for a facial or other beauty treatment was taken to Clarins, the cosmetics company, which subsequently set up the first facility providing beauty treatments at Heathrow. Similarly, the concept of 'Whiskies of the World' was developed by BAA in Heathrow Terminal 1 and now carries 280 different brands of whisky including Highland Queen, their own exclusive brand, allowing them to sell a bottle of whisky every six seconds at a BAA airport.

BAA offers the guarantee that landside prices will be no higher than found in the same store in the High Street and airside prices will be at least VAT free, with liquor and tobacco up to 50 per cent cheaper and perfume up to 30 per cent cheaper. A personal shopping service allows passengers to order goods in advance by a 24-hour freephone service and then to collect them on arrival from shopping-information desks. There is a no-quibble money-back guarantee whereby dissatisfied customers can return items by a registered freepost within the UK and the refund of postage outside the UK. In April 1995, the company offered the first ever airport loyalty scheme for customers at its airports. It has become the world's largest multi-retailer scheme involving more than 120 retailers. In the trial at Gatwick, 35 000 customers spent £6 million and collected bonus points every time they spent money on car parking, car hire, currency-exchange shopping, or eating. BAA has attracted 250 000 card holders within three years of the launch and membership is growing by almost 5 per cent per month, with a quarter of the members being non-UK residents. There have been more than two million bonus-point transactions to date and card holders are expected to increase their average spend by £6 per airport visit. The scheme is particularly effective with business travellers, who average a one-third higher spend than non-members. The database will prove invaluable for targeting frequent flyers with promotional offers.

Leisure facilities are also considered important, but care is taken to avoid the 'theme park' criticism being levelled at the facilities on offer. Whilst Schipol offers virtual-reality golf, gambling, and similar facilities, Gatwick has attempted to provide an educational theme to its leisure provision. Linked to the national curriculum, the airport is linking its exhibits to the history, future, and science of flight, from which local schools could benefit. With flight decks from old aircraft and plans for flight simulators in which passengers and visitors can land aircraft, there is a serious side to the amusements.

Duty- and tax-free (DTF) sales have become highly important for airports (and airlines) as a source of revenue, accounting for about 15–20 per cent of airports' income in Europe. The Commission originally envisaged abolishing DTF allowances for passengers travelling within the EU with the advent of the Single Market. Estimates of the impact of abolition concluded that landing and passenger charges would need to rise by 13–25 per cent to compensate airports for lost revenue. In turn, airlines would pass these higher charges on to the traveller in higher fares, possibly causing a negative effect on travel demand, particularly in the leisure market. The lost income to airlines, particularly charter companies, for on-board DTF sales would cause further upward pressure on fares. After strong lobbying from many sections of the international transport industry, the 15 finance ministers of the EU decided in 1991 that the abolition of DTF should be postponed until July 1, 1999. However, by 1998, most of the transport ministers had called for an urgent review of the decision, after estimates that there would be 145 000 job losses across the industry in Europe were published.[5] The study confirmed that the short-term job losses would only be replaced indirectly and over a long period as the result of the smooth running of the market. The total DTF market within Europe is estimated to be worth £3 billion. This figure is forecast to increase by 40 per cent by the end of the decade,[6] and almost double by the year 2005. Similar growth rates can be expected in the Asia Pacific region, whereas the Americas are forecast to see growth of approximately 50 per cent by the year 2005.

One of the major criticisms by the members of the International Duty Free Confederation (IDFC) is that there is little harmonisation of duty and tax across the EU at the moment. VAT ranges from 15 per cent in Germany to 25 per cent in Denmark and Sweden, whilst it is only a fifth of that in

Greece and Spain. Ken Berridge, of Allders International, is quoted as saying: 'The only common denominator in Europe is duty free.'[7]

In May 1996, Allders, who had held the DTF concessions at all BAA's airports, entered into an agreement with BAA to sell Allders International for £130 million in cash. In the proposed-sale circular to shareholders, it was reported that Nuance, a division of Swissair, had publicly stated that it was prepared to offer £145 million, but that, at that time, no formal offer had been made. When the formal offer was subsequently made BAA matched it, but withdrew when Swissair raised the offer to £160 million.

Allders International was the largest tax- and duty-free retailer in Europe and the second-largest worldwide, behind the American DFS. With 110 stores at airport locations, 84 stores on cruise ships and 28 off-airport stores, it had a total of 2112 employees. In the six months to March 1996, the company recorded a loss of £1 million compared to a profit of £3.5 million for the same period in the previous year. Allders had claimed that new contracts at Copenhagen and Brisbane had depressed the results of the European and Australasian regions, whilst North America had shown an overall improvement. With Europe contributing 62 per cent of turnover and 57 per cent of profit, the company's most significant contract was with BAA to manage the concessions at Heathrow, Gatwick, and Stanstead. The contract was due to run until June 30, 1999, with a BAA option to terminate at 9 months' notice. There was a joint venture with Air Portugal and established operations in Paris, Amsterdam, and Copenhagen. Australasia accounted for 20 per cent of turnover and 29 per cent of operating profit, with the balance being earned in eight US and Canadian airports.

Allders had recognised the problems of the abolition of duty-free allowances for intra-EU travellers, and also required capital to develop their department and out-of-town stores, however, it was acknowledged that:

> this planned growth has required, and continues to require, substantial investment . . ..
> The Board believes that in an increasingly competitive international environment, Allders International would benefit from access to greater resources.

As a result of the takeover of Allders by Nuance, BAA in 1996 formed their own 'World Duty Free' chain to take over the former Allders outlets from Spring 1997, the stores being managed by non-BAA staff, and the then retail director, Barry Gibson, saying: 'We made clear our strategic intention to win a significant position in the International DTF market some time ago. We took the decision then to take more control of our duty- and tax-free business as the first step, and we are now implementing that decision. We remain interested in pursuing opportunities to develop our business.'

World Duty Free runs DTF shops, specialist shops, and in-flight duty-free concessions. At BAA airports, it operates as a concessionaire paying a percentage of revenue to the operator. With over 8 per cent of the $20 billion world duty-free market, they are the world's number-one retailer of duty-free liquor and tobacco, and the second largest duty-free vendor of other products. The £429 million acquisition of the American based Duty Free International Inc., now renamed WDF Americas Inc., provided an opportunity to apply the core duty-free retail strategy to a non-EU environment. The company's demonstrated ability to improve sales performance and margins will be applied to the additional outlets and provide significant new distribution channels for the exclusive in-house brands and specialist duty-free retail formats. Additionally, the group will benefit from a greater geographical spread and enhanced buying power. By June 1999, with the natural expiry of contracts, BAA will operate all DTF retail outlets at its airports. World Duty Free In-flight leads the world as both concessionaire for the sale of DTF on board aircraft and wholesale supplier to airlines.

The group has also expanded away from airports by a joint venture with McArthur/Glen to develop designer outlet centres in Europe. The first such was opened at Cheshire Oaks, the second at Troyes in the Champagne district of France, and the third at Swindon. The Cheshire Oaks centre is the largest designer outlet in Europe and attracts 60 000 visitors a week, most of whom expressed the intention of visiting four times a year. There are over 60 concession holders at Cheshire Oaks, all of whom are well-known brands such as Benetton, Dak Simpson, Fruit of the Loom, Kurt Geiger, Nike, and Timberland. Similarly, there are 50 well-known brands represented at Troyes.

This cautious start has, as yet, contributed little to the fortunes of the group as the early results, although promising, have not covered the cost of developing the sites. However, given the retail-management skills of the group, it is an area which is being pursued at other potential sites such as Dartford in Kent, York, Bridgend in Wales, and Mansfield. All sites have been carefully chosen to be near easy transport links to major population centres.

Property management

In 1988, BAA acquired a major property development company, Lynton Property, valued at approximately £200 million. After a reorganisation, the company is now responsible for all BAA's property dealings off-airport, whilst on-airport property management is handled by the respective airport businesses. Property income in 1995–96 totalled £213 million, up 10.4 per cent on the previous year. The increase was mainly due to a renegotiation of major leases held by British Airways at Heathrow and to a general increase in lettable space. This level of income qualifies the company as one of the largest property companies in the UK. However, BAA enjoys somewhat of a unique position since it is, to a large extent, a monopolistic supplier to buyers of relatively limited power (tempered by the presence of the regulator).

Lynton's rental income declined from £25 million in 1993–94 to £23 million in 1998 as the disposal of off-airport property was accelerated. BAA aims to continue to dispose of this type of property and concentrate on the airport and near airport portfolio.

On airport rents are derived for the following types of accommodation:

- Terminal offices
- Perimeter offices
- Cargo warehouses
- Industrial storage
- Pier/ramp accommodation
- Commercially Important Passenger (CIP) accommodation

Rent is not received from retail or catering concessionaires; BAA pays them a management fee, with BAA effectively owning the business.

The rapid expansion of retailing has inevitably boosted the value of BAA's portfolio of property assets, which is currently valued at well over £4 billion. Since 1990, it has provided tenants with 100 000 square metres of additional space and the company is planning to add a further 150 000 square metres. At Glasgow, the terminal was expanded by 70 per cent in the 1990s at a cost of £60 million, and there are plans for further development. Southampton, a traditional small regional airport, has been completely rebuilt at a cost of £25 million.

BAA's strategy for property is to maximise the effective use of on-airport land. For example, BAA uses premium rents in the central terminal area to limit the area that tenants can afford. Although the MMC report contains assertions that rents at Heathrow are too expensive, BAA rejects this, claiming that the location of on-airport property demands higher rent, and that overseas airports show similar price differentials. Property rents at Heathrow continued to rise through the recession, Heathrow Airports Limited achieving increases of 30 per cent above 1989 levels by 1993, whereas commercial rents in the rest of the UK had declined by 30 per cent. However, in 1993 rents were frozen until March 1997.

In response to market research, BAA has introduced the 'Property Challenge', a charter of good management for its holdings. This includes:

- Provision of increased value for money
- A freeze on terminal rents at 1993 levels until March 1997. Future rent increases are dependent upon achievement of performance standards
- More openness for tenants to judge whether they are getting value for money
- Provision of more user-friendly legal documents

There is close liaison with clients to ensure that a customer focus is maintained and that needs are met, with performance standards, particularly in the area of fault repairs, tied to rental agreements. This, of course, is logistically easier with on-airport property. The performance standards introduced include: the resolution of 95 per cent of faults within four hours; all accommodation handed to new tenants to pass a standard 'property check'; to achieve a score of at least 3.5 in BAA's own cleaning quality monitor; to issue 95 per cent of standard legal documentation within five working days; and to deal with 95 per cent of applications for modifications to accommodation within ten working days. The close liaison with customers and tenants would include surveys as to quality and the properties' value for money. At the time of the 1996 Monopolies and Mergers Report, no other property company was going to these lengths to ensure customer satisfaction, and BAA's own surveys demonstrated that the bulk of the targets were being met.

Over the past 5 years, BAA has increased its supply of lettable space by 1.3 million square feet and has invested £10 million in improving quality and tenant choice. There are further plans to develop an additional 43 acres which have been released by British Airways. Over the foreseeable future, BAA expects rental income to increase at 40 per cent of the rate of increase of passenger numbers.

Lynton plc has recently been developing hotels near Heathrow, and has also completed office complexes adjacent to Heathrow and nearby Slough. The company normally seeks to work in partnership with existing and new clients to find opportunities where their combined efforts can add value. BAA and Lynton form 'Framework Partnerships' with selected suppliers of structural engineering, civil engineering, consulting services, and construction management. The intention is to create long-term partnership by involving selected suppliers from the beginning of projects, and sharing the benefits of cost-reduction efficiencies. By standardisation of design for buildings and equipment, they have brought about a major change in the process of designing, building, and managing their facilities. In general, these partnerships achieve better close-out prices on projects than the general UK building industry. At any point in time, the company is managing 100–150 construction contracts and in 1996 the capital spend was over £400 million. As there are usually close links between the construction projects and airport estates, BAA can be seen to be concentrating on a niche market by concentrating on those clients that need to be located on or near to an airport. This tends to mean concentrating on a market which is more commercially attractive than the general property development market, an area where prices fell soon after the acquisition of Lynton.

International operations

For a number of years BAA have generated *ad hoc* revenues from consultancy agreements with overseas airports mainly in Commonwealth countries. However, after privatisation the company moved away from consultancy, and has made concerted efforts to obtain equity involvement or enter management contracts with a view to developing equity involvement at a later date. With the core competencies of airport management and facilitating retail environments they have looked for opportunities abroad.

The airports of most other countries are in public ownership and are only slowly being privatised. Against stiff competition, BAA have won contracts to manage the shopping malls at Pittsburgh (1992) and the whole airport complex at Indianapolis (1996). Although in their own right these are relatively small, they represent a significant breakthrough in what is potentially an enormous market. The US market itself is difficult to enter with complex regulation and cross-interests, but with 4500 airports and airstrips it is by far and away the largest market in the world. Most US airports are production led, unimaginatively marketed, and somewhat spartan, any surpluses generated are ploughed back into building projects, topped up with grants and bond issues. Airport charges often have to be raised to make up for shortfalls in retail and other revenues.

At Pittsburgh, the 15-year contract is based on average retail spend and this has increased from $2.5 per passenger in 1992–93 to $8.10 in 1988, amongst the highest in the country, whilst at Indianapolis, there is a fixed fee with a 'bonus' based on the increase in retail spend. The recognised skills in retail management have helped BAA to attract over 100 retail and catering outlets to Pittsburgh, which has become America's largest and most successful airport retail complex at over 100 000 square feet. Despite the relatively small proportion of international traffic, sales per square metre are now running at over three times the usual level for typical US shopping malls. People come to the airport to watch planes, to eat, and to shop.

At Indianapolis, the airport complex – which consists of Indianapolis International, four reliever airports, and a heliport – is to be managed on a ten-year contract. The airport authority retains ownership and expects to gain £70 million from increased revenue and lower costs. New stores in the recently opened, $2.3 million purpose-built retail mall include Waterstones, Bath, Body Works, and Godiva Chocolates. Both local and expatriate staff have been involved in the management of contracts there, with the exchange of skills, expertise, and staff flowing both ways. Generally, human-resource management is very important to BAA, with such schemes as: self-development programmes, management development initiatives, profit-related pay, employee surveys, staff share purchases, and the 'Freedom to Manage' empowerment initiative.

In September 1994, after a number of delays in parliament, Australia announced the privatisation of its airports in three phases:

Phase 1	Brisbane, Melbourne, and Perth in summer 1997
Phase II	Remaining airports except Sydney
Phase III	Sydney

It is believed that 23 airports in total will be privatised, but under the current legislation any consortium with 15 per cent of any previous phase will not be able to bid for Sydney – considered to be the jewel in the crown.

BAA, as a 49 per cent member of the APAC consortium with State Superannuation Board of New South Wales (13%) and Australian Mutual Provident Society (38%), was selected to manage Melbourne airport, whilst Schipol is the member of the consortium selected to run Brisbane. Schipol is similarly a member of the consortium selected to design, build, and operate a new internationals arrival terminal at JFK airport in New York.

In June 1995, Italy introduced legislation allowing private operators to manage the country's airports. Aeroporti di Roma is controlled by the banks and SEA Aeroporti di Milano has been converted to a private company, it is the intention that both should be 100 per cent privatised. BAA, having signed a letter of intent in January 1996, has already purchased a majority stake in Naples' Capodichino and now manages the airport.

BAA was short-listed with six others by the airports authority of South Africa (ACSA), to modernise the facilities at Johannesburg airport, where the successful candidate would acquire a 20 per cent holding in ACSA, but was unsuccessful. Other groups compete in this lucrative arena: Aeroports de Paris has signed a contract to manage St Petersburg and Amsterdam Airport, Schipol, has a similar arrangement with Cartagena in Columbia.

Roger Kitley, managing director of BAA International is quoted as saying, ' we bring private sector disciplines and a sharper focus',[8] whilst Pat Cowell, president of the rival American Airports Group International, has said: 'What we're offering is the capital, expertise and flexibility of the business world.' There can be no doubt that there are a wealth of opportunities in this area, and it has been suggested that shareholders should sell their shares in airlines and invest in airports instead. As Mr Kitley added: 'The biggest barrier we face is politics. Privatisation is an offensive word in some countries, but there is real momentum. The train has left the station.'

In summary the critical success factors that the company bring to bear on the situation are those of:

- Competing for transfer passenger traffic
- Improving ground access and passenger throughput
- Promoting airports as destinations

- Retailing management
- Redefining the customer
- Leveraging expertise in the global arena

And these are all areas where they have demonstrated considerable success so far.

Notes

1 Key themes in the global service economy

1. E. Chell, J. M. Howarth, and A. S. Brearley, *The Entrepreneurial Personality: Concepts, Cases and Categories*, Routledge, London 1991.
2. Timothy Ferris, *Coming of Age in the Milky Way*, William Morrow, New York 1988.
3. R. Cantillon, *Essai sur la Nature du Commerce en Général* (1755), Institut National d'Études Demographics, Paris 1952.
4. Quoted in Authur H. Cole, 'An approach to the study of Entrepreneurship: A tribute to Edwin F. Gay', in *Exploration in Enterprise*, ed. Hugh G. J. Aitken, Harvard University Press, Cambridge, Mass., 1967, pp. 32–3.
5. Ibid.
6. Thomas C. Cochran, 'Entrepreneurship', in *International Encyclopaedia of the Social Sciences*, vol. 5, Free Press, New York 1968, pp. 88–9.
7. John Arndt, 'The Political Economy of Marketing Systems: Reviving the Institutional Approach', *Journal of Macromarketing*, vol. 1, Autumn 1981.
8. Joseph A. Schumpeter, *Capitalisation, Socialism and Democracy*, 3rd edn, Harper and Row, New York 1950, p. 132.
9. Edward F. Denison, *Trends in American Economic Growth, 1929–1982*, Brookings, Washington DC, 1985.
10. Author's estimates based on GNP trends and demographic changes.
11. Kenichi Ohmae, *The Mind of The Strategist*, Penguin Business Library, London 1985.
12. L. C. Thurow, *Head to Head*, Morrow, New York 1992.
13. Robert Heller, *The Super Marketers*, Sidgwick and Jackson, London 1987, p. 216.
14. John Ellis and David Williams, *Currency for Britain*, Penguin, London 1996.
15. Louis L. Stern, 'Consumer Protection via Self-Regulation', *Journal of Marketing*, July 1971, p. 53.
16. M. R. Cvar, 'Case Studies in Global Competition: Patterns of Success and Failure', in *Competition in Global Industries*, ed. M. E. Porter, Harvard Business School, Boston 1986.
17. T. J. Peters and R. H. Waterman, *In Search of Excellence*, Harper and Row, London 1982.
18. H. I. Ansoff, 'The Firm of the Future', *Harvard Business Review*, vol. 43:5, September–October 1965, pp. 162–78; Rosabeth Moss-Kanter, 'The Gurus', *Management Today*, February 1997, pp. 56–7; J. B. Quinn, H. Mintzberg, and R. M. James, *The Strategy Process*, Prentice Hall, Englewood Cliffs, NJ, 1988.
19. G. Johnson and K. Scholes, *Exploring Corporate Strategy*, 2nd edn, Prentice Hall, Englewood Cliffs, NJ, 1988.

20. J. L. Heskett, 'The Multinational Development of Service Industries: Managing in the Service Economy', *Harvard Business Review*, 1986.
21. R. C. Pozen, 'Is America Being Shut Out Again?', *The New York Times*, 10 January 1993.
22. Kenichi Ohmae, *The Borderless World*, Harper Business, New York 1990, pp. 1–9.
23. K. Kashani, 'Why Marketing Still Matters', *Financial Times*, October 1995, pp. 8–10.
24. Peter M. Chisnall, *Strategic Industrial Marketing*, 2nd edn, Prentice Hall, Englewood Cliffs, NJ, 1989, p. 301.
25. M. Boskin, quoted by Lester Thurow, in *The Future of Capitalism*, Morrow, New York 1996.

2 Defining service organisations

1. Peter M. Chisnall, *Strategic Industrial Marketing*, 2nd edn, Prentice Hall, Englewood Cliffs, NJ, 1989.
2. Christopher H. Lovelock, 'Classifying Service to Gain Marketing Insights', *Journal of Marketing*, vol. 47, Summer 1983, pp. 1–20.
3. G. Hollins and B. Hollins, *Total Design*, Pitman, London 1991, p. 111.
4. W. Regan, 'The Service Revolution', *Journal of Marketing*, vol. 27:3, 1963.
5. R. Judd, 'Similarities or Differences in Product and Services', *Journal of Retailing*, vol. 44:4, 1968.
6. R. Zemke, *The Service Edge: 101 Companies that Profit from Customer Care*, New American Library, New York 1989; R. L. Desatnick, *Managing to Keep the Customer: How to Achieve and Maintain Superior Customer Service throughout the Organisation*, Jossey-Bass, San Francisco 1987; P. Kotler, *Marketing Management: Analysis, Planning, and Control*, Prentice Hall, Englewood Cliffs, NJ, 1980.
7. V. Zeithamel, 'How Consumer Evaluation Processes Differ between Goods and Services', in *Marketing of Services*, 1981.
8. C. Gronroos, 'A Service-Oriented Approach to the Marketing of Services', *European Journal of Marketing*, vol. 12:8, 1978.
9. P. Kotler, *Marketing for Non-Profit Organisations*, 2nd edn, Prentice Hall, Englewood Cliffs, NJ, 1982.
10. D. E. Bowen, 'Managing Customers as Human Resources in Service Organisations', *Human Resources Management*, Autumn 1986, pp. 371–83.
11. V. Zeithamel, A. Parasuraman, and L. Berry, 'Problems and Strategies in Service Marketing', *Journal of Marketing*, vol. 49, Spring 1985.
12. T. Levitt, 'Marketing Intangible Products and Product Intangibles', *Harvard Business Review*, vol. 59:3, 1981.
13. A. Rushton and D. Carson, 'The Marketing of Services: Managing the Intangibles', *European Journal of Marketing*, vol. 19:8, 1985.
14. W. Sasser, 'Match Supply and Demand in Service Industries', *Harvard Business Review*, vol. 57:6, 1979.
15. B. Nicoulaud, 'Problems and Strategies in the International Marketing of Services', *European Journal of Marketing*, vol. 23:6, 1989.
16. C. Voss et al., *Operations Management in Services Industries and the Public Sector*, Wiley, London 1985.
17. R. J. Schonberger, *Building a Chain of Customers*, Hutchinson, London 1990.
18. Quoted in *Planning the Service Encounter*, ed. J. A. Czepial et al., Lexington Books, Lexington 1985.

19. V. A. Zeithamel et al., *Delivering Quality Service*, Free Press, New York 1990.
20. T. J. Peters, *Thriving on Chaos*, Pan and Macmillan, London 1987.
21. J. Teboul, *Managing Quality Dynamics*, Prentice Hall, London 1991.
22. J. J. McManus, *Resisting Change (Selected Readings in Process Management)*, Lakewood Research Publications, Mass., 1994.
23. W. S. Smith, *The Quest for Quality*, Quest Quality Consulting, London 1989.
24. Quoted in *Planning and Management Change*, ed. B. Mayon-White, Harper and Row, London 1986.
25. G. Johnson, *Strategic Change Management Process*, Basil Blackwell, Oxford 1987.
26. A. Pettigrew and R. Whipp, *Managing Change for Competitive Success*, Basil Blackwell, Oxford 1991.
27. S. Dawson, *Analysing Organisations*, Macmillan, London 1985.
28. M. Harper, 'A New Profession to Aid Marketing', *Journal of Marketing*, 1961.
29. J. A. Rosier, 'The Coming Crisis in Bank Management, II', *The Banker's Magazine*, August 1973.
30. S. M. Davies and B. Davidson, *2020 Vision*, Simon and Schuster, New York 1991.
31. Alvin Toffler, *Future Shock*, Random House, London 1970; Herman Kahn and Anthony Wiener, *The Year 2000: A Framework for Speculation on the Next 33 Years*, Macmillan, New York 1967.
32. John Kay, *Foundations of Corporate Success*, Oxford University Press, Oxford 1993.
33. Bernard Catry and Michael Chevalier, 'Market Share and the Product Life Cycle', *Journal of Marketing*, October 1974, pp. 29–34.
34. Robert D. Buzzell et al., 'Market Share – A Key to Profitability', *Harvard Business Review*, January 1975, pp. 97–106.
35. M. S. Williams, 'The Impact of Market Share on Return on Investment', in *Handbook of Business Strategy, 1989/90 Yearbook*, ed. H. E. Glass, Warren, Gorham, and Lamont, Boston 1989, pp. 331–6.
36. B. T. Gale, 'Advertising Profitability and Growth for Consumer Business', *The PIMS Letter on Business Strategy*, vol. 43, The Strategic Planning Institute, Cambridge, Mass., 1989, p. 9.
37. Michael Porter, *The Competitive Advantage of Nations*, Macmillan, London 1994.
38. J. J. Boddewyn et al., 'Service Multinationals: Conceptualization, Measurement and Theory', *Journal of International Business Studies*, Autumn 1986.
39. The concepts of physical evidence, participants, and process have been taken from, R. G. Murdick, B. Render, and R. S. Russell, *Service Operations Management*, Allyn and Bacon, London 1990, pp. 536–7.
40. Porter, *Competitive Advantage*, p. 232.
41. These terms were developed by SRI International (formerly the Stanford Research Institute).
42. P. Kotler, *Marketing Management Analysis, Planning and Control*, Prentice Hall, Englewood Cliffs, NJ, 1980.
43. Igor Ansoff, *Corporate Strategy*, McGraw Hill, New York 1965, pp. 122–38.
44. David Kollat, Roger Blackwell, and James Robeson, *Strategic Marketing*, Holt, Rinehart and Winston, New York 1972, pp. 21–3.
45. D. I. Cleland and W. R. King, 'Competitive Business Intelligence Systems', *Business Horizons*, December 1975, p. 20.

3   The development of strategic planning

1. G. Hamel and A. Heene, *Competence-Based Competition*, Wiley, London 1994.
2. A. Toffler, *Future Shock*, Pan, London 1970.

3. G. Thompson, *The Foreseeable Future*, Viking, London 1960.
4. J. Diebold, *Beyond Automation*, McGraw Hill, New York 1964.
5. L. Bagrit, *The Age of Automation*, New American Library, New York 1965.
6. S. Makradakis, *Forecasting, Planning, and Strategy for the 21st Century*, Free Press, New York 1990.
7. R. F. Vancil, 'The Accuracy of Long-Range Planning,' in *The Truth about Corporate Planning*, ed. D. E. Hussey, Pergamon Press 1983.
8. R. N. Anthony, *Planning and Control Systems: A Framework for Analysis*, Irwin, Homewood, IL, 1956.
9. H. D. Koontz and O'Donnell, *Principals of Management*, McGraw Hill, New York 1959.
10. P. F. Drucker, *The Practice of Management*, Pan, London 1968.
11. A. D. Chandler, *Strategy and Structure*, MIT Press, Cambridge, Mass., 1962.
12. A. P. Sloan, Jr., *My Years with General Motors*, Doubleday, New York 1964.
13. G. A. Steiner, *Top Management Planning*, Macmillan, London 1969.
14. R. M. Cyert and J. G. March, *A Behavioural Theory of the Firm*, Prentice Hall, Englewood Cliffs, NJ, 1963.
15. P. F. Drucker, 'Business Objectives and Survival Needs: Notes on a Discipline of Business Enterprise', *The Journal of Business*, vol. 31:2, April 1958, pp. 81–90.
16. J. Argenti, *Systematic Corporate Planning*, Van Norstrand Reinhold, New York 1974.
17. T. L. Wheelan and J. D. Hunger, *Strategic Management and Business Policy*, Adison Wesley, Reading, Mass., 1991.
18. B. D. Henderson, *The Logic of Business Strategy*, Ballinger, 1984.
19. Quoted in J. I. Moore, *Writers in Strategy and Strategic Management*, Penguin, London 1992.
20. R. D. Buzzell and B. T. Gale, *The PIMS Principles – Linking Strategy to Performance*, Free Press, New York 1987.
21. M. E. Porter, *Competitive Strategy : Techniques for Analysing Industries and Competitors*, Free Press, New York 1980; and M.E. Porter *Competitive Advantage: Creating and Sustaining Superior Performance* The Free Press, New York 1985.
22. D. F. Abell, *Defining the Business: the starting point of strategic planning*, Prentice Hall, Englewood Cliffs, NJ, 1980.
23. S. S. Mathur, 'How Firms Compete', *Journal of General Management*, vol. 14:1, Autumn 1988.
24. K. Ohmae, *The Mind of the Strategist: The Art of Japanese Business*, McGraw Hill, New York 1982.
25. H. Mintzberg, *The Rise and Fall of Strategic Planning*, Prentice Hall, Englewood Cliffs, NJ, 1994.
26. G. A. Steiner, *Strategic Planning, What every Manager Must Know*, Free Press, New York 1979.
27. H. Mintzberg, *The Rise and Fall of Strategic Planning*, Prentice Hall, Englewood Cliffs, NJ, 1994.
28. Y. Allaire and M. Firsirotu, 'Coping with Strategic Uncertainty', *Sloan Management Review*, vol. 33:3, Spring 1989, pp. 1–16.
29. R. M. Hogarth and S. Makridakis, 'Forecasting and Planning: an Evaluation', *Management Science*, vol. 27:2 (Feb), 1981.
30. S. Makradakis and M. Hibon, 'Accuracy of Forecasting: An Empirical Investiga-

tion', *Journal of the Royal Statistical Society*, ser. A, vol. 142:2, 1979.

31. P. N. Pant and W. H. Starbuck, 'Review of Forecasting and Research Methods', *Journal of Management*, vol. 16:2, June 1990.

32. I. Ansoff, *Implanting Strategic Management*, Prentice Hall, Englewood Cliffs, NJ, 1984.

33. H. A. Simon (1973), quoted in Henry Mintzberg, *The Rise and Fall of Strategic Planning*, Prentice Hall, Englewood Cliffs, NJ, 1994.

34. R. M. Grant *Contemporary Strategic Analysis*, Basil Blackwell, Oxford 1991.

35. M. Friedman, 'The methodology of positive economics', in *Essays in Positive Economics*, University of Chicago Press, Chicago 1953.

36. M. T. Hannan and J. Freeman, *Organisational Ecology*, Havard University Press, Cambridge, Mass., 1988.

37. T. Peters, *Liberation Management*, Macmillan, London 1992.

38. R. Sanchez and D. Sudharshan, 'Real-time market research: learning by doing in the development of new products', in *Proceedings of the International Product Development Conference*, ed. C. Karlsson, European Institute for Advanced Studies in Management, Brussels 1992.

39. O. E. Williamson, 'Strategising, economising and economic organisation', *Strategic Management Journal*, vol. 12, pp. 75–94, 1991.

40. R. Whittington, *What is strategy and does it matter?*, International Thomson, London 1993.

41. D. N. McCloskey, *If you're so smart; the Narrative of Economic Expertise*, University of Chicago Press, Chicago 1990.

42. D. Miller, 'The Icarus Paradox', *Business Horizons*, January–February 1992.

43. T. Peters and R. H. Waterman, *In Search of Excellence*, Harper Collins, London 1982.

44. D. Miller, 'Architecture and Simplicity', *American Management Review*, vol. 18:1, 1993, pp. 116–38.

45. R. Stacey, 'Strategy as Order Emerging from Chaos', *Long-Range Planning*, vol. 26:1, 1993, pp. 10–17.

46. P. Pelikan, 'Evolution, economic competence and the market for corporate control', *Journal of Economic Behaviour and Organisation*, vol. 12, 1989, pp. 279–303.

47. S. Slatter, *Corporate Recovery*, Penguin, London 1984; P. Grinyer, D. Mayes, and P. McKiernan, *Sharpbenders: The secrets of unleashing corporate potential*, Basil Blackwell, Oxford 1988.

48. P. Burrows, 'A peek at Steve Jobs' plan', *Business Week*, 17 November, 1997.

49. D. J. Ravenscraft and F. M. Scherer, *Mergers, Sell-Offs and Economic Efficiency*, The Brookings Institution, Boston 1987.

50. K. M. Eisenhardt, 'Agency theory; an assessment and review', *Academy of Management Review*, vol. 14:1, 1989, pp. 57–74.

51. J. R. Kimberley and E. J. Zajac, 'Dynamics of CEO/Board Relationships', in *The Executive Effect*, ed. D. C. Hambrick, JAI Press, Greenwich, CT, 1988.

52. J. A. Byrne, 'For a So-So CEO, $95 million in cash', *Business Week*, 20 October, 1997.

53. M. Goold and A. Campbell, *Strategies and Styles*, Basil Blackwell, London 1987.

54. H. A. Simon, *The New Science of Management Decisions*, Prentice Hall, Englewood Cliffs, NJ, 1960; R. M. Cyert and J. G. March, *A Behavioural Theory of the Firm*, Prentice Hall, Englewood Cliffs, NJ, 1963.

55. L. Hrebiniak and W. Joyce, *Implementing Strategy*, Macmillan College Publishing, London 1984.
56. C. E. Lindblom, 'The science of muddling through', *Public Administration Review*, vol. 19, 1959, pp. 79–88.
57. R. D. Stacey, *Strategic Management and Organisational Dynamics*, Pitman, London 1996.
58. A. Pettigrew, 'Some limits on executive power in creating strategic change', in *Executive Power*, ed. S. Srivasta and Associates, Jossey-Bass, San Francisco 1986.
59. J. Pfeffer, *Power in Organisations*, Ballinger Publishing, London 1981.
60. R. M. Kanter, *The Change Masters, Innovation and Entrepreneurship in the American Corporation*, Simon and Schuster, New York 1985.
61. H. Mintzberg, 'Crafting Strategy', *Harvard Business Review*, July–August 1987, pp. 65–75.
62. J. B. Quinn, Strategies for Change, *Logical Incrementalism*, Irwin, Homewood, IL, 1980.
63. H. Mintzberg, *The Rise and Fall of Strategic Planning*, Prentice Hall, Englewood Cliffs, NJ, 1994.
64. H. Mintzberg and J. A. Waters, 'Of strategies, deliberate and emergent', *Strategic Management Journal*, vol. 6, 1985, pp. 257–72.
65. K. E. Weick, 'Cartographic myths in organisations', in *Mapping Strategic Thought*, ed. A. S. Huff, Wiley, London 1990.
66. G. Johnson, 'Rethinking incrementalism', *Strategic Management Journal*, January–February 1988.
67. L. Heracleous and B. Langham, 'Strategic change and organisational culture at Hay Management Consultants', *Long-Range Planning*, vol. 29:4, 1996.
68. R. M. Grant, 'The resource based theory of competitive advantage: implications for strategy formulation', *California Management Review*, vol. 33:3, 1991, 114–22.
69. C. K. Prahalad and G. Hamel, 'The core competence of the corporation', *Harvard Business Review*, July–August 1990.
70. J. Kay, *Foundations of Corporate Success, How Strategies Add Value*, Oxford University Press, Oxford 1995.
71. J. Kay, *Financial Times*, 29 October 1996.
72. G. Hamel, 'Competition for competence and interpartner learning within international alliances', *Strategic Management Journal*, vol. 12, 1991, pp. 83–103.
73. G. Hamel and C. K. Prahalad, 'Strategy as stretch and leverage', *Harvard Business Review*, March-April 1993.
74. P. Senge, *The Fifth Discipline, the Art and Practice of the Learning Organisation*, Century Business, London 1992.
75. K. Ayas, 'Design for learning and innovation', *Long-Range Planning*, vol. 29:6, 1996.
76. G. Stalk, 'Time – the next source of competitive advantage', *Harvard Business Review*, July–August 1988.
77. G. Hamel and C. K. Prahalad, *Competing for the Future*, Harvard Business School Press, Mass., 1994.
78. M. Weber, *The Theory of Social and Economic Organisations*, ed. and trans. A. M. Henderson and T. Parsons, Free Press, New York 1947.
79. R. Mead, *International Management*, Basil Blackwell, Oxford 1994.
80. M. Aiken and S.B. Bacharach, 'Culture and organisational structure and processes: a comparative study of local government administrative bureaucracies in the Walloon and Flemish regions of Belgium', in *Organisations Alike and Unalike: international and institutional studies of the sociology of organisations*, ed. C. J. Lammers and D. J. Hickson, Routledge, London 1979.

81.   G. Hofstede, *Culture's Consequences: international differences in work-related values*, Sage, Beverley Hills, CA, 1984.

82.   J. K. Fukuda, 'Japanese and Chinese management practices: uncovering the differences', *Mid-Atlantic Journal of Business*, vol. 21:3, Summer 1983, pp. 35–44.

83.   D. Bork, *Family Business, Risky Business*, AMACOM, New York 1986.

84.   S. C. Brandt, *Entrepreneuring: the ten commandments for buiding a growth company*, Addison Wesley, Reading, Mass., 1982.

85.   C. A. Bartlett and S. Ghoshal, *Managing across Borders: the transnational solution*, Hutchinson Business Books, London 1989.

86.   R. T. Pascale, 'Our curious addiction to corporate strategy', *Fortune*, vol. 25, January 1982, pp. 115–16.

87.   R. Whittington, *What is Strategy and does it Matter?*, International Thompson, London 1993.

4   Strategic management models, tools, and techniques

1.   Alfred D. Chandler, *Strategy and Structure*, MIT Press, Cambridge, Mass., 1962.

2.   Igor Ansoff, *Corporate Strategy*, rev. edn, Penguin Business, London 1987, p. 27; (first publ. McGraw-Hill, New York 1965).

3.   K. R. Andrews, *The Concept of Corporate Strategy*, Irwin, Homewood, IL, 1971.

4.   Ansoff, *Corporate Strategy*, p. 196.

5.   Igor Ansoff, *Implanting Strategic Management*, Prentice Hall, Englewood Cliffs, NJ, 1985.

6.   M. Goold and A. Campbell, *Strategies and Styles*, Basil Blackwell, Oxford 1990, p. 222.

7.   C. West Churchman, *The Systems Approach*, Delacorte Press, New York 1968.

8.   Peter F. Drucker, *Management, Tasks, Responsibilities, Practices*, Heineman, London 1974.

9.   James E. Lynch, 'Only Connect: The Role of Marketing and Strategic Management in the Mordern Organisation', *Journal of Marketing Management*, 1994, p. 531.

10.   P. Kotler, *Marketing Management: Analysis, Planning, and Control*, Prentice Hall, Englewood Cliffs, NJ, 1980.

11.   S. Tilles, 'Making Strategy Explicit', in *Business Strategy*, ed. H. Igor Ansoff, Pelican, 1972.

12.   G. Johnson and K. Scholes, *Exploring Corporate Strategy*, 2nd edn, Prentice Hall, Englewood Cliffs, NJ, 1988, p. 53.

13.   D. Hurd, 'Vulnerability Analysis in Business Planning', *SRI International Research Report*, no. 593, 1977.

14.   David Georgoff and Robert Murdick, 'Managers Guide to Forecasting', *Harvard Business Review*, February 1986, pp. 110–20.

15.   Herman Kahn, *On Thermonuclear War*, Oxford University Press, London 1960.

16.   J. C. Dupperin and M. Godet, 'SMIC – a method for constructing and ranking scenarios', *Futures*, vol. 7, August 1975, pp. 302–12.

17.   R. E. Linneman and H. E. Klein, 'Using scenarios in strategy decision making', *Business Horizons*, vol. 28, February 1985, pp. 64–74.

18.   Pierre Wack, 'Scenarios: uncharted waters ahead', *Harvard Business Review*, October 1985, p.77.

19.   Ibid., pp. 73–89.
20.   Peter Schwartz, *The Art of the Long View*, Doubleday, New York 1991.
21.   M. E. Porter, *Competitive Strategy*, Macmillan, New York, 1980.
22.   K. Cool and I. Dierickx, Rivalry, 'Strategic Groups, and Firm Profitability', *Strategic Management Journal*, vol. 14, 1993.
23.   M. E. Porter, *The Competitive Advantage of Nations*, Macmillan, London 1990, p. 506.
24.   Richard Tanner Pascale and Anthony G. Athos, *The Art of Japanese Management*, Penguin, London 1987, p. ix.
25.   Sidney Schoeffler, Robert D. Buzzell, and Donald F. Heany, 'Impact of Strategic Planning on Profit Performance', *Harvard Business Review*, March–April 1974.
26.   Sidney Schoeffer, 'Nine Basic Findings on Business Strategy', *The PIMS Letter on Business Strategy*, no. 1 The Strategic Planning Institute, Cambridge, Mass., 1984, pp. 3–5.
27.   George Day, 'Diagnosing the Product Portfolio', *Journal of Marketing*, vol. 41:2, April 1977.
28.   D. C. Hambrick, I. C. MacMillan, and D. L. Day, 'Strategic Attributes and Performance in the BCG Matrix – A PIMS-based Analysis of Industrial Product Businesses', *Academy of Management Journal*, September 1982, pp. 510–31.
29.   N. Piercey and W. Giles, 'Making SWOT Analysis Work', *Market Intelligence and Planning*, vol. 7:5–6, pp. 5–7.
30.   M. E. Porter, *Competitive Advantage*, Free Press, New York 1985, p. 38.
31.   Porter, *Competitive Advantage*, p. 40.
32.   R. G. Murdick, R. H. Eckhouse, R. C. Moor, and T. N. Zimmerer, *Business Policy: a framework for analysis*, 2nd edn, Grid, 1976.
33.   Ansoff, *Corporate Strategy*,
34.   G. Newman, 'The Anatomy of a Suicide: Strategies, Scapegoats and Culprits in the Postderegulation Airline Industry', *Advances in Applied Business Strategy*, vol. 1, 1984.
35.   D. Riley, 'Competitive Cost Behaviour Investment Strategies for Industrial Companies', *Manufacturing Issues*, Booz, Allen and Hamilton 1987.
36.   J.K. Shank and V. Govindarajan, *Strategic Cost Management*, Free Press, New York 1993.
37.   W. E. Deming, *Quality, Productivity and Competitive Position*, MIT Centre for Advanced Engineering Study, Cambridge, Mass., 1982.
38.   J. Juran, *The Quality Edge: A Management Tool*, PIMA, 1985.
39.   J. Simpson and D. Muthler, 'Quality Costs: Facilitating the Quality Initiative', *Journal of Cost Management*, vol. 1:1, 1987.
40.   S. Ghoshal and D. E. Westney, 'Organizing Competitor Analysis Systems', *Strategic Management Journal*, 1991, pp. 17–31; also see, Henry Mintzberg, *The Rise and Fall of Strategic Planning*, Prentice Hall, London 1994, p. 374.
41.   G. Day and D. Reibstein, 'Keeping ahead in the Competitive Game', *TIMES, Mastering Management*, pt. 18, 1995; R. M. Grant, *Contemporary Strategy Analysis*, 2nd edn, Basil Blackwell, Oxford 1995; B. J. Quinn, 'Strategic Change: logical incrementation', *Sloan Management Review*, vol. 20, 1978, pp. 7–21.
42.   P. Selznick, *Leadership in Administration*, Harper and Row, London 1957, pp. 135–9.
43.   J. A. Pearce and F. David, 'Corporate Mission Statements: the bottom line', *Academy of Management Executive*, May 1987, pp. 109–15.

44. G. Donaldson and J. W. Lorsch, *Decision Making at the Top*, Basic Books, 1983.
45. W. Bennis, *On becoming a Leader*, Addison Wesley, Reading, Mass., 1989.
46. Richard Tanner Pascale and Anthony G. Athos, *The Art of Japanese Management*, Penguin, London, 1987, p. 185.
47. A. Campbell and S. Yeung, *Do You Need a Mission Statement?*, Economist Publications, London 1990.
48. Steiner et al., *Management Policy*, p. 233.
49. T. R. Dye, *Understanding Public Policy*, Prentice Hall, Englewood Cliffs, NJ, 1976, p. 26.
50. G. Johnson and K. Scholes, *Exploring Corporate Strategy*, 2nd edn, Prentice Hall, Englewood Cliffs, NJ, 1988, pp. 135–6.
51. Goold and Campbell, *Strategies and Styles*, p. 65.
52. G. Hamel, Y. Doz, and K. C. Prahalad, 'Collaborate with your competitors and win', *Harvard Business Review*, January–February 1989, pp. 133–9.
53. R. Hall, 'The concept of bureaucracy: an empirical assessment', *American Journal of Sociology*, vol. 69, 1963, pp. 32–40; J. Child, 'Organisation structure, environment and performance: the role of strategic choice', *Sociology*, vol. 6, 1972, pp. 1–22.
54. R. Daft and N. Macintosh, 'The nature and use of formal control systems for management control and strategy implementation', *Journal of Management*, vol. 10, 1984, pp. 43–66.
55. J. E. Skivington, and R. L. Daft, 'A Study of organisational framework and process modalities for the implementation of business-level strategic decisions', *Journal of Management Studies*, vol. 28, January 1991, pp. 45–65.
56. Alfred D. Chandler, *Strategy and Structure*, MIT Press, Cambridge, Mass., 1962.
57. O. E. Williamson, 'The Multidivisional Structure', in *Markets and Hierarchies*, Free Press, New York 1975.
58. F. M. Scherer and D. Ross, *Industrial Market Structure and Economic Performance*, 3rd edn, Houghton Mifflin, Boston, Mass., 1989; R. E. Miles and C. Snow, 'Organisations: new concepts for new forms', *California Management Review*, vol. 28:3, 1986, pp. 62–73; W. Boeker, 'Strategic Change: The Effects of Founding and History', *Academy of Management Journal*, vol. 32:3, September 1989, pp. 489–515.
59. H. Mintzberg, *The Structure of Organisations*, Prentice Hall, Englewood Cliffs, NJ, 1979.
60. W. H. Davidson and P. C. Haspelagh, 'Shaping a global product', *Harvard Business Review*, July–August 1982.
61. J. G. March and J. P. Olsen, 'Organisational learning and the ambiguity of the past', *European Journal of Political Research*, vol. 3, 1975, pp. 147–71; J. P. Walsh and L. Fahey, 'The rule of negotiated belief structures in strategy making', *Journal of Management*, vol. 12, 1986, pp. 325–38.
62. R. Johansen and R. Swigart, *Upsizing the Individual in the Downsized Organisation*, Century Business Books, 1994, p. 86.
63. Johnson and Scholes, *Exploring Corporate Strategy*, pp. 83–4, 94–5.
64. Bain et al., *Managing the Management Tools*, Institute of Management, London 1996.
65. Goold and Campbell, *Strategies and Styles*, p. 39.
66. C. K. Prahalad and G. Hamel, 'The core competence of the corporation', *Harvard Business Review*, May–June 1990.
67. J. B. Quinn, T. L. Doorley, and P. C. Paquette, 'Beyond products: services-based

strategy', *Harvard Business Review*, March–April 1990.
68. Prahalad and Hamel, 'Core competence', pp. 79–91.
69. Tony Proctor, 'Establishing a strategic direction: a review', *Management Decision*, vol. 32:2, 1997, p. 149.

5 The application of strategic management

1. D. Schwartz, 'How to be a global manager', *Fortune*, March 1988.
2. J. Solomon, 'Managing', *The Wall Street Journal*, July 1989, p. B1.
3. Row, Mason, Dickel, Mann, and Mockler, *Global Business Drivers from Strategic Management*, p. 313.
4. H. Itami, *Mobilising Invisible Assets*, Harvard University Press, Cambridge, Mass., 1987.
5. Michael Porter, *Competitive Advantage*, The Free Press, New York 1985.
6. Ibid., p. 13.
7. Michael Porter, *The Competitive Advantage of Nations*, Macmillan, London 1990, p. 39.
8. S. S. Atchison, 'A Perfectly Good Word for WordPerfect: Gutsy', *Business Week*, 2 October 1989, pp. 99–102.
9. S. S. Mathur, 'Talking Straight about Competitive Strategy', *Journal of Marketing Management*, 1992, pp. 199–217.
10. D. K. Clifford and R. E. Cavanagh, *The Winning Performance: How America's High and Midsize Growth Companies Succed*, Bantam Books, New York 1985.
11. J. S. McClenahen, 'Get Used to 2%', *The Economy (USA)*, April 1996, p. 26.
12. P. Verdin and P. Williamson, 'Sucessful Strategy: Stargazing or Self-Examination?', *European Management Journal*, vol. 12, 1994, p. 13.
13. X. Gilbert and P. Strebel, 'Developing Competitive Advantage', in ed. J. B. Quinn, H. Mintzberg, and R. M. James, *The Strategy Process*, Prentice Hall, Englewood Cliffs, NJ, 1988, p. 76.
14. W. E. Fulmer and J. Goodwin, 'Differentiation: Begin with the Consumer', *Business Horizons*, vol. 31:5, October 1989, pp. 55–63.
15. R. E. Miles and C. C. Snow, *Organisational Strategy, Structure, and Process*, McGraw Hill, New York 1978.
16. E. Segev, 'A Systematic Comparative Analysis and Synthesis of Two Business-Level Strategic Typoligies', *Strategic Management Journal*, October 1989, pp. 487–505.
17. D. Miller and P. H. Friesen, 'Porter's Generic Strategies and Performance: An Empirical Examination with American Data. Parts 1 and 2', *Organisational Studies*, 1986; C. Hill, 'Differentiation Versus Low Cost or Differentiation and Low Cost: A Contingency Framework', *Acadamy of Management Review*, vol. 13, 1988.
18. A. L. Murry, 'A Contingency View of Porter's Generic Strategies', *Academy of Management Review*, vol. 13, 1988, pp. 390–400.
19. C. Bowman and Simon Carter, 'Organising for Competitive Advantage', *European Management Journal*, vol. 13:424, 1995.
20. C. Edwards and J. Peppard, 'Forging a link between Business Strategy and Business Re-engineering', *European Managemt Journal*, vol. 12, 1994, p. 409.
21. Ibid., p. 410
22. R. Pitts and D. Lei, *Strategic Management*, West Publishing, USA 1996.
23. G. Hamel and C. K. Prahalad, 'Strategic Intent', *Harvard Business Review*, May–June 1989, pp. 63–76.

24. Eileen Shapiro, 'Managing in the Age of Gurus', *Harvard Business Review*, March–April 1997, p. 145.

25. L. Miller, 'The New Professionals', *World Executive Digest*, vol. 14:5, 1993, pp. 14–16.

26. Gary Hamel, 'Strategy as Revolution', *Harvard Business Review*, 1996, p. 76.

27. S. Ghoshal and C. Bartlett, 'Building the Entrepreneurial Corporation: New Organisational Processes, New Managerial Tasks', *European Management Journal*, vol. 13, 1995, p. 145.

28. D. Muzyka, A. De-Koning, and N. Churchill, 'On Transformation and Adaptation: Building the Entrepreneurial Corporation', *European Management Journal*, vol. 13, 1995, p. 352.

29. R. Davies, 'Making Strategy Happen: Common Patterns of Strategic Failure', *European Management Journal*, vol. 11, 1993, p. 202.

30. J. O. Eastlack and P. R. McDonald, 'CEO's Role in Corporate Growth', *Harvard Business Review*, vol. 48, May–June 1970.

31. A. Kakabadse and A. Myrers, 'Board Room Skills for Europe', *European Management Journal*, vol. 14, 1996, p. 198.

32. E. Gummesson, 'Nine Lessons on Service Quality', *Total Quality Management*, February 1989.

33. G. A. Pauli, *The Second Wave – Japan's Global Attack on Financial Services*, Waterlow, 1987.

34. C. W. Hofer and D. Schendel, *Strategy Formulation: Analytical Concepts*, West Publishing, St Paul, MN, 1978, p. 11.

35. Ibid., p. 24.

36. J. I. Moore, *Writers on Strategy and Strategic Management*, Penguin, London 1992.

37. I. Ansoff, *Corporate Strategy*, Penguin Business, London 1987, p. 182.

38. J. B. Quinn, *Strategies for Change: Logical Incrementalism*, Irwin, Homewood, IL, 1980, p. 140.

39. A. Kenyon and S. S. Muthur, *Getting to the Meaning of Business Strategy: Reflections on the Designed v Emergent Dispute*, Working Paper no. 131, City University Business School, London 1991.

40. G. Johnson and K. Scholes, *Exploring Corporate Strategy*, Prentice Hall, Englewood Cliffs, NJ, 1988, p. 38-9.

41. H. Schwartz and S. M. Davis, 'Matching Corporate Culture and Business Strategy', *Organisational Dynamics*, Summer 1981, p. 43.

42. L. J. Bourgeois and D. Brodwin, 'Putting Your Strategy into Action', *Strategic Management Planning*, March–May 1983.

43. L. G. Hrebiniak and W. Joyce, *Implementing Strategy*, Macmillan College Publishing, London 1984.

44. L. D. Alexander, 'Successfully Implementing Strategic Decisions', *Long-Range Planning*, June 1985, p. 92.

45. See, for example, Quinn, *Strategies for Change*; and Hrebiniak and Joyce, *Implementing Strategy*.

46. A. J. Rowe et al., *Strategic Management: A Methodological Approach*, 4th edn, Addison Wesley, Reading, Mass., 1994, p. 483.

47. S. Bungay and M. Goold, 'Creating a Strategic Control System', *Long-Range Planning*, vol. 24, June 1991, pp. 32–9.

48. P. Drucker, *The Practice of Management*, Harper Row, New York 1954.

49. Peter Doyle, 'Setting Business Objectives and Measuring Performance', *European Management Journal*, vol. 12, 1994, p. 129.

50. Hamel, 'Strategy As Revolution', p. 72.

51. W. Chan Kim and Renee Mauborgne, 'Value Innovation: The Strategic Logic of High Growth', *Harvard Business Review*, January-February 1997, p. 104.
52. R. G. Eccles and N. Nitin, *Beyond the Hype*, Harvard Busines School Press, Boston 1992.
53. Bungay and Goold, 'Creating a Strategic Control System'.
54. P. Lorange, M. F. Scott, and S. Ghoshal, *Strategic Control*, West Publishing, St Paul, MN, 1986.
55. W. G. Ouchi and M. A. Maguire, 'Organisational Control: Two Functions', *Administrative Science Quarterly*, December 1975, pp. 559–69.
56. Bungay and Goold, 'Creating a Strategic Control System'.

6 Future trends in strategic management

1. P. F. Drucker, *Post Capitalist Society*, Harper Collins, London 1993.
2. W. P. Summers, J. Nemec, and J. M. Harris, 'Repositioning with Technology: Making it Work', *Journal of Business Strategy*, Winter 1987, pp. 16–28.
3. W. Orlikowski and D. Gash, *Changing Frames: understanding technological change in organisations*, Centre for Informations System Research Working Paper, MIT, Cambridge, Mass., 1992.
4. K. Fletcher, C. Wheeler, and J. Wright, 'Success in Database Marketing', *Marketing Intelligence and Planning*, vol. 10:6, pp. 18–23.
5. 'Top 100 IT users', *Computing*, 2 October 1997, pp. 41–56.
6. D. Thwaites, 'Forces at work: the market for personal financial services', *International Journal of Bank Marketing*, vol. 9:6, pp. 30–5.
7. S. Caulkin, 'The Knowledge Within', *Management Today*, August 1997, p. 28.
8. M. E. Porter and V. E. Millar, 'How information gives you competitive advantage', *Harvard Business Review*, July–August, pp. 149–60.
9. J. Lambeth, 'News Analysis: Banking on the Internet', *Computer Weekly*, 30 January 1997.
10. S. Dutta and Y. Doz, 'Case Study: linking information technology to business strategy at Banco Comercial Portugues', *Journal of Strategic Information Systems*, 1995, pp. 89–110.
11. T. Jelassi, 'Gaining Business from Information Technology', *European Management Journal*, vol. 11:1, 1993, p. 68.
12. R. Butler, R. Turner, P. Coates, R. Pike, and D. Price, 'Investing in New Technology for Competitive Advantage', *European Management Journal*, vol. 11:3, 1993, p. 372.
13. C. F. Kemerer and G. L. Sosa, 'Barriers to Successful Strategic Information Systems', *Planning Review*, September–October 1988, pp. 20–46.
14. G. W. Keen, *Shaping the Future: Business Design Through Information Technology*, Harvard Business School Press, Boston 1991.
15. G. Premkumar and W. R. King, 'Assessing Strategic Information Systems Planning', *Long-Range Planning*, vol. 24, October 1991, pp. 41–58.
16. V. Grover and J. T. C. Teng, 'How Effective is Data Resource Management', *Journal of Information Systems Management*, Summer 1991, pp. 16–20.
17. C. Hagmann and C. S. McCahon, 'Strategic Information Systems Competitiveness', *Information and Management*, Elsevier Science Publishers, Oxford 1993, pp. 183–92.
18. B. S. Neo, 'Factors Facilitating the Use of Information Technology for Competitive Advantage: an Exploratory Study', *Information and Management*, vol. 15, 1988, pp. 191–201.

19. J. Naisbitt, *Global Paradox*, Nicholas Brealey Publishing, London 1995, p. 70.
20. G. Hamel and C. K. Prahalad, 'Competing in the New Economy: Managing Out of Bounds', *Strategic Management Journal*, vol. 17, 1996, p. 242.
21. C. J. Choi and M. Kelemen, *Generic Cultural Competencies: Managing Co-operatively Across Cultures*, Dartmouth Publishers, London 1994.
22. M. F. Wolff, 'Forging Technology Alliances', *Research Technology Management*, May–June 1989, pp. 9–11.
23. J. C. Camillus and A. L. Lederer, 'Corporate Strategy and the Design of Computerised Information Systems', *Sloan Management Review*, vol. 26:3, 1985.
24. H. Bjornsson and R. Lundegard, 'Corporate Competitiveness and Information Technology', *European Management Journal*, vol 10:3, September 1992, pp. 341–7.
25. *The Economist*, 13 December 1997.
26. S. Ghoshal and C. A. Bartlett, *The Individualised Corporation*, Heinemann, London 1998.
27. R. H. Hayes, S. C. Wheelwright, and K. B. Clark, *Dynamic Manufacturing*, Free Press, New York 1988.
28. T. Hope and J. Hope, *Competing in the Third Age, the Ten Key Management Issues of the Information Age*, Harvard Business Press, Boston, Mass., 1997.
29. R. M. Kanter, *When Giants Learn to Dance*, Unwin, London 1989.
30. K. Grint, *Fuzzy Logic*. Oxford University Press, Oxford 1997.
31. R. Kaplan and D. Norton, 'The balanced scorecard: measures that drive performance', *Harvard Business Review*, vol. 70:1, 1992.
32. S. Ghoshal and C. A. Bartlett, 'Beyond the M form: towards a managerial theory of the firm', *Strategic Management Journal*, forthcoming.
33. P. Ward, 'A 360 degree turn of the better', *People Management*, 9 February 1995.
34. R. Jacobs and M. Floyd, 'A bumper crop of insights', *People Management*, 9 February 1995.
35. B. J. Nalebuff and A. M. Brandenburger, *Co-opetition*, Harper Collins Business, London 1997.
36. P. M. Senge, *The Fifth Discipline*, Century Business, London 1990.
37. R. M. Kanter, *The Change Masters*, Simon and Shuster, New York 1985.
38. S. R. Barley and G. Kunda, 'Design and devotion, surges in rational and normative ideologies of control in managerial discourse', *Administrative Science Quarterly*, vol. 37, 1992, pp. 363–99.
39. S. Ghoshal and C. A. Bartlett, *The Individualised Corporation*, Heinemann, London 1998.
40. Grint, *Fuzzy Logic*.
41. D. Mercer, *Futures Shape of Organisations*, Open University Futures Forum, Milton Keynes, ongoing.
42. C. Handy, *The Age of Unreason*, Business Books, London 1989.
43. F. Kinsmann, *The Telecommuters*, Wiley, London 1987.
44. 'In defence of international relations', *Financial Times*, 31 October 1997.
45. C. Johnson, 'A matter of trust', *Management Accounting*, vol. 71, 1989, pp. 12–13.
46. J. Smythe, C. Dorwood, and J. Reback, *Corporate Reputation: managing the new strategic asset*, Century Business, London 1992.
47. Arthur Ashe, *Days of Grace*, Alfred Knopf, New York 1993.
48. 'The UK Banking System', *IBCA Credit Rating Agency*, London March 1977.
49. J. Stein, *The Banking System in Germany*, 21st edn, Bank Verlag, Bonn 1997.
50. 'The German Banking System', *IBCA Credit Rating Agency*, May 1976.
51. *Banking System Outlook – United Kingdom*, Moody's Investor Service, Global

Credit Research, London 1997.

52. G. Bowley, 'Compuserve services to remain separate', *Financial Times*, 11 September 1997.
53. 'Internet soll Freihandelszone Werden', *Hannoverische Allgemeine Zeitung*, 8 July, 1997.
54. 'Banking online hat Nachteile', *Neue Presse*, 16 October 1997.
55. 'Banken und Sparkassen drangen ins Internet', *Berliner Morgenpost*, 27 August 1997.
56. A. Wallis, 'Internet Banking', MBA thesis, University of Westminster, 1997.
57. George Graham, 'The difficulty of banking on the world', *Financial Times*, 29 October 1997.
58. *The Wall Street Journal*, 6 August 1987.
59. 'New Boss New Plan', *Business Week*, 2 February 1998.
60. 'Erasing old Frontiers', *Financial Times*, 1 October 1997.
61. Simon Beavis, 'Gates Nightmare for BT Regulator', *The Guardian*, 20 January 1998.
62. Bill Gates, *The Road Ahead*, Viking, London 1995.
63. 'Fear of Finance, Survey of the World Economy', *The Economist*, 19 September 1992.
64. R. Reich, *The Work of Nations*, Alfred A. Knopf, New York 1991.
65. *The Economist*, 6 December 1997.
66. M. Emerson, 'One market, one money', *European Economy*, vol. 35, October 1990.
67. 'A balance sheet for EMU', *Europe Business*, 12 March 1997.
68. C. Johnson, *In with the Euro, out with the Pound - the Single Currency for Britain*, Penguin, London 1996.
69. J. Quatremer, 'L'euro sera a l'heure, avec ou sans la France', *Liberation*, 8 July 1997.
70. 'Small but perfectly formed', *The Economist*, 3 January 1997.

7   The case material

Case Study 1: Competitive strategies in the world airline industry

1. M. A. Brenner, O. J. Leet, and E. Schott, *Airline Deregulation*, ENO Foundation for Transportation, Westport, Conn., 1985.
2. S. Vandermerwe and C. H. Lovelock, *Singapore Airlines: Using Technology for Service Excellence*, European Case Clearing House, Cranfield, 1991.

Case Study 2: BAA plc

1. R. Doganis, *Flying Off-Course, the Economics of International Airlines*, MMC Report, 1991.
2. *Financial Times*, 30 April 1996.
3. *Financial Times*, 28 November 1996.
4. *Financial Times*, 5 February 1998.

5. *Daily Telegraph*, 21 March 1998.
6. *Duty Free International*, October 1996.
7. *Financial Times*, 26 November 1996.
8. *Financial Times*, 28 November 1996.

Person Index

Topic Index

087063

COMPETITIVE STRATEGIES FOR SERVICE ORGANISATIONS